FREEMASONRY IN LONDON
From 1785

The Arms of y^e most Ancient & Honorable Fraternity. of Free and Accepted Masons.

Holiness to the Lord.

The Arms of the Operative. or Stone Masons.

Locken. Sculp

Frontispiece of Ahiman Rezon, *1764 edition*

FREEMASONRY IN LONDON
From 1785

ROY A. WELLS

LONDON
LEWIS MASONIC

© 1984 Roy A. Wells

First published in England in 1984
Published by LEWIS MASONIC
Terminal House, Shepperton, Middlesex
who are members of the
IAN ALLAN GROUP OF COMPANIES

Printed and bound in England by
Butler & Tanner Ltd, Frome, Somerset

Printed for masonic circulation.
Previous titles by the same author
  Some Royal Arch Terms Examined
  The Tyler or Outer Guide (Prestonian Lecture 1977)

British Library Cataloguing in Publication Data
Wells, Roy A.
  Freemasonry in London from 1785.
  1. Freemasonry—England—London—History
  I. Title
  366'.1'09421   HS596.L6

ISBN 0 85318 138 1

TABLE OF CONTENTS

ILLUSTRATIONS

Line Illustrations

FOREWORD

Bro Roy Wells' book will be of great interest not only to those who wish to study the history of Domatic Lodge, No 177 (which was how it was originally conceived) but also to a wider readership, its author having taken the opportunity to extend his coverage to give a broader picture of Freemasonry in London over the last two centuries.

It is refreshing to have this presented as seen through the life of a London lodge of Antients origin and through the personalities connected with it, whose influence on the Craft in general was of such importance in the last years of the eighteenth century, those of the early nineteenth leading to the Union and those following in its aftermath.

As might be expected of one closely associated for many years with the Domatic Chapter of Instruction, the history of the Royal Arch is given equally comprehensive treatment by the author, whose other activities in London masonry are also reflected in later sections.

It gives me much pleasure to commend his book to the Craft.

Terence O. Haunch, *1984*
PAGSupt Wks
(*Librarian and Curator, Freemasons' Hall, London 1973-1983*)

ACKNOWLEDGEMENTS

The author gratefully appreciates permission granted by the Board of General Purposes of the United Grand Lodge of England, and the Committee of General Purposes of Supreme Grand Chapter of Royal Arch Masons of England. Also a similar permission from the Council of Management of Quatuor Coronati Correspondence Circle Limited to quote from their records. Warm thanks are now tendered to Terence Haunch, former Librarian and Curator (since retired) at Freemasons' Hall, to John Hamill his successor but previously Assistant Librarian, and to John Groves, Assistant Curator, for patient assistance willingly given during the period of research. Thanks also to the Librarian and staff of the Maritime Museum at Greenwich, and to the many authors of lodge and chapter histories where references have been made, but far too numerous to mention.

ABOUT THE AUTHOR

Roy A. Wells was initiated in Five Orders Lodge No 3696 at the Holborn Restaurant on 26 January 1938, and became Master in 1952. He was exalted in Five Orders Chapter reaching the office of First Principal in 1957.

During active service with the Royal Navy from 1941 to 1945 he spent part of 1942/3 in Israel to his considerable advantage as a masonic student with biblical interest. Early associations with the Domatic Chapter of Instruction No 177 stimulated his thirst for knowledge in the Royal Arch and he was elected Scribe E of that teaching authority in 1956 which office he still occupies. In that capacity he has provided terms of reference for a countless number of Companions. Upon his retirement from business life in 1968, he was invited to become Personal Assistant to the late Harry Carr at Quatuor Coronati Lodge No 2076, the premier Lodge of Masonic Research. Five years later he succeeded as secretary/editor and became Master of that distinguished lodge in 1973 but, on medical advice, handed over those clerical duties in December 1975.

His qualities as a masonic researcher, writer and personality have become widely known and appreciated. Numerous essays and articles from his pen have appeared in the world masonic press, research lodge publications both home and overseas, and in 1978 his first book was published, *Some Royal Arch Terms Examined*, being a valuable source of reference. He was appointed Prestonian Lecturer in 1977, his chosen subject being *The Tyler or Outer Guide* which proved immensely popular.

He has travelled widely overseas, giving masonic talks and lectures and in 1980 at the Masonic Lodge of Research of Connecticut he was invested with the James Royal Case Medal of Excellence for 'outstanding contributions in the field of masonic research', only the ninth recipient of the award and the second English brother to be so honoured, the first being the late Bro Harry Carr.

Roy Wells was honoured with London Grand Rank in 1965 and became President of the London Grand Rank Association in 1982. He received active rank as a Grand Officer in Supreme Grand Chapter in 1966 (the bi-centenary year) and in the United Grand Lodge of England in 1971. Having been promoted in both he now holds ranks as Past Grand Standard Bearer in the Royal Arch and Past Assistant Grand Director of Ceremonies in the Craft. .

Freemasonry in London From 1785

Introduction

The most critical period in masonic history must surely surround the time in which the two well-established Grand Lodges worked as separate authorities and eventually joined together in 1813 as The United Grand Lodge of England. The anomalous position of the 'Antients' is indicated by the fact that they came into existence forty-four years after the 'Moderns' who were styled thus for having departed from original forms of ritual and procedure. The following pages will not only furnish a study of that period and the pursuit of Freemasonry in London thereafter, but will relate the experiences of brethren who were associated with Domatic Lodge and its Chapter. It is not an individual history of those two bodies as such but will provide an interesting means through which the development may be examined.

From a geographical situation Domatic Lodge came into being at the very heart of London Freemasonry, and whilst it cannot be said to have had a major influence in the course of Freemasonry as a whole, its associates rather more than its membership, were frequently to be found near the centre of important activity in Freemasonry from 1785 for the next sixty years, and its Chapter of Instruction from 1850 onwards.

The initial stages for Domatic commenced in December 1785 with a Dispensation that was granted by the Antients Grand Lodge in accordance with Regulation No 8 of *Rules and Orders* that had been adopted in their General Assembly on 17 July 1751:

> No admission or Warrant shall be granted to any Brothers to hold a Lodge until such time they shall have first form'd a Lodge of Ancient Masons and sit regularly in a Credible House and then to Apply by Petition and such Petition to be Attested by the Masters of three Regular Lodges who shall make a proper Report of them.

The first Minutes for the Dispensation meetings are headed:

> The Minutes of the Dispensation Granted to Br Charles Fenwick to be held at Br William Smiths the Sign of the Ship in Little Turn Stile—Holburn for the Purpose of Making And forming a Lodge of Opporitave Masons on December 21 1785 . . .

In the twelve meetings held under that Dispensation a total of forty brethren were Initiated, Passed, and Raised, during which time frequent visits were paid by senior Grand Officers presumably to ensure that the meetings were actually 'in a Credible House'. Just six weeks later, on 7 February 1786, Laurence Dermott, Deputy Grand Master, assisted by Thomas Harper, Junior Grand Warden, and others of distinction Constituted the brethren as Lodge No 234 and it was in those Minutes that the name Domatic was brought into use.

The word 'Domatic' derives from Scotland and was used there to describe those who were engaged in the mason craft. The best examples of its use, and of relative descriptions in Freemasonry in the eighteenth century are to be found in three references from *History of the Lodge of Edinburgh* by Murray Lyon (Glasgow, 1900):

> A strong proof of the jealousy with which the operative or 'Domatic' element in the Lodge guarded itself

against being subordinated to the Speculative element may be perceived in the tenacity with which it clung to the distinctive appelation of the two classes into which its intrants were wont to be divided; viz., Honorary Members, those who were not Operative masons; and Operative Members those who were handicraft masons by profession, a classification which continued to be observed from the year 1728 till 1761. (p 88)

... non-professionals connecting themselves with the Lodge by the ties of membership would, we believe, be actuated partly by a disposition to reciprocate the feelings that had prompted the bestowal of friendship.... The class of members ... became known, to wit, Gentleman Masons, Theoretical Masons, Architect Masons, Honorary Members. (p 87) ... Its constitution was remodelled in 1793, when, out of deference, it may be supposed, to its Operative origin it was resolved that the office of Senior Warden should always be filled by a domatic mason. (p 449)

Another worthy reference is from R.F. Gould's comments on the Lodge of Edinburgh No 1 (*History of Freemasonry*, 1884 edn, vol 1, p 408):

Many of the operatives did not view the introduction of the speculative element with favour, and at one time the promoters and the opponents of the innovation were divided into hostile camps, but eventually those who supported the Gentlemen or Geomatic Masons won the day, the Domatics having to succumb to the powerful influences arrayed against them. In No. 1, however, the latter held the balance of power in their hands.

In the Domatic Lodge Minute Book the name is spelt in that form for the first two occasions but from then on variations appear. The most common form is Deomatick, with occasional returns to Domatick, or similar. Whilst considerable licence in word forms is appropriate to that period it cannot be ruled out that a brother may have fastened upon the idea that by altering the prefix to Deo he could compound a meaning to link with the Almighty; but we are denied any reason for its use.

Occupations for the founders and the new entrants were not recorded, which raises the question whether or not every member was actually engaged in the mason craft as a stone-cutter, carver, or setter. One may be given to pondering on whether the term 'Opporitave Masons' was employed to include workers in allied building trades such as carpenters, joiners, bricklayers, slaters, tilers, plasterers, painters, etc. It is difficult to accept that all forty-one entrants in those twelve Dispensation meetings prior to Constitution and those who were admitted in the three and a half years covered by the first Minute Book were all operative stonemasons. The earliest Return from Domatic Lodge, preserved in the archives of Grand Lodge, is dated in the year 1801 and occupations shewn in that are 'mason, carpenter, plasterer, bricklayer, smith, printer, bookbinder, tailor, undertaker, victualler, gent'. Nevertheless, how jealously they guarded their intention to restrict the membership to operative masons was demonstrated only five meetings after the Constitution. It stands as a harsh example of ingratitude which might have been circumvented quite easily if the traditional art of compromise had been exercised, but, the full story appears within.

Domatic Lodge may count itself fortunate in that the first Minute Book has survived, as well as the first Minute Book of the Lodge of Instructions, as it was called when formed on 30 October 1808, five years before the Union. Although the Domatic Chapter qualified for a seniority to date from 1793, unfortunately its surviving records date only from 1827. The Chapter of Instruction has Minutes, with small breaks at times, from its formation on 15 February 1850.

From their inception the Antients practised the Royal Arch degree, indeed it was classified by them as a Fourth Degree, but as it was restricted to those who had presided as Master of a lodge only a percentage of the membership qualified. The Royal Arch itself, at lodge level, was far less organised and the degree performed much less regularly than the Craft degrees; assistance from qualified brethren outside the lodge membership was often called upon. On 4 August 1786 it was announced in the Grand Lodge of Ireland:

... it is highly improper for a Master Mason's Lodge, as such, to enter upon their Books any Transactions relative to the Royal Arch.

2

As the roots of those who founded the Antients Grand Lodge were embedded in *Regulations* and directives issued from Ireland, and their procedure modelled on such forms, we are denied details or records of what would have been most useful information. The foregoing directive was probably reaffirming a condemnation of those who were mixing the records, but separate Minutes for occasional meetings for Royal Arch purposes meant a paucity of recording that has been constantly deplored by masonic historians. Fortunately, considerable detail was placed on record by the Grand Chapter of the Moderns, from 1766, and their subordinate Chapters.

The Royal Arch was not only another point of difference between the two Grand Lodges in England, the Order, or Degree, was simply just not recognised by the Moderns Grand Lodge. Their members, however, were not to be denied, they participated privately and individually to such an extent that those brethren meeting in a chapter in Gerrard Street, Soho, erected a Grand Chapter as a controlling body separate and apart from their Grand Lodge. Their records have provided a wealth of information.

Efforts aimed at uniformity in ritual and ceremonial in the Craft occupied considerable attention for the first twenty-seven years of the nineteenth century, focus for a similar purpose had then to be switched to the Royal Arch. It is a matter for regret that in both cases no official manual was ever printed and the recommended ritual and procedure promulgated only at special meetings, although relayed from then on through those who had been thus informed. It is generally agreed that posterity is indebted to George Claret, a ritual printer whose work at that time and onwards came to be accepted as authentic. He supplied details in manuscript for the Royal Arch in the same period as his Craft publication in 1838; his printed Royal Arch ritual appeared in 1845.

It is in this field of activity that a major achievement for Domatic is represented. The Domatic Chapter of Instruction was founded 15 February 1850, a mere five years after the appearance of Claret's printed Royal Arch ritual. It has kept up a comparatively unbroken sequence of meetings since that date, as shewn by its Minute Books and magazine reports of its activity, and therefore is the oldest Royal Arch teaching authority. The Working which bears its name conforms to what was set down by Claret and could well form a link with that unmistakeably firm announcement made in Grand Chapter in November 1835:

> Some misconception having arisen as to what are the ceremonies of our Order it is hereby resolved and declared that the ceremonies adopted and promulgated by special Grand Chapter on the 21st and 25th Nov. 1834, are the ceremonies of our Order which it is the duty of every Chapter to adopt and obey.

Printed rituals are commonplace nowadays, but it was not until 1960 that the Domatic Chapter of Instruction published the ritual as it is taught by them, and then only because an unauthorized printed manual bearing their name had been in use for many years and was being widely used. It had spread errors and was causing great difficulties for the Preceptors and it was some years before the nuisance was eradicated. The authentic ritual bears the title *The Ritual of the Holy Royal Arch as Taught by Domatic Chapter of Instruction No 177* and its weekly meetings are held at Freemasons' Hall, London. Who could possibly have predicted that from the first meeting of those few Companions at the Falcon Tavern, Fetter Lane, Holborn, on 15 February 1850 that 'Domatic Working' was to become known and practised in Chapters under the English Jurisdiction worldwide, and was to form the basis upon which recommended rituals in Holland and France, to name but two other countries have been compiled.

The selected, but co-ordinated records that are available from each branch of Domatic, that is, the Lodge itself dating from 1785, the Lodge of Instruction from 1808, the Royal Arch Chapter from 1793, and the Chapter of Instruction from 1850, have been set within against a background of the development of Freemasonry in London from that time. It may well give real perspective to some minor entries and references that, if taken by themselves, would have had very little meaning.

In order to portray the spirit of the period and

to reflect the character of those concerned, the quaint spelling and style of expression of all extracts used have been faithfully copied from the originals. Where it has been thought helpful for the reader who may wish to pursue an individual subject, or a facet of the same, mention in context has been made of relative work of masonic scholars and, in so doing, footnotes have been avoided.

It might well be said that the small snippets from incidents in which brethren or Companions from Domatic were involved, or those with whom they were associated in some form or other, could be deemed to be tesserae which have now been set into the wider picture of Freemasonry in London, but have helped to make a clearer mosaic. They include items reflecting integrity, intrigue, fidelity, fellowship, mystery and mastery, in fact all the qualities and failings of human nature that one would expect to find in any large organisation, but this time they have been clothed with a masonic apron.

Part 1—The Craft

The Dispensation of 1785

It is a matter for regret that we have no trace of the Dispensation granted to Charles Fenwick and unfortunately there is no mention of it in the Minutes of the Grand Stewards nor those in that period of Grand Lodge. It is unusual that it was not recorded because from as early as 1753 in the records of the Antients there is mention of that form of licence as the following examples will shew:

> 19 June 1753. Order'd a Dispensation for M. John Doughty for the purpose of congregating and making of Freemasons at the One Tun in the Strand from this day unto the first Wednesday in July next.
>
> 4 July 1753. Order'd that Alexander Clarke shall have a Dispensation to form a lodge and make Masons for the space of one month.

In order to bring such 'Makings' under proper control and to maintain regularity, the following was passed in Grand Lodge on 1 March 1757:

> The Grand Secretary made a Motion for a New Regulation concerning the making of new Masons. After many debates it was Agreed and Order'd that no person shou'd hereafter be made a Mason in an Antient Lodge under the sum of One pound five shillings and sixpence and Cloath the Lodge if required. And also that every person Made under a temporal Dispensation shall pay as much as those made in Warranted Lodges. On default hereof the Transgressors shall be dealt with according to the Eight General Regulation. This Regulation to extend to all Masons whether Members or Visitors if found Makeing or Assisting to make in a Clandestine Manner.

By the time Bro Charles Fenwick had been granted his Dispensation the charge for 'Making'

1 *Title page of the first edition of* Ahiman Rezon, *1756*

5

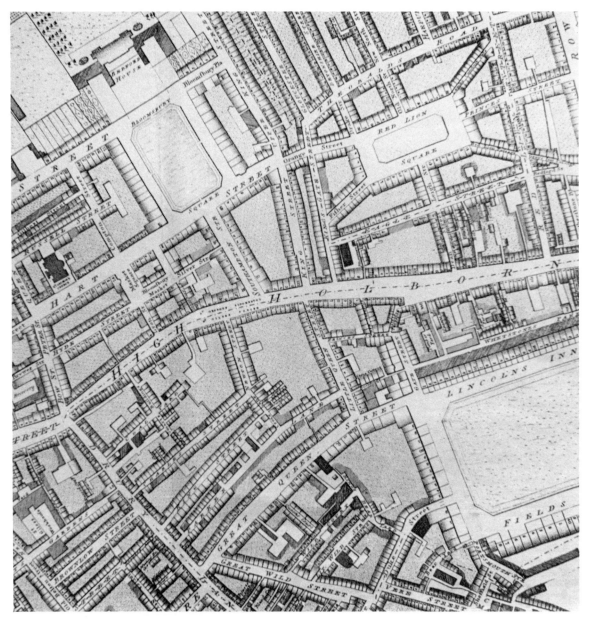

2 *Section of a map of central London in 1790. Great Queen Street and Gate Street are prominent*

had been raised to £2.2.0. With regard to the format there is no reason to think that it differed in any way from that which is recorded in *Appendix A* which although dated ten years earlier than the one for Domatic is the nearest to that date available to us. With a few amendments we would have all the details. However, the thirty-day limit imposed by the Dispensation proved too short for Fenwick as we find an item dated 23 January 1786 in the accounts section of the Minute Book: 'To Dispensation renewed 1.6d.'

The Antients Book of Constitutions was compiled by Laurence Dermott and published in London in 1756 under the title *Ahiman Rezon: or Help to a Brother.*

The First Meeting Place

The first meeting place for Domatic Lodge was The Ship Tavern an establishment which takes its rightful place in the history of Holborn itself. It was, and still is, situated at the junction of Little Turnstile and Gate Street at the rear of Holborn Underground Station. Reference to the map by R. Horwood (*c* 1790) will shew that some street names have been altered and others have disappeared. New roads that are familiar today had not then been constructed. What is now West Central postal district has for centuries been the centre of London Freemasonry.

According to records the first building as a

4 *The Ship Tavern as it is today. It was rebuilt in 1923*

3 *An early print of The Ship Tavern which was built in 1549*

tavern on that site was erected in 1549 and some idea of what it looked like can be gathered from an early print reproduced as Plate No. 3. The present establishment was built in 1923 and Plate No. 4 will shew how well the style was preserved and the traditional aspect maintained. On the exterior south wall a plaque has been fixed shewing its connection with Freemasonry in general and Lodge No 234 in particular, the number allocated to Domatic at its Constitution. The plaque has this to say:

THE SHIP TAVERN

This Tavern was established in the year 1549. During the proscription of the Roman Catholic religion, it was used as a shelter for Priests and Services were held here secretly. The neighbourhood was once notorious for the gambling houses of Whetstone Park. Famous visitors have been Richard Penderell, who aided King Charles' escape, Bayford, shoemaker and antiquarian, the woman Chevalier d'Eon who lived as a man, and Smeaton the builder of the first Eddystone Lighthouse. It was the centre of Freemasonry and a Lodge with the number 234 was consecrated here by the Grand Master the Earl of Antrim in 1786.

Although he was Grand Master of the Antients Grand Lodge at that time, the statement that the lodge was consecrated by the Earl of Antrim is not correct. Chevalier d'Eon's personal state was the exact reverse of what has been stated for he was a male transvestite; a Frenchman initiated in 1768 in a Moderns lodge No 376 under the name *La lodge de l'Immortalite* meeting at the Crown and Anchor, in the Strand. According to Henry Sadler, d'Eon served that lodge as Junior Warden between 1769 and 1770 but his name does not appear in their records thereafter. Chevalier d'Eon received a commission in a cavalry regiment in 1757, was an acknowledged expert fencer, and for his valuable work in the Secret Service was made a Chevalier of the Royal and Military Order of Saint Louis, an honour from Louis XV. Later in an English court he testified that he had been masquerading as a man for forty years but that actually he was a woman. He returned to London in November 1785 to settle some financial affairs and

5 *The wall plaque outside The Ship Tavern with masonic inscription. Lodge 234 was the number allocated to Domatic Lodge at its constitution, however, the Lodge was not consecrated by the Earl of Antrim as stated*

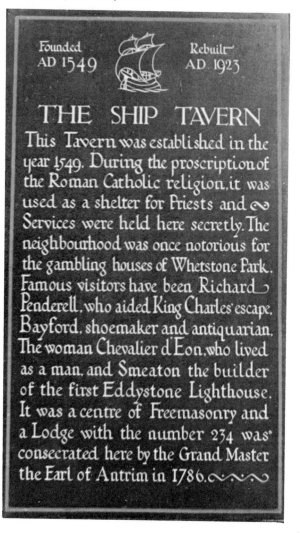

6 *Chevalier d'Eon: A man who lived as a woman. He was initiated into freemasonry in 1768*

stayed for the remainder of his life. He died 21 May 1810 in seclusion and penury then an autopsy conducted by eminent surgeons revealed that he was, without question, male and a death Certificate to that effect was issued.

Other items on the plaque give some idea of its background but in order to have a proper assessment of the part that it played we need to look a little deeper. It comes into the history of Holborn as a result of the efforts of Lord George Gordon (1751-93), a Protestant fanatic who rebelled against the Catholic Relief Bill of 1778 and then organised actions which led to the 'Gordon Riots'. From various items, including newscuttings from that period, preserved in the archives of Holborn Reference Library, we learn that in 1780 the rioters attempted to burn down the Catholic Chapel in Lincoln's Inn Fields, and for protection the communion plate was removed to 'The Ship' and Mass was then held there in great secrecy. At that time those who professed and officiated in the Catholic faith were in grave danger of being treated as felons, the extreme penalty for which was hanging, to be cut down whilst still alive and then to be quartered. One rather imaginative account of the Mass had this to say:

... in the long room on the first floor, a priest, under the protection of the Sardinian Embassy on the west side of the Fields, was wont to assemble a limited congregation twice each Sunday by stealth. Entering singly from the four different ways, namely Holborn, Gate Street, Whetstone Park, or Lincoln's Inn. The worshippers called for a mug of ale and passed into the parlour. If it sometimes happened a warning was given, all signs of worship were removed and the priest went into hiding. In 1780, when Lord George Gordon's rioters were trying to burn down the Duke Street Chapel in Lincoln's Inn Fields, sacred plate from the Sacristan was removed to the 'Ship' and Mass was served there.

It is highly probable that in an emergency the celebrant took refuge in a 'Priest's Hole' access to which would have been gained through a secret panel.

An interesting account that bridges the distance from that period to the present era appeared in the *Westminster Gazette* on 7 July 1909:

The Bishop's Beer

Close by the new Roman Catholic church in Kingsway, opened yesterday by the Archbishop of Westminster, is an ancient hostelry, the Ship Tavern, where history is linked with that of the old Sardinian Chapel, which is now to be demolished. In the penal times, when Bishop Challoner—whose saintly career was referred to by Father Bernard Vaughan in his sermon yesterday—was forbidden, under pain of felony, to preach in public, he gathered around him at the Ship Tavern a small flock of his co-religionists. The meetings took place at night in an apartment known as the club room, the door of which was guarded by a brawny Irishman, who admitted none but with the appointed password. To disarm suspicion, Dr. Challoner had also set before him a pint of porter, and this, known as "The Bishop's Beer", the assemblage sipped while his Lordship delivered his exhortation.

It was but a mere five years from the Gordon Riots that Charles Fenwick of Lodge No 194 was prevailed upon to obtain a Dispensation 'to make and form a lodge', a rather special lodge, at 'The Sign of the Ship'. One of the two others assisting in that task was the landlord, William Smith also of Lodge No 194, the other was Charles Sinclair of Lodge No 8. In December 1785 the first meeting took place, one might even be tempted to say that a voyage commenced. Another forty meetings were held in that establishment until circumstances arose to cause the brethren to change course and seek other accommodation.

Twelve Meetings by Dispensation

The first Minute Book of the lodge consists of forty-four leaves of which thirty-four have the proceedings dating from 21 December 1785 to 30 June 1788, then there is one plain leaf separating the nine leaves on which accounts for the same period have been written. Verbatim Minutes will not be inflicted upon the reader but it is proper that certain items should be quoted in detail and the first entry in the Minute Book should be no exception:

The Minutes of the Dispensation Granted to Bʳ Charles Fenwick to be held at Bʳ William Smiths the Sign of the Ship in Little Turn Stile—Holburn for the purpose of Making And Forming a Lodge of Opporitave Masons on December 21 1785
Opened at 6 o clock in the first Part when we proceeded to make Mʳ John Wood, John Perkins Juner, Charles Broad, Joshua Perkins Siner, Richard Mekin, John Edwards, William Vale, Edward Cook, James Crow, Richard Hall, and Robert Crow as apprentice Masons when Bʳ Sinclair Gave a lecter in the first Part when all Paid there Dues and Agreed to meet on Monday 26 Inst when Bʳ Wood Proposed Joshua Parker, Bʳ Perkins Proposed George Crouch & William Lawerence to be mead neaxt meeting Night and Closed at 11 in Good Hearmony.

It was thus, in accordance with the official edict from the Antients Grand Lodge, a new lodge was formed and given the opportunity to establish itself prior to the application to be Constituted and entered on the Register of that Grand Lodge.

It should be noted that only three brethren appear in their own right, Charles Fenwick to whom the Dispensation was granted, William Smith the landlord of the Ship Tavern, and Bro Sinclair who gave the Lecture. We are reminded that 'three form a lodge, etc' Charles Fenwick is shewn in the Antients *Register* of 1783 as 'Admitted in 1782' and 'PM 194', Charles Sinclair as 'Admitted in 1780' and 'P.M. No 8' and it is established that William Smith was a member of lodge No 194. Although Bros Fenwick and Sinclair did not exactly rise to eminence in Grand Lodge they were undoubtedly close to the hierarchy. During the Dispensation period of Domatic Lodge, Sinclair gave lectures in First and Second degrees and acted as Secretary, he is presumed to have written the first Minutes, but more of that later. The quaint spelling that appears in all written work is typical of the period, it reflects the phonetic approach and from that we have some idea of the pronunciation of a particular recorder as one word may appear in several forms according to the manner of the writer.

From that first meeting on 21 December 1785 to and including 3 February 1786, a total of twelve meetings were held under the authority of the Dispensation. Forty-one Candidates were Initiated and during that time the Minutes were all headed by the words 'Dispensation Lodge held on ...'. All the Candidates can be accounted for as having been Passed, two names are missing from those who were Raised but among those recorded for that Degree one name appears at two successive meetings! The lodge was usually 'Open'd at 6 o clock in the first Part ...' but on January 15 was 'Open'd at 4 pm in the Second Part to make B^{rs} Makin & Edwards Craft Masons then opened in the third Part to Pass the following B^{rs} to that of a Master Mason ...'

The charge for 'Making' was £2.2.0 and all the names appear in the accounts section of the book under the heading 'Monie paid to the Dispensation'. Those payments afforded the capital from which the various payments were made. The actual cost of the Dispensation is not shewn, but amounts of £1.1.0 each to Charles Fenwick and Charles Sinclair may be relevant. One month later an item occurs: 'To Dispensation renewed 0.1.6.'

The twelve Dispensation meetings were visited on four occasions by John McCormick, Grand Secretary, twice by Henry Westley, Grand Pursuivant, and once each by John Feakins, Senior Grand Warden and Thomas Harper, Junior Grand Warden. Six other visitors are named in the Minutes for those meetings.

The final meeting was quite a busy one and mention is made of the receipt of a favourable reply from Laurence Dermott, Deputy Grand Master, to their application for the all-important Constitution as a Regular lodge:

Despensation Lodge Feb. 3 1786
Open'd at 6 o clock in the first Part to make John Knight apprentice and Paid his Dues open'd in the Second Part to Craft the same then opened in the Third Part to Pass Robert Crow & John Knight to Master Masons when B^r Sinclair Gave a Lecter in the first Part when the Depety Grand Masters answer was red and joyesly Received when the Members of the Despensation with the assistance of there instructers Chose there Officers that no time may be Losed on the Day of Installation when B^r John Woods was chose Master B^r Broad S.W. B^r Perkins J.W. B^r Joshua Perkins Siner [Senior] Treasurer, Chas Sinclair Sec. for the time being B. Vale S.D. B. Hall J.D.

Called to Refreshment at 10 Called on at Half after. Closed at 11 in Good Harmony.

Three degrees in one meeting, one Candidate in all three, a Lecture, agreement upon who should be the first Officers of the lodge, and 'Refreshment', all in the space of five hours, it was a busy meeting indeed! It ended the period of 'Making and Forming a Lodge of Opporitave Masons', Charles Fenwick, Charles Sinclair, and William Smith had completed that task, and four days later the new brethren were Constituted to take their place as Lodge No 234 on the Register of the *Grand Lodge of England According to the Old Institution*, otherwise known as the 'Antients' and, it was on that occasion, they adopted the title 'Domatic Lodge'.

The allotted number was really no indication of the number of Warrants that had been issued by the Antients Grand Lodge because some, as a result of dormancy having been returned, had been re-issued. The total number of lodges at that time was approximately 160 under the Antients jurisdiction and 180 under the premier Grand Lodge, or Moderns. That comparison shews how rapidly the former had flourished; a situation which was due in no small measure to Laurence Dermott their indefatigable Grand Secretary from 1752-71 but by this time a very well experienced Deputy Grand Master.

Constitution by Laurence Dermott

The history of Domatic Lodge, as such, must commence with the record of proceedings under Dispensation dating from 21 December 1785, but those twelve meetings are not taken into consideration for its dating on the Register which is determined by the date of the Warrant of its Constitution. (See *Appendix B*) The event was recorded in the Minute Book as follows:

The Domatic Lodge Constituted Febr^y 7 1786
Opened at 20 Minutes before three as the Grand Lodge the Right Worshipfull Lau. Dermott Esqr D.G.M. in the Chear the Right Worshipfull B^r Tomas Harper J.G.W. & the Grand Treasurer with there Pursuivant and Tyler present—After some seremonies

7 *The warrant of Domatic Lodge constituted in 1786*
   [*see* Appendix B]

B^r Wood was called as Master and fully approved of by the body who was then to be constituted when he received his Regular Charges Rules and Regulations Received a serimony which Cannot be mentioned here after which he caled his wardens B^{rs} Broad & Perkins which was fully approved of as before when they receive Each of them a serimony According to there Degree when the Dicons was chose B^r Veal & Hall and recived there Charge of attending the Treasurer and Sec^y left to the pleasure of the Brethren on next Lodge night when the Grand Lodge Closed 20 minutes before 6 and Lodge No. 234 was opened in Due form and on account of Refreshment it was Closed—During Pleasure in Good Harmony—Visited by B^r Dixon S, Dixon T, Allen, Silverwood, Deavy, Lurham, Barradine, Hardy, Mason, Smith, Corby, Johnston, & Swan, when B^r Hugh Knight proposed William James to be made a mason next Lodge Night.

An interesting comparison may be made between that record and what was entered in the Minutes of Grand Lodge for the event:

Grand Lodge Open'd in Due Form at the Sign of the Ship, Little Turnstile, Holborn, Feb^{ry} 7 1786
The Right Worshipfull Lau. Dermott Esq in the Chair.
Present The R. W^{ll} Thomas Harper J.G. Warden
      The W^{ll} John McCormick G.S.
      The W^{ll} Robert Galloway G. Treas.
John Dixon 231. Edward Silverwood 231. Richard Dixon 231. Thomas Lulham 231. Thomas Allen 72. Charles Sinclair 8. James Swan 8. Charles Fenwick 194. G. Hardie 3. Thomas Mason 3. John Smith 3. Thomas Corby 3. Wilfred Johnston 3. W^m. Smith 194. W^m. Barradine 63. Wm Davy 128.
Installed according to Ancient Usage:
      John Wood   Master
      Charles Broad S. Warden
      John Perkins   J. Warden
All matters relative to this Constitution being Compleated the G. Secretary in the Name of the Most Noble and Right Honourable Earl of Antrim Grand Master Proclaimed the New Lodge Duly Constituted No. 234. Registerd in the Grand Lodge Vol. 6 Letter F to be held at the Sign of the Ship little Turnstile Holborn Upon the last Monday of each Callender month. Closed and Adjourned to the General Grand Lodge.

From those two accounts we get a clear picture of how Domatic Lodge came into being, as well as a little of the format for such an event. The old maxim assures us that a man is known by the company that he keeps so let us see what and where were the meeting-places of lodges of those who attended.

The Grand Lodge of the Antients was then meeting at The Pauls Head Tavern, Cateaton Street (now Gresham Street), London.

No 3 met at the Ship, Tower Street (now St. Georges & Cornerstone Lodge No 5)

No 5 met at Castle Eating House, St. Michael's Alley, Cornhill (now Albion Lodge No 9)

No 6 met at Bricklayers' Arms, Bristol Street, Blackfriars (now Enoch Lodge No 11)

No 8 met at Coopers' Arms, Kent Street, Southwark (now Kent Lodge No 15)

No 10 the meeting-place is not shewn in the records for that year but in 1790 it met at The Griffin, Villiers Street. (it is now Royal Athelstan Lodge No 19)

No 63 the meeting-place for 1786 is not shewn but in 1789 it met at Three Crowns, Old Jewry. (it is now St. Mary's Lodge, and by a strange co-incidence despite the several closing-up of numbers on the Register has the same No 63 today)

No 72 met at Freemasons' Hall, Paradise Square, Sheffield, Yorkshire (lapsed c 1788)

No 128 not shewn for 1786 but in 1789 met at Black Friar, Playhouse Yard, Blackfriars. (lapsed c 1793)

No 194 met at White Hart Tavern, Holborn (now Middlesex Lodge No 143)

No 231 met at Swan Inn, Blackman Street, Southwark (now Phoenix Lodge No 173

In attendance upon the senior Grand Officers were Bros. Henry Westley, Grand Pursuivant, and Benjamin Aldhouse, Grand Tyler, both holding paid position as such in the Antients establishment.

The cost of the Constitution was listed in the accounts section of Domatic Minute Book as follows:

To Feast at Installment	£13. 2. 7	
To Grand Secretary, Warrant, Registry, books etc.	5.15. 6	
To Tyler	4. 0	

That account was to become the subject of investigation and the Minutes of the next meeting have that reference. But first we recall that the appointment of Secretary and Treasurer had been deferred at the Constitution and, presumably Bro Sinclair was still acting as 'Secretary for the time being':

Domatic Lodge No. 234 Feb.ʸ 14 1786
Opened at 7 O Clock on Emergency to settle the accounts of the Lodge and other matters that was transacted when a Despensation, when the Secretary and Treasurer with their Assistant was ordered to do the same and lay the report of the estimate before the Lodge in the interval. Bꞏ Willᵐ James was made an Apprentice Mason and paid all Dues, he being properly reported last Lodge night, when the Worshipfull Master gave a lecture in the first part. Call'd to refreshment at 9 o Clock. Call'd on at ten when the Sect. and treasurer with his assistant Proclaimed their Accounts when Bꞏ Hall Beg'd to See the Bill of the day of Constitution but the treasurer had forgot it therefore that inquiry was dispenced with till next Lodge Night and Clos'd at 11 in good Harmony. Visited by Bꞏ Bland of No. 8 and Bꞏ Davy of 128 and Bꞏ Sinclair of No. 8.

It was not until 26 June 1786 that we find John Chadwick as Treasurer and Joshua Parker as Secretary, when 'Bro. Joshua Perkins was raised Master in the Chair for the half-year ensuing ...'

Whilst the heading for the Minutes for the inaugural meeting was quite specific in that it stated the grant of the Dispensation was to be 'for the purpose of Making and forming a Lodge of Opporitave Masons', it is almost certain that such was not the case. Such a state of affairs could have been only a verbal and mutual agreement among those who were to become the first members of the lodge, bearing in mind that they became a lodge, formed as such by their three sponsors at that first meeting, in December 1785. Nothing of that purpose was stated in the Warrant (see *Appendix B*) received by them after Constitution by Laurence Dermott on 7 February 1786; it was no

different from any other Warrant issued by the Antients Grand Lodge in that period. (Compare the details of the two Warrants shewn in *Appendices B and C*)

The work of the brethren who had supervised, guided, instructed, and participated during the Dispensation period and shortly afterwards, however, had been brought to fruition. One might be tempted into saying that they had cared for it from conception to Constitution. How well their work had been done was demonstrated by one of those initiated at the inaugural meeting when, after Constitution, the newly installed Master, Bro Wood 'gave a lecture in the first Part' and repeated that performance at the following meeting; one of their proteges had become a worthy exponent of ritual in such a short time. The members of the lodge soon proved themselves to be entirely self-supporting in that respect and any mention of Bros Fenwick and Sinclair afterwards in the Minutes is as visitors to the lodge, of which they must have felt some degree of pride, and with which they sought to be identified as Joining Members. That unfortunate event at the fifth meeting is recorded in the following terms:

Deomatick Lodge No. 234 Aprꞏl 24—1786
Opened at 7 o clock When two Brethren was propos'd to Join the Lodge but not being operative Masons where Rejected. Call'd to refreshment at 9 o clock Call'd on at 10. Visited by Bꞏ Gallaway G.T. Bꞏ McCormack G.S. Bꞏ Westley G.P. Bꞏ Davy 128. Bꞏ Ranger of -do-. Bꞏ Sinclair No. 8. Bꞏ Fenwick 194. Bꞏ McLean No. 23. Bꞏ Malvin of -do-. When Bꞏ Fenwick & Sinclair when [sic] away and paid nothing. Closed at half past 10 in good harmony.

The two brethren who had done so much for the 'opporitave masons' were thus rejected. Although the lodge is stated to have closed 'in good harmony' the feeling before then must have been somewhat intense for those two brethren to have left without paying what must have been their dues for refreshment. However, they were not to allow the matter to rest as the Minutes for the next meeting will shew:

Deomatick Lodge 234 May 15 1786 on Emergency
Opened at 7 o clock when it was unanimously agreed

by the majority to make good all deficiencies of payments within six months from the date as above. When B͏ͬ Fenwick & B͏ͬ Sinclair sent a Note to the Worshipful Master endeavouring to disturb the Harmony of the Lodge and desiring an answer For which they receive a Blank paper. When afterwards B͏ͬ Wood gave a lecture in the Apprentice. Clos'd at half past 10 in good Harmony. B͏ͬ Stavely Tyler.

That is the last time we see the names Fenwick and Sinclair in the Minute Book, but the matter was still pursued as they reported it to Grand Lodge for their consideration, only to attract an official censure on their cause:

Grand Lodge 7 June 1786
... The Right W. Deputy Grand Master Order'd the Grand Secretary to Read a Petition of Brother Charles Fenwick of No. 194 and Charles Sinclare of N͏ͦ 8 with a complaint against Brother Wood Master of N͏ͦ 234 and the Rest of the Brethren of Sd N͏ͦ This Cause could not be Discussed no other way than what mony͏ˢ they had Received from Sd Lodge 234 and not that sum with any propriaties. The Deputy Grand Master gave them a Severe reprimand for their Misconduct and Charged them to behave for the future.

'Blow, blow thou winter wind, thou are not so unkind as man's ingratitude'—how appropriate are Shakespeare's immortal words in this instance; obviously it was a situation that had grown out of all proportion. In the hindsight of modern practice it would have been so simple to have elected all three brethren concerned in that 'Making and Forming' period as Honorary Members—'For services rendered to Freemasonry in general and to Domatic Lodge No 234 in particular.' However, that complaint now causes us to look at the Accounts to see 'what monys they had Received from Sd Lodge 234'. The relative items are listed below:

1785		
21 Dec	To Charles Fenwick	1. 1. 0
26 ,,	To Charles Sinclair	1. 1. 0
28 ,,	To Fenwick—1 doz aprons	10. 0
1786		
15 Jan	Paid Charles Fenwick towards Hangers	10. 6
,, ,,	Paid Charles Sinclair towards regalia	10. 6
17 ,,	To Fenwick remainder for Hangers	4. 7. 2

22 Jan	To Extra expence to Fenwick & Sinclair	10. 0
30 ,,	Paid Mr. Sinclair the remaining sum for Columns, Gavels, etc.	1.14. 6
23 ,,	To Dispensation renewed	1. 6

Although the first two items are not detailed there is hardly anything that can be challenged in those accounts. The payment of £1. 1. 0 made to Fenwick on the first meeting, and a similar amount to Sinclair on the second, may have been in the nature of payment 'for services rendered'. No payment is shewn for the initial cost of the Dispensation and although the amount of 1.6d for renewal was made it is shewn as having been paid to Fenwick who probably had paid the first cost. According to Henry Sadler who compiled a 'Table of the Grand Secretary's Fees, AD 1751' an item appeared for 'Dispensation for forming a new Lodge and making Masons under the Grand Seal, 2.6d'. It gives some idea of the initial cost.

It is noteworthy that in those days aprons were often of full length, reaching from chest to knees. They were left in the 'Apron Box' which was in charge of the Tyler or the landlord who was frequently one and the same. When they became soiled a replacement was made by the Candidate an action which was known as 'Cloathing the lodge'. The item in the accounts for 'Hangers' relates to collars, customarily referred to as 'Hangers' or 'Ribbands'. The Collar jewels of office for Domatic Lodge were supplied by John McCormick, the Grand Secretary, who was a silversmith by trade, and the sum of £7.10. 0 in settlement was debited on 23 January 1786.

The Antients Grand Stewards

In March 1754 the Antients Grand Lodge set up a Charitable Committee to inspect petitions from needy brethren and to relieve any that may be found worthy. In November the Committee was renamed the Stewards Lodge. All their transactions came under the scrutiny of Grand Lodge to whom their Minutes were submitted and read out for approval.

Charles Sinclair is mentioned in the Minutes of 18 September 1782 being recommended to Grand Lodge as one of the approved undertakers. At various times his name, linked with a number of lodge petitions reached the Grand Stewards, two outstanding examples of which are of interest:

19 Sept. 1787. Heard the petition of Charles Sinclare of Lodge No. 2 setting forth his case to be greatly Distressed and in fear of haveing his goods seized and his family turned out into the Street. Order'd him .... 5 Gns.

On 16 February 1791 he was paid £5. 5. 0 and on 15 August 1798 the following appeared:

Charles Sinclair of Lodge No. 10 Distressed family by Sickness upwards of two months and having no Employ as his business was greatly thereby reduced. Relieved £5. 5. 0.

In 1793 'being found on examination duly qualified Sinclair was appointed Under Tyler of Royal Lodge' and in 1800 appointed Tyler of that Lodge.

It is also of interest to note that on 16 March 1785, earlier in the year in which he obtained the Dispensation, Charles Fenwick petitioned for relief and was granted the sum of £4. 4. 0; in October 1794 he was also awarded £3. 3. 0.

Benjamin Aldhouse and Henry Westley, Grand Tyler and Grand Pursuivant respectively holding those paid positions in Grand Lodge were both in attendance upon the Grand Officers for the Constitution of Domatic Lodge, are also mentioned in those records. In January 1785 Aldhouse petitioned for assistance and was paid £4. 4. 0. His masonic record is truly remarkable in that he was initiated in 1777 in Lodge No 63 and was Master in 1789 and 1798; was appointed Grand Tyler 1782 and held that position for nine years; he was then appointed Grand Pursuivant in 1791 and held that until the Union in 1813; at the Union he was invested as Grand Usher, an entirely new office and he was the only brother ever appointed to it; he became Secretary to the Charity 'For Clothing and Educating the Sons of Indigent Free Masons according to the Old Institutions', the forerunner of what became The Royal Masonic Institution for Boys. Throughout his masonic

career he was much in demand for lectures on Freemasonry and for guidance on ritual and ceremonial. Amongst other lodges he was Tyler of Mount Moriah Lodge (now No 34) for fifty years; he died in 1843, aged 99, having been an active Freemason for 67 years.

Henry Westley was a Past Master of Lodge No 6 but was a member of several others. In the records it is noted that he was paid £2. 2. 0 'for binding Ahiman Rezon' the Antients Constitutions (see Plate No 2 for title page of 1st Edition dated 1756) and on that same day 20 April 1785 was paid £3. 3. 0 from the charity by the Grand Stewards; in September of that year he was paid £2. 2. 0 'for bad health' and again in 1789 another £3. 3. 0 for the same reason.

Westley and Aldhouse both applied to the Grand Stewards for an increase in salary but were 'order'd to do their duties better and G.L. would take it into consideration'.

Various members of Domatic Lodge applied for assistance among them the names of brethren already mentioned and some who will appear in later pages, for example: R. Meakin, J. Snellgrove, W. Whitehead, John Knight, R. Crow, J. Sellars, W. Robinson, J. Taylor, J. Orchard, S. Ricknell. Specimen entries appeared as follows:

6 Nov. 1787	Thomas Abbott 'Great distress through Sickness Relieved 3 Gns.
16 Jan. 1788	George Crouch 'In work and in health—rejected'
19 Oct. 1791	Emanuel Richmond of No. 234 'confined for debt in Newgate—Relieved £2. 2. 0 to be left with Treasurer and paid to his family 5s 3d p.week'
21 June 1797	James Taylor 'for his funeral—£3.10. 0'

The case of John Perkins is complex but it has a significant masonic ending which deserves mention here:

16 May 1792   Petition of John Perkins of Lodge No. 234 not considered a Proper object and was unanimously Rejected.

2 Aug. 1792	John Perkins of 234 P.M. of said Lodge being Rejected in May last and not signed by any of the person or officers nor any of them attending was Rejected and for the said reasons as mentioned in May last.
19 Sept. 1792	John Perkins of Lodge No. 234 unanimously Rejected being deemed unworthy of Relief & being also rejected in May, June, last.
21 Nov. 1792	John Perkins for Drawing for the Gd. Lodge Royal Arch Cert. £2.2.0.

An entry dated 4 March 1801 has the following:

Thoṣ Napier of Lodge No 234 for Misconducting himself in Grand Lodge was Order'd to quit the Lodge and Unanimously Suspended all his Masonic Rights for 12 months.

This brother occupied the Chair of the lodge for the first half of 1798 and because of his good services to the lodge and the various lectures he had given the brethren of Domatic lodge 'resolved that he be presented with a jewel as Past Master', but that Resolution did not arise until 19 September 1803. A jewel to a Past Master was not an automatic gift but an award for outstanding services beyond that office. This one was probably a tangible 'Vote of confidence' following the above mentioned suspension. Five years later Napier was relieved by payment of £6.6.0 by the Grand Stewards, a very high sum which tends to shew his standing by that date.

In the year 1806 the brethren of Domatic considered the action of a Past Master and recorded 'that this member be erased from the books' and the Secretary was ordered to report his name to the Grand Secretary. The relevant portion of his letter had these words:

... John Allison for Conduct highly Reprehensible During the time he fill'd the Chair as Master & by Receiving two pounds for the Use of Charity & Converting it to his own [lasey]? easy Purpose & deserting the Lodge it is therefore the Unanimous wish of the Lodge No. 234 that his Name be Regularly Circulated in so doing will oblidg

	Yours Respectfully	
Bṛ Ward	Bṛ Vale	
Master	Secretary	10 June 1806

Another incident two years later was to be examined by the Grand Stewards apparently to the satisfaction of all concerned:

20 July 1808. Received and Read the Complaint of the Master & Wardens of Lodge 234 London Agst Broṛ John Marden late Past Master of said Lodge for Receiving and Converting to his own use the Sum of Five pounds granted for the funeral Expenses of Broṛ Taylor of said Lodge. Order's that all parties Attend the Meeting of next Stewards Lodge.

17 August 1808. Lodge 234 The Master thereof upon the Complaint of said Lodge agst Broṛ Marden produced two sevḷ letters from the widow of Brother Taylor dec'd declaring she was now satisfied and has received satisfaction for the money Rec'd by Bro. Marden on Account the Funeral of her late Husband dec'd which letters the Master of said Lodge requested might be given to him to make some further inquiry into the Matter or bring the same before the Stewards' Lodge.

No other reference appears in the Minutes.

From the few instances quoted it will be seen that the work of the Grand Stewards Lodge prior to the Union extended far beyond the bounds of just administration of the charity funds. They acted as arbitrators, adjudicators, and to use a modern term, 'troubleshooters'. Literally they were the precursors of the many and wide-ranging Committees which function so well under the Board of General Purposes of today. They are the authorities who, after full deliberations, make suitable recommendations to Grand Lodge which is the final authority.

Complete Severance From Sponsors

We have followed the development arising from the rejection of Charles Fenwick and Charles Sinclair, two of the three who were responsible in the formation of the lodge and nursing it through the Dispensation period, we now turn to the third brother. The meetings were 'to be Held at Bṛ William

Smiths the Sign of the Ship in Little Turn Stile
...' and they continued there for eighteen months
although, it would appear, not without some stress
in the latter period.

First of all we have to identify the landlord and
this is done in the list of visitors at the Constitution meeting as recorded in the Minutes of Grand
Lodge. There we find 'William Smith 194' and not
only is that the name of the landlord but is shewn
as a member of the same lodge as the unfortunate
Charles Fenwick. There is nothing to suggest any
disharmony until the dramatic entry almost one
year after the Constitution:

> Deomatick Lodge N⁰. 234. Jan 29–1787
> Open'd at 7 O Clock proceeded to Business when it
> was agreed By a Majority present that Bʳ Smith of
> 194 Shou'd never by admitted as a Visiter into our
> Domatick Lodge N⁰. 234 for Disrespect paid to Ma-
> sonry. Visited by Bʳ Wade of 192 Bʳ Brett 194 Bʳ
> Banks of St. John. Call'd to Refreshment at 9 o
> Clock. Call'd on at half past 9. Clos'd at 10 in good
> harmony.

The next meeting, called for February 26, however, was not held as the Minute Book states—
'Lodge not opened upon the occasion the Land-
lady being sick'. It not only shews that the brethren had consideration for Mrs Smith but the hia-
tus brought a cooling-off period for all. Seven
more meetings were held at the Sign of the Ship
but on the seventh the following was recorded:

> Deomatick Lodge No. 234. July 30 '87
> Open'd at 7 o Clock in the Apr. when Bʳ J. Mecalle
> of Sᵗ Jn⁰ Producing a Proper Certificate was Propos'd
> & Admitted a Member of this Lodge. Also a Motion
> was made by Bʳ Wood Past Master & Seconded by
> Bʳ Cooke Past Master that this Lodge be mov'd to
> any Centerall & Reputable House that any Bʳ or Bro-
> thers shall know to be Convenient & Worthy this
> Motion. Pass'd Unanimously & Agreed to ...

Relationships between the landlord and the members had become strained to breaking point and
that meeting was the last to be held at that venue.
An Emergency meeting was called on August 8
and the brethren moved at once to 'the Sign of the
French Horn, Holborn, Agreeable to the Motion

made & agreed to last Lodge Night.' In one year
and seven months the brethren had held a total of
forty-one meetings at 'the Ship', all of which,
according to the Minutes had 'Closed in Good
Harmony', but in reality enough had happened to
cause the brethren to sever completely the connection with those three who had 'formed the lodge'.
They certainly had more than 'five to hold the
lodge' and more than 'seven to make a perfect
lodge'—but time was yet to tell!

The Lodge met at the Sign of the French Horn
only until December 18 of that year and then it
moved to the Sign of the Sun, Gate Street, Lincolns Inn Fields, adjacent to Little Turn Stile and
their original meeting-place. (See Plate No 2 for
map).

Certain Rules and Orders (Antients)

Unfortunately, early By-laws of Domatic Lodge
have not survived but we do have the opportunity
of seeing how well the brethren kept within the
guidelines laid down by the Antients Grand
Lodge. In 1751 Laurence Dermott compiled *Rules
and Orders* for private Lodges and in 1771, slightly
amended, they were published for general use. A
copy of that issue in possession of No 4 then meeting at the Sun Tavern, Ludgate Street, London,
has been preserved and from it we are able to
ascertain the composition and operation of an Antients lodge in that period and to determine how
well Domatic conformed. The following extracts
are of some interest:

> 1. THAT a Lodge of Free and Accepted Masons
> aforesaid shall be held at ...... the said Lodge shall
> consist of One Master, Two Wardens, Two Deacons,
> One Secretary, One Treasurer, and as many Members
> as the Master and Majority shall think proper; and
> that every Brother shall appear in clean decent Ap-
> parel, with proper [masonic] Clothing, and observe a
> due decorum while the Lodge is engaged in what is
> serious and solemn; and for the better Preservation of
> Secrecy, and good Harmony, a Brother well-skilled in
> the Master's Part, shall be appointed and paid for
> Tyling in the Lodge-door, during the Time of Com-
> munication.

When the officers for Domatic Lodge were selected at the meeting prior to Constitution, the offices of Secretary and Treasurer were not filled; remembering that Bro Sinclair was requested to act as Secretary 'for the time being'. Seven meetings afterwards Bro John Chadwick was elected Treasurer, Bro Joshua Parker as Secretary and both invested at the following meeting on St. John's Day, 24 June 1786. It is noteworthy that Deacons were specified by the Antients whereas that office is rarely to be found in lodges under the premier Grand Lodge thus making a point of difference which was resolved at the Union of 1813. A few lodges, formerly under the Antients Jurisdiction have retained the collar jewels of the Deacons representing the winged figure of Mercury, and Domatic Lodge is no exception.

The appointment of a Tyler was an exception by those brethren but no reason is supplied. *Rules and Orders* contain this directive on that subject:

> xx. THAT the Tyler shall receive one Shilling for every Mason that shall be made in this Lodge, and Sixpence for every old Mason that shall become a Member of this Lodge. And the said Tyler shall take particular Care not to admit any Person (not even a Member) without the Knowledge and Consent of the Presiding Officer; neither shall he admit any Visitor (that is not a member of a Warranted Lodge) a second Time. Sojourners producing Certificates excepted.

The first item in the accounts for payment 'to Tyler' is dated 17 January 1786 and it would appear that the three shillings entered for that was for three meetings held on 12th, 15th, and 17th. The next entry is for a similar amount and

8 *A Deacons collar jewel as worn by lodges under the Antients Grand Lodge*

apparently covered the three meetings held on 18th, 22nd, and 25th of January; all of those meeting being prior to Constitution. It is not until May 15 that there is any mention of Tyler in the Minutes and then Bro Stavely is shewn in that capacity but no payment appears to have been made for his services, although he was not a member of the lodge. In the total of sixty meetings recorded in the first Minute Book, twelve under Dispensation and forty-eight onwards from the Constitution, covering the period from 21 December 1785 to 30 June 1788, there are only eight references to Tylers and in the accounts section only thirteen entries for payments during that time. From 2 June 1788 the 'going rate' for payment to the Tyler had become two shillings and it is quite possible that Bro Westley Grand Pursuivant, and Bro Aldhouse Grand Tyler had something to do with that.

The *Rules and Orders* were equally specific with regard to the admission of Candidates:

IX. ANY Person desirous of being made a Free-Mason in this Lodge shall be proposed by a Member hereof; that is to say, his Name, Age, Description of his Person, Title or Trade, and Place of Residence. That such a Proposal shall be made in Lodge Hours, at least one Lodge Night before the Initiation, in order that the Brethren may have sufficient Time and Opportunity to make a strict Inquiry into the Morals, Character, and Circumstances of the Candidate. And the Brother that proposes him shall at the same Time, deposit such a sum (of the Candidate's Money) as the Majority shall think sufficient (not less than One Crown) to insure the Lodge that the Candidate will attend according to the Proposal, And if the Lodge approve his Person, Age, Character and Circumstances, and therefore Initiate him into the Mystery, &c. he shall pay whatsoever Sum the Brethren shall think proper (not less than Two Guineas) and cloath the Lodge if required. But if the Lodge think the Candidate unworthy and refuse to make him, his Money shall be faithfully returned to him. But in case the Lodge approve his Person and Character, &c. and he refuse to be made, then he shall forfeit his Money for the Benefit of distressed Free-Masons.

9 *Andrew Montgomery 'Garder of ye Grand Lodge'* (1738)

Whilst items of finance have changed considerably since those days, it is still the custom in many lodges for Candidates to be proposed in open lodge before completion of an Application Form preparatory for interview by an appointed lodge Committee. Domatic Lodge have maintained that practice. To 'Cloath the Lodge' in those early days meant the provision of new aprons where needed, at a cost of one shilling each, to replace any that may have become soiled. Whilst there was no difference between the apron worn by a stonemason at work and that used in lodge in the early period, brethren were not permitted to use a working apron on a lodge night or attendance. One case is on record of a brother being fined sixpence for wearing his working apron when attending a lodge meeting in Maiden Lane, Covent Garden.

The term of office for the Master and Wardens was also governed by the *Regulations*, as follows:

THAT on S? Johns day the 24th of June and S? Johns day the 27th of Decem? the Master of every Lodge shall deliver into the Secretary of Grand Lodge the Names of the Master & Wardens that are appointed to serve for the ensueing Half Year.

That *Regulation* was maintained by the brethren in Domatic Lodge until December 1811 when the Master who was elected for the period to June 1812 remained in office for a second term thus being the first Master to occupy the Chair as Master for the full period of one year; that was the period agreed at the Union which became the normal practice from then on. It is of some interest to note that the name of the Senior Warden who served with that Master, according to the official Return, was 'Sinclair' but no initial shewn thereon. Was it just plain co-incidence? Could it perhaps have been a family connection with Charles Sinclair who was so prominent in the Dispensation period and shortly afterwards?

Another *Regulation* of some interest concerns visitors:

THAT in order to preserve good Harmony, and encourage Master Masons, it is hereby Ordered and Declared, that no Brother under the Degree of a Master Mason, shall be admitted to visit this Lodge, upon any pretence whatsoever.

With that *Regulation* in mind we find an interesting set of circumstances arising from the following entry:

Deomatick Lodge N? 234 Nov?? 27—1786
Opened at half past 7 o clock When proceeded to raise B? Joseph Blicks to an Apprentice Mason .. paid 10.6d ...

The next time Bro Blicks name appears is on March 26 and then he is shewn as a 'visitor from Lodge 192' Of the fifty-eight names listed in the accounts section of the book fifty one are shewn as having paid £2.2.0, Bro. Blicks paid 10.6d, and one brother 5.0 which was probably his first instalment or deposit amount. The remainder were obviously paying by instalments and had not reached their total of £2.2.0 by the end of the accounting period. From those details it would be reasonable to assume that Bro Blicks was initiated as a Serving Brother, particularly as he was then the landlord of the Sun Tavern, Gate Street, Lincoln's Inn, an establishment to which the lodge was to move in December 1787. It would seem that he followed up his Freemasonry by being Passed and Raised in Lodge 192 in which he became a full member.

Items from the Early Accounts

Meeting-places for lodges in general were taverns or coffee houses the landlords of which were usually made as Serving Brethren to act as Tylers, messengers for the delivery of summonses or 'letters' from the Master, and as caterers. In the case of Tylers for Domatic Lodge, it has already been pointed out that they received scant mention in Minutes or Accounts and it is fairly evident that the duty was performed by the members, and often without payment. Bro John Perkins, one of the eleven initiated at that first Dispensation meeting, is one of the eight names mentioned as Tyler in the first Minute Book, but it seems that he was a handyman in every sense of the term. We find him as Treasurer for one period in 1787 and as Secretary for the following session and in the accounts section the following appears:

15 Nov. 1786	Paid to John Perkins for one days labour	2s 6d.

A sword, obviously for use of the Tyler, was purchased for the sum of three shillings just one week after Constitution. But another entry appears later:

2 June 1788	Sword	8. 0
	Ribband for -do-	1. 6

As the payment was made to the Grand Secretary who had supplied the Officers' jewels two years earlier, that entry would have been for a silver collar jewel and a suspending ribbon or collar.

Items concerning summonses are as follows:

31 July 1786	To Summons	£0. 0. 6
16 Aug. ,,	,, ,, ...	5
15 Sept ,,	To Br Cormack to Hundred Summons	3. 0
18 Dec. ,,	To Summons	2. 8
8 May 1787	For summonsing the Members	3. 0
-do-	½ Hund. of Blanks -do-	1. 3
14 Sept	For Summonsing the Lodge to attend Funeral of a Br of Lodge No. 4 ...	3. 0
-do-	½ Quire of Paper for the Use of the Lodge	0. 6
2 Oct.	For Summoning of Br Mardon to the Lodge & Br Gilbert	0. 3
-do-	For a Writing Desk for the Use of the Lodge & Porterage	16. 0

As the members of the lodge would have been resident within easy access to the meeting-place the delivery of summonses would not have been too arduous a duty. The Tyler, by that period was usually paid an extra shilling for that task. The 'Hundred Summons' supplied by Bro McCormick, Grand Secretary, may well have been specially printed for general use, requiring only the time and date of the meeting to be inserted by the Secretary and that supply would have lasted several meetings. The '½ Hundred of Blanks' would have related to a supply from a printing plate of stereotype design available to any lodge. The earliest summons, printed especially for Domatic Lodge, to have survived the test of time, is dated 1848 and has been reproduced as Plate No. 10. The

acquisition of a writing desk and supply of paper was quite a step forward in the secretarial field.

Bro McCormick, his name often spelt incorrectly as 'McCormack,' was the Grand Secretary of the Antients Grand Lodge but he was, in business life, a silversmith with premises in Horsehoe Alley, Moorfields. His masonic activity provided considerable scope for him as a supplier in general and for masonic jewels in particular, as the following item will show:

23 Jan. 1786	To McCormick for Jewels	£7.10. 0
7 Feb.	To Grand Secretary to Warrant Registry Books etc.	5.15. 6

We do not have a breakdown of the sum which included payment for the Warrant, but to arrive at the cost of the Constitution of the Lodge a comparison may be made with the details given in the chapter 'The Additional Warrant' below.

Some of the other items listed in the accounts section are also worthy of attention, for example in March 1786 the amount of £6. 6. 0 was entered for Candlesticks. At that cost they must have been ornate. Also, it would seem that some kind of bargain was struck regarding the following item:

31 July 1786	A Box the gift of Br James for which the Worshipful Master and the rest of the Fraternity in return raised Br Gilbert to the Degree of Master	£1. 1. 0

John Gilbert was initiated on February 17 1786, was Passed on May 29 and whilst there is no record in the brief Minutes for July 31, that entry in the accounts provides evidence of his raising.

Another item of some interest is the entry—'For a Stamp for Receipt ... 4d' dated 8 August 1787. As that amount would not in any way coincide with a levy for excise payment and there is no entry in the Minutes to complement it, probably it refers to a hand stamp then to be used for receipt purposes.

That year also, the members must have given thought to personal apparel of the Candidates during the ceremony of initiation and their action in that connection is reflected by the following:

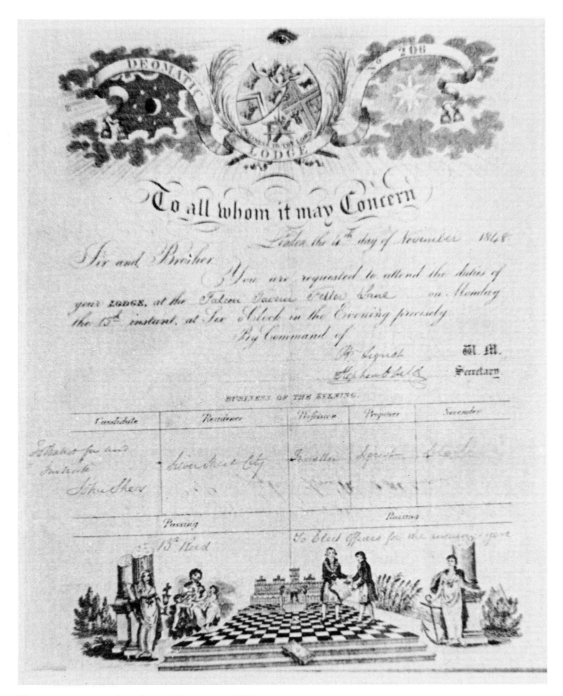

10 *An early summons from Domatic Lodge, dated 1848*

21 Dec. 1787   Paid for a flannel frock and
Drawers 12. 0

the expression 'properly prepared' certainly took on a different meaning at that juncture.

A quaint entry indicates that attention was also being paid to the appearance of the lodge itself:

23 Jan. 1788   For Quishen (Cushion) &
Cover £1. 10. 0

We do not have details of that but judging from the cost it might well have been a cushion, suitably braided upon which the three Great Lights of Freemasonry would have been placed, and maybe a fall to the front bearing the lodge number.

A term that appears now and then is 'Borrowed of the Benefit' which indicates that the brethren afforded temporary relief as loans from funds set aside for such purpose.

Another frequent item appearing in the accounts related to the obligation imposed upon the three principal officers of the lodge by another Regulation in the Antients *Rules and Orders*:

> THAT the Master and Wardens of the lodge shall attend the Grand Lodge, and the Stewards Lodge, when summoned by the Grand Secretary (if within Twenty Miles of London); and when in the Grand or Stewards Lodge he, they or either of them, shall have full Powers and Authority to transact all Matters relative to the Lodge, as well, full, and truly, as if they the whole Body were there present.

It accounted for such entries as:

15 May 1786   Paid to Master & Wardens
for attending Grand
Lodge & Stewards Lodge   £0. 7. 0
31 July   To Expences attending
Grand Lodge   2. 0
13 Sept   Paid to Master & Wardens
to attending Grand Lodge
on Quarterly Night   2. 0
30 July 1887   Paid to Br. Wilcox for attending the Grand Lodge   4. 0
-do-   Paid to Br. Cook for Attending the Grand Lodge &
Stewards Lodge   6. 0
23 Jan 1788   Pd to Br. Wilcox for Attending Grand and Stewards
Lodge   2. 6
    -do- to Br. Vale   3. 0
    -do-   Br. Abbot   3. 0
    -do-   Br. Wood   1. 0

The members deemed that to be a justified liability to be met from the general fund until there was a change of heart exemplified by a Resolution passed on 14 June 1795:

> It was agreed that in future the Master and the Wardens pay their own expenses when attending Grand Lodge and the Stewards Lodge.

It is of interest to note that the first reference to a floorcloth for masonic purpose does not arise until 1793 and one can only conclude that Domatic Lodge had been using whatever was available to them at landlord's premises. Independence, however, came to the fore on the 28 May of that year:

> A Motion was made and seconded and unanimously carried, that this Lodge should be provided with a proper Cloth painted for making Masons and that Bro. Thos. Butler, Painter, P.M. of 194 shall be ordered to prepare forthwith.

Two years later, either that item failed to withstand the amount of use, or alternatively the brethren wanted a design with different symbols thereon; another entry appears:

> 31 March 1795 Bro. Jarvis produced a Making Cloth for which he was paid £5. 5. 0.

It was in that year we find the only instance of the Master serving two consecutive terms of office arising from the default of a brother elected and then declining to serve. Although there is no reference in the Minutes, a penalty for such inaction is shewn by the following:

> Bro. Edward Shore, Jun. Warden, chose to fine according to the 5th Bye-law rather than to serve. Fined 2s. 6d.

Fines on members for a variety of offences were common but perhaps one of great interest is one relating to processions:

> 23 June 1793 A Motion was made and carried that each member attending the Procession on St. John's Day shall pay 2s. 6d. towards paying the Music and Expenses during the day at Bowling Green House and each attending member of the Lodge leaving the Procession to drink with any person or by themselves so as to interrupt the Grandeur of the Procession shall pay 6d for each such offence.

The Mystery of Missing Pages

The first Minute Book of Domatic Lodge is an interesting means of measuring the construction of the lodge and its behaviour pattern in relation to the Antients Grand Lodge, not only so far as it had developed by that period but also for the personalities who had emerged and risen to prominence. Yet, how much more would we have been assisted if certain leaves had not been cut from the book? What had been written on those leaves that caused someone to 'lose' them and, in the case of the first few meetings to re-write the Minutes?

The first six leaves have been cut from the book leaving narrow strips still bound in it which shew traces of writing proving they had been used. There were three meetings by Dispensation in the month of December 1785 and the date has been used four times, but on each occasion the year has been written as '1786' then to be followed by meetings in January, *et seq*, also with the year written as 1786. It would not be unreasonable to assume that the re-writing had taken place after the turn of the year and the brother concerned, in all probability Bro Sinclair, had failed to realise his aberration. It poses the question, 'What was the need to occasion such an exercise?'. Pencil corrections have been made in those dates but when that was done cannot be determined.

There is ample reason to involve Charles Sinclair in this as he was one of the three concerned in the formation of the lodge and was appointed to act as 'Sect. for the time being' when the officers for the new lodge were chosen at the meeting prior to the Constitution on 7 February 1786. In January of the previous year he had actually been voted as Grand Secretary elect for the Antients Grand Lodge, a nomination from which he withdrew in a regrettable mix-up which was straightened out by Laurence Dermott and finalised, conveniently, as the following extract from the Minutes of 2 March 1785 will shew:

Grand Lodge. The R.W. Bro. Lau. Dermott having also hinted in the above letter that he w^d support Bro^r. John McCormick as Grand Secretary to this R.W. Grand Lodge Bro^r. Charles Sinclair having resigned and no other Bro^r. being Candidate for the Office the Question being put he was thereupon Chosen Grand Sec^y. for the present year and accordingly enter'd upon the duty of his said Office.

The first Minute Book for Domatic Lodge covers meetings from 21 December 1785 to 30 June 1788 and in that period other pages have also been 'lost' in like manner. One leaf has been cut out between the meetings held on 22nd and 25th January 1786; the next occurs between May 28 and June 21 1787, one between September 25 and October 30, and two more between 30 October and November 27 of the same year. Traces of writing can still be seen on the strips remaining in the book in nearly all cases and that, to say the least, is complete frustration for any historian. An illustration of the point may be gathered from this item in the accounts section:

1787 Oct. 2.   For Summoning B^r. Mardon
                 to the Lodge and B^r.
                 Gilbert 0. 3d

The Minutes for the meeting appropriate to that item would have appeared in the book between those of September 25 and October 30 but the page has been cut out; we are denied any knowledge of that incident and it does seem that the Minute Book was at the mercy of whoever was involved in any 'cover-up operation' also that it was not an isolated case in the early days of the lodge.

The Additional Warrant No 258

We now come to what must be acknowledged as a unique event in the history of Freemasonry. In the development and progress of the Antients Grand Lodge it was not uncommon for Warrants to change hands, quite officially, and for lodges seeking a senior position on the Register to purchase a redundant Warrant with higher status than their own. An example of this activity may be seen from the following:

Grand Lodge. 6 December 1758.

Lodge Warrant No. 13 was purchased for Two Guineas by Lodge No. 63 who assumed the Name & Number and rank of L⁰. N⁰. 13.

The acquisition of Warrants for that purpose became the subject of a Resolution passed in Grand Lodge on 5 September 1792:

> RESOLVED AND ORDERED—THAT the R.W. Grand Master or his Deputy do grant Warrants as are vacant to Lodges making application for the same giving the preference or choice to senior Lodges: And that the sum of Five Guineas, to be paid into the Fund of Charity, shall be the established fees for taking out such senior Warrant.

It is on record for a lodge to possess a second Warrant, but only for a short period. In the case of Domatic Lodge it was done for a purpose other than for seniority as the number was junior to their own, yet they actually held meetings under both Warrants and made official Returns to Grand Lodge for each lodge. They kept the second Warrant alive in that manner for six years before disposing of it to other brethren who were responsible for what is now the thriving Lion and Lamb Lodge No 192.

Two factors must be taken into consideration in an examination of this strange behaviour. The first arises from the stated intention that headed the Minutes of their first meeting by Dispensation—'Making and Forming a Lodge of Operative Masons'—which was rigidly upheld by their rejection of those two capable brethren, Fenwick and Sinclair, a few months later. Yet it must be emphasized that the wording of the Warrant for their Lodge No 234 was in all respects similar to others then being issued by the Antients Grand Lodge (See Appendices B and C for comparison). However, it may well have been that the intended restriction although self-imposed, produced a sense of inhibition that caused the brethren to acquire a second Warrant with an open membership in mind that would bring them some social advantage. In the event it proved to be a case of opportunism that was screened in the Minutes for 15 December 1789:

The Worshipful Master proposed to add a new Warrant for the use of the members of this Lodge, to be under the denomination of a Working Warrant which proposal was agreed upon by a majority present, when Bᵣ Edwᵈ Cook, Bᵣ John Wood, Bᵣ Thoˢ Abbott, were chosen as Broʳˢ to get this new Warrant for the above use.

Before pursuing the subject we must pass on the second factor, which concerns Sir Watkin Lewes, member of Parliament for the City of London, an Alderman, and former Lord Mayor of London in 1780. Sir Watkin Lewes was initiated on 5 November 1781 in Lodge of Emulation No 12 on the Register of the premier Grand Lodge (Moderns), it is now No 21. On 20 June 1788 he was described as 'Modern re-made in No 1' which was the Antients Grand Masters Lodge No 1, a number retained after the Union purely by chance. All three degrees for that 're-making' were conferred. In the Antients Grand Lodge in 1789 he became Junior Grand Warden designate and, by Resolution of Grand Lodge was 'to be Passed the Chair unless in the meantime he was installed Master of a Lodge'. It was an opportunity for the brethren of Domatic Lodge to obtain the new Warrant and the three brethren who had been Masters of the lodge in the years 1786/87/88 respectively were well chosen for the project, lost no time in the discharge of that duty. Only nine days were to pass and the new Warrant No 258 was in their possession—the Master Designate written into it was Sir Watkin Lewes, with Edward Cook as Senior Warden and Thomas Abbott as Junior Warden; Bro John Wood, the first Master of Domatic Lodge stood down in favour of the distinguished London brother.

The only record of the Constitution of Lodge No 258 is that which has been written in Vol One of *Athol Grand Lodge and Stewards Rough Minutes* carefully preserved in the archives at Freemasons Hall, London. That record has been annotated 'This Report is not in the G.L. Minutes':

24 Dec. 1789. Constitution of Lodge No. 258 at the Sun, in Gate Street, Lincoln's Inn Fields.

11 *A typical 'Making-Cloth' as used by lodges during the eighteenth and nineteenth centuries*

Grand Lodge mett at two o Clock and open'd in Due form The Right Wor! James Perry Esq D.G. Master in the Chair, The Right Worshipfull Tho? Harper Esq. S.G. Warden, The Right W!! James Agar Esq. J.G. Warden, The R! Worshipful John Feakins Esq. G. Treasurer The W!! John McCormick G. Secretary who in the Name of the most Noble Marquis Earl of Antrim Proclaimed the New Lodge No. 258 Duly Constituted.

Grand Lodge Closed and Adjourned from this day to Monday the 28 day of December and to meet at the hour of 12 o Clock.

Visitors		Members	
B: Joshua Perkins	234	Sir Watkin Lewes Kn!	M
B: John Perkins	,,	Edward Cook 234	S.W.
B: John Taylor	,,	Tho? Abbott ,,	J.W.
B: Pat Donnaly	81	W!! Robinson	,,
		George Crouch	,,

The report is followed by a breakdown of the charges made in connection with the Constitution and it does help us to review the bulk figure entered in the accounts for the Constitution of Domatic Lodge a few years earlier:

G. Secretary's Charges to No. 258		
Petition	0. 2. 6
Warrant	1.14. 0
G. Secretary's Fees	10. 6
Book of Constitutions or Rules	10. 6
Pursuivant & Tyler	10. 0
	3. 7. 6

Grand Pursuivant and Tyler were salaried positions but on occasions of this nature they received additional payment, as shewn above.

At the meeting of Grand Lodge held at the Crown and Anchor Tavern, in the Strand, on 28 December 1789, Sir Watkin Lewes was duly installed as Junior Grand Warden, and listed among those present were:

Lodge 234 Master & Wardens & 8 Members
Lodge 258 Master & Wardens & 6 Members

The only brother in Lodge 258 who was not a member of Domatic Lodge No 234 was Sir Watkin Lewes, but it is surprising how easily Domatic brethren came to wear two hats according to whatever occasion. At a meeting on 25 January

1790, a little more than one month after the second Warrant had been obtained and Lodge 258 had been Constituted, the following members of the lodge were described as 'Visitors':

W. Robinson W.M. 258	Edward Cook P.M. 258
Thos Abbott P.M. 258	Sam Meeks 258
John Spence 258	John Marden 258

All were members of Domatic Lodge, but 'P.M.' placed after the names of Cook and Abbott was an entitlement achieved in the mother lodge, whereas 'W.M.' after the name of Bro Robinson is quite significant in that he assumed the Chair following Sir Watkin Lewes who, although Master Designate in the new Warrant, in effect, had only 'Passed the Chair' to qualify him for investiture and installation as Junior Grand Warden. Support for that view is to be found in the Minutes of the new lodge for their meeting of 11 February 1790, just one month later:

Opened at Seven-o-clock, the Worshipful Master and all Officers present. Proceeded to grant Sir Watkin Lewis Pass Master his recommendary Certificate to pass the Holy Royal Arch. . . .

We do not have a record of when or where Sir Watkin Lewes was Exalted in the Royal Arch but, because of his near association with Domatic Lodge it may well have been at the hands of those brethren who were qualified and formed into a Chapter for that purpose. Evidence of that nature, supported by the meeting known to have been held for a similar purpose at the Hercules Pillars in 1789, would have given strength to an earlier date for seniority of Domatic Chapter than 1793 which was allowed.

The paucity of records for the new lodge is most regrettable but there is no reason to think that it served any real purpose beyond what was achieved in passing its Master Designate through the Chair. Nevertheless, over the years that the Warrant was held, dues were paid by its members and Returns to Grand Lodge were made, until the following stage was reached on 27 October 1795:

The Worshipful Master ordered the Lodge to be summoned (again) on Friday, October 30, to take into consideration the disposal of the Lodge No. 258.

12 *Sir Watkin Lewes, Lord Mayor of London in 1780-1*

The Minutes for that Emergency Meeting recorded:

> The Worshipful Master informed the Lodge that he had ordered the Secretary to summons the Brothers for this Evening to take into consideration the disposal of the Warrant of the Lodge 258 as it being found that the Members not attending to the support of the two Warrants it being found that the Lodge 258 by this means was become burthensome, it being thought best to dispose of it, as an application has been made by a respectable company of gentlemen, when a Committee was appointed ... to have full power to dispose of the same in such a manner as they think meet for the good of the Lodge.

The Warrant was sold for one guinea and the Minutes of 26 January 1796 have these details:

> Bro. Wight presented the Lodge with the sum of One Pound one from Bro. Clark of 244, for having purchased the Warrant of 258 and afterwards relinquishing the same, which was put to the moneys for decorating the Lodge by unanimous consent of the members present.

The matter was finalised in April when it was stated:

> Bro. Wight informed the Lodge that the Committee appointed for the disposal of the Warrant 258 had disposed of the same and to be moved to the Bear and Wheatsheaf in Lower Thames Street and that the

Secretary do acquaint the Grand Secretary of the same.

and, according to the Register, printed in the June *Quarterly Communication Proceedings* of the Antients Grand Lodge, the meeting-place for Lodge 258 was The Bear and Wheatsheaf, as stated by Bro Wight.

Thus we find a small niche in masonic history for those brethren of Domatic Lodge who, for a period of just over six years, actually possessed and were actively engaged in the administration of two Craft Warrants, Nos 234 and 258, both of which were couched in similar terms but serving vastly different purposes by their design. Not all the brethren in Domatic Lodge joined Lodge 258, and it would seem that the interest of those who did flagged a little in due time, but the records prove that the acquired Warrant was, at all times, under the direct control of the brethren of Domatic Lodge whether or not they had taken up membership of Lodge 258. By general voice, and at their whim, without reference to the Grand Lodge, or to the Grand Stewards Lodge, the disposal was effected at their behest, the transfer was made and then officially approved. It underlines the fact that those outside the membership of Domatic Lodge were not in any way concerned with the affairs of Lodge No 258 during that period.

Thomas Abbott, who was Junior Warden Designate for No 258, was subsequently elected Treasurer of Domatic Lodge and held the office from June 1793 to June 1796. George Wight, who disposed of the Warrant 'for the sum of One Pound one', and is described in the records as 'W.M. 258', was appointed Secretary of Domatic Lodge which office he held from June 1793 to December 1797. He was twice selected by Grand Lodge to be one of the 'Nine Excellent Masters for preserving the Craft free from innovation', otherwise known as 'Nine Worthies', and served for the years 1797 and 1798. There is no mention of Past Masters' Jewels in Domatic records until 1796, it would seem that occupation of the Master's Chair for just six months was not a sufficient qualification but, in July of that year, we find:

Motion was made by Br Burton [Treasurer] and seconded, That Br Wight should be presented with a Past Master's Jewel at the expense of the Lodge.

The strange part of that is, Bro Wight did not serve as Master of Domatic Lodge but had been Master of Lodge 258, the second Warrant. The only office he ever held in Domatic was as Secretary so we may conclude that it was given for his valuable work in general.

In 1799 the Statute on the subject of Secret Societies was enacted and was then construed to place a ban on the forming of new masonic lodges. At that time the re-issue of Warrants from lodges that had become dormant, or that had lapsed, became even more necessary and indeed fashionable. They met the need when entirely new Warrants could not be granted and the transfer of an existing Warrant was deemed to be a continuance of the lodge. However, nowhere else do we find an instance of one lodge holding two Warrants, paying dues simultaneously under both to Grand Lodge, and conducting meetings under each in the same period, but in this case. it went on for six years. After the disposal of the second Warrant it is noticeable that among the visitors listed in Domatic records most of them came from No 258 shewing that an affinity did build up between those brethren and the brethren who acquired No 258.

In the eighteenth century lodge banners were far from being just a decorative asset, items for display at lodge meetings, they were functional for the purpose of processions whether masonic or public; brethren at that time were, literally, ranged under their respective banners. From Domatic records it may be seen that it took only four years for those brethren to reach the stage of adding that item to their equipment and whilst they did not supply a description of the banner itself we have to admire the businesslike manner in which the money for it was raised:

7 June 1970. When a motion was made by the Worshipful J. Chadwick, which was the most proper and advantageous method to pay for the flag or Bill delivd When it was agreed that each member on the Book was equally to pay share and share alike and it appeared there are 41 members and that each was to

pay by monthly Payment at 1s and the first Payment to begin in July, and it was agreed that none whose name are enrolled should have their Certificates untill their subscriptions and all dues are paid up.

In his *History of the Domatic Lodge No 177*, written for the Centenary Festival of the lodge, 12 February 1886, George Blizzard comments:

To understand the allusion in this Minute it must be explained that the 'Antient' brethren, unlike their 'Modern' rivals, during certain periods of their existence, had an annual procession on St. John Baptists Day, when G. Lodge attended Divine Service in state and afterwards held a summer feast, much as sundry of our Provincial Grand Lodges do nowadays. After the passing of the Act of 1798 [the Act is dated one year later] for the Suppression of Secret Societies— from the operation of which, however, the Freemasons were exempt, the practice of having a public procession was discontinued for a few years, but it was revived and continued in force to the year before the Union.

13 *Jewel of the 'Nine Worthies' or 'Excellent Masters' 1792-1813. The reverse side of the jewel is on the right and shows a figure levering the keystone from the arch*

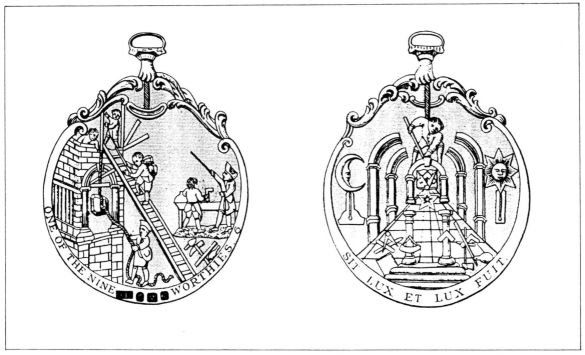

Brother Dermott produced a Certificate (signed by Edw. Spratt G.S.) under the Seal of the Grand Lodge of Ireland of his good behaviour and servitude &c &c &c.

Craft Certificates

In 1870 Richard Spencer, masonic publisher and supplier, of Holborn, published a reprint of some *Old Constitutions* which included one purported to have been *'taken from a Manuscript wrote about Five Hundred Years since'* as it was published by J. Roberts in 1722; it was known as the *Roberts Manuscript* and in that we have the earliest mention of certification and enrolment in masonic organisation:

> Additional Orders and Constitutions made and agreed at a General Assembly held at—
> on the Eighth Day of December, 1663.
> III. That no Person hereafter which shall be accepted a *Free-Mason* shall be admitted into any Lodge, or Assembly until he hath brought a Certificate of the Time and Place of his Acception, from the Lodge that accepted him.
> IV. That every Person who is now a *Free-Mason*, shall bring to the Master a Note of the Time of his Acception, to the end the same may be enrolled in such Priority of Place, as the Person deserves, and to the end the whole Company and Fellows may the better know each other.

In a comprehensive study with excellent Plates of specimen English Craft Certificates (*AQC* Vol 82) Bro T.O. Haunch, librarian and Curator of Freemasons' Hall, London, at that time, stated:

> However sceptical one may be of this tradition of an annual assembly of masons before 1717, it does seem that the seed of documentary proof of a man's being a mason (and the idea, too, of registration), was sown in operative masonry, and Anderson's copying of the Roberts *Constitutions* transplanted it into speculative freemasonry where it was to grow and flourish.

Craft Certificates, however, had been in use in the Irish jurisdiction before the Antients Grand Lodge came into being in 1751, indeed, in answer to certain irresponsible charges made against him in Grand Lodge on 2 March 1757—the following was written in the Minutes:

The *General Register* of the Antients Grand Lodge was compiled in 1751 and ruled in columns to shew details of individual membership. Next to the column headed 'Time of Discharge' is one headed 'Reason Why' and the entries in that are varied, having such comment as: 'Gone to Scotland by Certificate'—'Gone to Ireland by Certificate from ye Grand'—'Declared off by Certificate'—'Certificate'—etc. In the same year in Rules and Orders adopted by the Antients Grand Lodge, the subject was brought under proper control:

> THAT no Old Mason be admitted a Member of any Lodge except he hath been made in a Regular Lodge and hath a proper Certificate of his good behaviour and his not owing any thing in such Lodge and in Case a Member of any Regular Lodge shall be desirous to become a Member of any such Lodge he sues to come into must be assur'd that he is not Indebted to the Lodge he then belongs to — — Regist^y 6^d

> In the margin   All good men Accept^d upon proper Recommendation. No ReRegistery p^d to ye G. Sec. Except the B^r Absolutely quit his former Lodge.

The item produced the conditions for Joining Members well under control ensuring that only brethren who had been Initiated in a Regular lodge could be considered. The matter was taken a step further for Registration purposes by another item:

> 14. THAT if any Member of a Private Lodge shall be desierous of leaving the Lodge he belongs to to Join another, he must have a proper Certificate from the Master of that Lodge and Notice to be given to the Secretary of the Grand Lodge of his leaving the same, and the Mast^r of Lodge and the s^d Brother shall join shall report him to the Grand Lodge in Order to have him Register'd in the Grand Lodge Book to ye Number of the Lodge he is then removed to and to pay for the same the sum of Sixpence.

The sum of sixpence was increased to one shilling in 1753.

It seems out of character that the Antients should be credited with being ahead of the Moderns in administrative matters, but it was indeed so in this case as the first reference to Certificates from the Moderns did not occur until 22 July 1755. It implies that certificates, of a kind, probably letters given to serve the purpose, had been in use by their members but were then to be brought under official supervision:

Ordered that every Certificate granted to a Brother of his being a Mason shall for the future be sealed with the Seal of Masonry & signed by the G.S. for which Five Shillings shall be paid to the Use of the General Charity.

When that Regulation became known it produced a scathing comment from Laurence Dermott who added the following comment to his Minutes of the Antients Grand Lodge meeting on 27 December 1755:

MEMORANDUM
This Year 1755, the Modern Masons began to make use of Certificates though the Ancient Masons had granted Certificates time immemorial.

The Regulation was reinforced by a Resolution passed on 13 August the following year:

Ordered that a Copper Plate be engraved for printing the Certificates to be granted to a Brother on his being a Mason & that a Dye be cut & an Engine made wherewith to Seal the same ...

The influence of the Grand Lodge of Ireland on the practices of the Antients was apparent throughout their behaviour and the subject of Certificates was no exception. From the Annual Report given to Grand Lodge of Ireland on 21 December 1775, the following edict set the pattern:

Annexed is a Form of a Certificate for a Master Mason, which it is expected for the future you will make use of, to intitle the Bearer thereof to a Grand Lodge One, or Admission into any other Lodge, and as it will be the means of abolishing many absurd Expressions frequently inserted in Lodge Certificates:

Form of a Certificate for a Master Mason
To all whom it may concern. We do hereby certify, that Brother   is a regular Master Mason, in the Lodge No.   and has during his Stay with us, behaved himself as an Honest Brother
Given under our Hands and Seal of our Lodge, in this   Day of

	Sec	Master
		Sen Warden
(SEAL)		Jun Warden

Admitted on the Day of
Declared off on the   Day of

Prior to the Union in 1813 it was not the general practice for either of the two Grand Lodges to issue Certificates to their members except for specific reasons, and then only against what might well be termed a Clearance Certificate from the lodge to which the brother belonged and had been paying dues. On this subject, T.O. Haunch commented:

In the Grand Lodge pre-Union archives there are more than twice as many files of papers of Ancients Lodges as there are for those of the premier Grand Lodge, and this is partly accounted for by the great number of lodge certificate 'returns'. These range from scraps of paper with the necessary details scribbled on by hand (although still in the wording and form of a certificate) to elaborate documents and even engraved certificates complete with ribbons, seals, etc. (op cit p 176)

It is in the light of the development by that period that we turn to a few of the references to Certificates that appear in Domatic records. The first mention is in the Minutes of 15 November 1786 stating: 'Br. Broad drew his Certificate' and, one month later on December 18 we find: 'Br. Brooks drew his Certificate' No reasons are stated, but as they were both early members of the lodge would not have had occasion to obtain one from Grand Lodge, but it now appears that a clearance certificate from the lodge was granted in order to obtain one from Grand Lodge which would be needed to join another lodge in the same jurisdiction. The earliest Certificate from Domatic Lodge to have survived the test of time is dated 20 April 1801 and was issued to Bro Grainger; it is exact in every particular to the form we have seen which was required by the Grand Lodge of Ireland.

It seems that Bro Broad who 'drew his Certificate' in November 1786 did so in order to join another London lodge because he was actively engaged in Domatic Lodge for the meeting on St. John's Day, 27 December: 'proceeded to raise Br. Cook to the Master Chair for the ensuing half year ...' the officers being then named with their various offices, and then the Minutes continue: 'Likewise to past Br. Broad the Chair.' That matter will be dealt with later when the Royal Arch comes under review, but it shews that Bro Broad had not left London at that stage. Maybe he joined another lodge to enable him to make quicker progress as his name appears twice in later Minutes, 28 April and 24 May 1788 as: 'Visited by Br. Broad Master of 192'.

Another useful comment made by T.O. Haunch (*op cit* p 175) was:

> Members of the Antients Grand Lodge seldom seem to have retained possession—if they ever had it—of the Lodge Certificate issued in their name. It was sent either direct to Grand Lodge to be exchanged for a Grand Lodge Certificate or (often in cases of emergency) presented by hand to the Grand Secretary with an endorsement or covering note authorizing him to deliver a Grand Lodge Certificate against it. ...

The following entry in Domatic Minutes, 30 July 1787, shews how a brother was quite acceptable if, having demitted from his lodge, he produced the right kind of Certificate:

> Br. James Mecalle of St. Johns Producing a Proper Certificate was Proposed & Admitted a Member of this Lodge.

The title 'St. Johns' meant that the brother was a sojourner without current membership of a lodge, but having clearance from his last lodge had applied to the Grand Secretary and had been provided with a 'Proper Certificate' of registration which was the means of access to membership of another lodge and with whom such a Certificate had to be lodged—in this case Domatic Lodge. In the Minutes of 23 February 1789 that requirement is clearly stated regarding another joining member:

> ... Bro. Sam Mecho, previously of Lo. 168, Bath, was admitted as a Joining Member and deposited his G. Lodge Certificate in our trust.

Two cases of refusal to deposit such Certificates, touching Domatic Lodge, eventually were to lead to a directive from Grand Lodge on that subject. It will be remembered that at the end of 1787 Domatic Lodge changed their venue to the Sun Tavern, Gate Street, and Initiated Bro Blicks the landlord. He took only that one degree from them appearing in the Minutes four months later described as 'visitor 192'. In November 1788 he was proposed as a Joining Member in Domatic Lodge but in April the following year it is recorded:

> Br. Blicks the landlord was called upon to show cause why he would not deposit his Grand Lodge Certificate in our hands, when he refused.

Such behaviour may well have provided grounds for complaint and the matter was raised officially to the Grand Stewards Lodge when it was repeated by another brother later on. It also affected Charles Sinclair who, together with the offender was ordered to attend the Grand Stewards Lodge on 21 July 1790 for the matter to be sorted out. It caused the following to be Minuted in those records:

> The dispute between Sinclair and Ranger when Ranger was ordered to deposit and leave with the lodge he now belongs to his G.L. Cert. and in future do not nor any other brother retain possession of a G.L. Cert. while continuing a Member of any private Lodge.

Bro Ranger made his first appearance in Domatic Lodge as a visitor from Lodge 128 on 24 April 1786, only four meetings after the Constitution.

Reluctance to deposit Certificates with lodge Secretaries is also balanced by a similar attitude or inaction on the part of the latter in meeting requests for clearance certificates. The following is an early instance of that in Domatic records, although Minuted in the Grand Stewards Lodge:

> Stewards Lodge. 17 Dec.ᵣ 1790
> Upon hearing the Complaint of Richard Hall against the Lodge 234 Order'd that said Lodge grant him a Certificate of date June 1786 the time he declar'd off from said Lodge and in Case of their not doing so the Grand Secretary to grant said Bᵣ. Hall his G.L. Cert. to join any other Lodge thereon.

Because of its mention of a certificate we now come to what must be regarded as a classic of the age, a masterpiece by the Secretary of the lodge and well worthy of reproduction for other material of interest:

> Deomatick Lodge No. 234 May 26th 1788
>
> Opin'd at seven o clock in the printice when proceed to make Tomas Jones Boulter an apprintice Mason affter being preporly prepar'd by Br. Cook in emergency E going in the contrey call'd to refreshment at nine and call'd on at 10 when procedde to chuse officers when Br. Abbott was chose Master Br. Brockett senr. Warden Br. Cellers junr. Warden Br. Marden Secty. Br. Lumb Treasurer Br. Wilcox Tyler when Wm. Hawk stands prepos'd by Br. Lumb Jno. Burgess prepos'd by Br. Cole and visited by Br. Brode [Broad] Mastr. of 192 and Br. Connor by is desire drew is sertificate and clos'd at 10 o clock in good harmony.

In that account it should be noted that the Candidate was properly prepared by Bro Cook who was his proposer; it was a custom that linked with very early behaviour and even in the present era it is only the duty of the Tyler to 'see' that the Candidate is properly prepared. The record of Wm Hawk is of some interest in that he was proposed in lodge in December 1787 by a Bro Atkins, again on 31 March 1788 by Bro Cook, that was repeated on 28 April, on 26 May proposed by Bro Lumb and that is as far as it goes for his name does not recur and no Ballot was ever taken. The records shew Bro Lumb was Secretary for the first half of 1788 and Treasurer for the latter half which tends to shew that those offices in that period were being treated as a means of progression from Deacons to Warden. The Tyler, who is rarely mentioned, for the first half of that year was Bro Burnett followed in the next half by Bro Wilcox showing how well that duty was being treated as one for the members; Bro Wilcox had already been Master of the Lodge.

A strange set of circumstances surrounds an item in the Minutes for 29 September 1788: 'Br. Chadwick delivered his Grand Lodge Certificate and joined'. Very strange in fact because in company with others on 25 January 1786, whilst the lodge was still meeting under Dispensation, Chad-

wick was among those listed as 'made Apprentices and paid all Dues'. Even more interesting in that the lodge 'Open'd in the Second Part to Craft the Same and Open'd in the Third Part to Pass to that of Masters'; all three degrees taken on the same night. The progress in the lodge made by Chadwick can be traced, as Treasurer for the latter half of 1786, Junior Warden for the first half of 1787, again for the first half of 1789, Senior Warden for the latter half of that year, finally reaching the Chair as Master for the first half of 1790. There is no record that he 'drew his Certificate', but, as he was not in office for 1788 we may assume that he left London returning in September when he lodged his Certificate 'and joined' in time to be elected as Junior Warden for the first half of 1789.

In due course Domatic Lodge followed the style of others who possessed an engraved plate for printing the private lodge certificate, as well as a plate of similar form for printing the summonses. The earliest Domatic Certificate to have survived, now carefully preserved in Grand Lodge archives, is one that was issued to Bro. Thomas Barraclough and dated 21 January 1805, but for what purpose is indeterminate as that brother served offices in the lodge in an unbroken sequence to become Master in the second half of 1806. That Certificate is accompanied by another issued in July of the same year to Bro. George Nelson.

Antients and Moderns

In order to appreciate what would otherwise be insignificant entries in Domatic records and to assess the value of some rather bare references, it is necessary to set them against the broad spectrum of what was happening in Freemasonry in that era, in the general sense, but in London in particular. We can then determine how deeply they were involved or whether major events passed them as they flowed with the trends that evolved. Whilst brethren or companions having membership in Domatic did not themselves achieve historic prominence, there is little question that many of them are to be found in company with masonic

To All Whom it may Concern
We do hereby Certify that Brother
Richard Granger was made a
Regular Master Mason Feby 17th; 1800
And has During his Stay, Amongest
us Behaved Himself as Became an
Honest Brother. Given Under
Our Hands,
This 20th Day of April 1800.

John Gill   Master
Wm Mennell Senior Warden
Thos Bell   Junior Warden

John Barker Secretary Pro Tempore

14 *A Craft Certificate, hand written and dated 1800*

leaders who influenced the course taken by the Craft, the Royal Arch, and the administrarion of Freemasonry in the English jurisdiction.

The Antients Grand Lodge came into existence with the stated aim of preserving ancient forms of Freemasonry. They charged the premier Grand Lodge with the creation and adoption of innovations, as well as the neglect of established practises, and the alteration of what they deemed to be masonic landmarks. The exact differences between the ceremonial forms have not been detailed, for obvious reasons, but items have appeared in various records to guide us. From inception the Antients were in amity with the Grand Lodge of Ireland, the Grand Lodge of Scotland, and later by virtue of military lodges holding ambulatory Warrants they established a similar amity with various Grand Lodges set up the Americas and other overseas Districts. Within a short time they gained parity with the premier Grand Lodge, which, having been formed since 1717 and therefore was thirty-four years senior, remained an entirely separate organisation; the authority for each was self-contained. The membership, however, was not entirely loaded with partisanship, and individual reaction was comparatively masonic unless fanned into opposition by events. In 1777 an official stand was declared by the premier Grand Lodge:

18 April 1777. Resolved. THAT the Persons who assemble in London and Elsewhere in the Character of Masons, calling themselves 'Ancient Masons' by virtue of an Authority from a Pretended Grand Lodge in England, and at present said to be Under the Patronage of the Duke of Athol, are not to be Countenanced or Acknowledged as Masons by any Regular Lodge or Masons under the Constitution of England; nor shall any Regular Mason be present at any of their Conventions to give Sanction to their Proceedings, under the Penalty of forfeiting the Privilegies of this Society, neither shall any Person Initiated at these Irregular Meetings be Admitted into any Lodge without being re-Made and paying the usual Making Fees. Resolved. THAT this Censure shall not extend to any Lodge or Mason Made in Scotland or Ireland under the Constitution of either of these Kingdoms, or to any Lodge or Mason Made abroad Under the Patronage of any Foreign Grand Lodge in Alliance with

the Grand Lodge of England, but that such Lodges and Masons shall be deemed Regular and Constitutional.

It drew from Laurence Dermott a statement concerning the cleavage and the reasons which led thereto, and the mild manner in which he expressed himself at that stage shewed that he was prepared to turn the other cheek. In *An Address to the Fraternity* which he published the following year he stated:

... concerning the difference between Ancient and Modern, I think it my duty to declare solemnly that I have not the least antipathy to the gentlemen, members of the Modern Society but, on the contrary, love and respect many of them, because I have found the generality to be worthy of receiving every blessing that good men can ask, or Heaven bestow. I hope that this declaration will acquit me of any design of giving offence ...

In the body of that *Address*, Dermott made many points, amongst which he stated that Freemasonry as practised in Antients Lodges was universal, whereas what was called Modern Masonry was not; that a Modern mason could make his secrets known to an Antient, but not vice-versa without further ceremony; that it was not possible to initiate or introduce a Modern Mason into a Royal Arch Lodge—'the very essence of Masonry'—without making him go through the ancient ceremonies; that the present Modern Lodges were not to blame for so much deviation because innovations were made in the reign of King George the First (1714–1727) and the new forms had been received by them as orthodox. After a brief review of Clubs and Societies imitative of Freemasonry, or otherwise, Dermott added:

In this we are to view the fraternities of Ancient and Modern Free-Masons, who are now become the two greatest communities in the universe; the Ancients, under the name of Free and Accepted Masons, according to the Old Institutions; the Moderns under the name of Free-masons of England. And although a similarity of names, yet they differ exceedingly in makings, ceremonies, knowledge, Masonic language, and installations; so much, that they always have been, and still continue to be, two distinct societies, totally independent of each other.

The 're-Making' on both sides was common practice and the following are typical entries in the Minutes of lodges in that early period:

> Neptune Lodge (now No. 22) an Antients Lodge
> 24 June 1754. Lodge open'd at two—at *Noon* being at the Festival of St. John. Call'd off to Refreshment at three, Call'd on in order to make Bro!. Robert Whitehall an Antient Mason, he being a Moddren Mason before, Made him in all parts. Master enstall'd & Wardens, Call'd off the Second time to Refreshment. Call'd on to work. Clos'd at 10 with Good Harmony.
>
> Grenadiers Lodge (now No. 66) A Moderns Lodge
> 11 June 1766. B!. Cann proposed M!. Will!. Graham to be Re-made a Mason from ye Ancient to ye Modern in this Lodge which was agreed to nem con.

The greater the distance from London the process was easier and local friendships proved stronger ties than those forged by Craft Warrant. Lodges themselves were known to change allegiance or even to appear on the lists of both. We have an excellent example of such behaviour in a letter dated 8 August 1792 from Thomas Dunckerley, Provincial Grand Master in and over Hampshire, to William White, Grand Secretary of the premier Grand Lodge (Moderns). Dunckerley stated:

> ... At the request of the Corporation of Southampton I laid the first Stone of All Saints Church in that Town last Friday, for which purpose I had summoned the Lodges of the County to attend.
>
> I have the pleasure to acquaint you that a Lodge of *Antient* Masons of Southampton, near 60 in number, requested to join ye Procession, which I refused, unless they would come under authority of our Grand Lodge. In two hours time I received their Petition for a Constitution, and immediately granted them a Dispensation....

Brethren who were 're-Made' did not of necessity become members of the lodge in which the conversion took place, but often obtained a Certificate from that lodge to confirm their status. If, however, they did join then a Certificate from the lodge allowed them to apply for one from their new Grand Lodge affording them the facility of wearing any one of two hats according to fancy. We find various expressions for the 're-Making'

and they include 'apostatised', 'translated', 'healed' and others.

Domatic Lodge was slightly more than one year old when it dealt with its first application for 're-Making' and the event was recorded in the following terms:

> Deomatick Lodge No. 234. 16 April 1787
> Open'd at 8 o clock in the Apprentice. When proceeded to make Stephen Hackett and Apprentice mason likewise from that to a Fellow Craft and from that to the Sublime Degree of Master Mason he being a modern before. Call'd to refreshment at 10 o Clock Call'd on at half past. Visited by B!. Wade of 192 Clos'd at 11 in Good Harmony.

A directive on the subject had already been promulgated by the Grand Lodge:

> Antients Grand Lodge. 29 September 1785
> The proper Sum for Making Modern Masons Antient was carried in Majority to be one pound one shilling and a fine lay'd on Each Warrant if not Strictly observed the sum of one pound one shilling.

Such leniency, however, was not afforded by Domatic brethren for they treated the exercise as if the brother was a non-mason and made their 'going rate' a charge of £2. 2. 0. Nevertheless they had a fair share of 'conversions', with no favours conferred, always the fee they charged was £2. 2. 0.

Death of Laurence Dermott

In December 1787 Laurence Dermott retired as Deputy Grand Master being, at that time, sorely afflicted with attacks of gout. Great tribute was paid to him by his successor, RW Bro James Perry who stressed the distinguished service to Freemasonry that had been given by Dermott over his forty-seven years in the Craft. Laurence Dermott remained comparatively active, although severely handicapped at times, but there is a sad lack of information regarding his death and the place of burial. It is known that his last residence was in Mile End, Old Town, Stepney; that he died in June 1791 in the Parish of St. Dunstan, Stepney, but the location of his grave is unknown. The manner of the man may well be judged from one sentiment expressed in his Will:

15 *A printed Clearance Certificate dated 1805*

... I bequeath my inmost Soul to the immortal Creator of all things, my body to the earth; and all my worldly riches I bequeath to my dearly beloved wife, Elizabeth Dermott ...

Probate of his Will was obtained in London on 15 July 1791 by his dearly beloved wife, and so departed from this life, and the masonic scene, one who may be deemed to have had the greatest single influence in the shaping of Freemasonry throughout the world. Amongst the many lodges that he brought into being, he Constituted Domatic Lodge No 234 on 7 February 1786 in company with Thomas Harper and others of distinction.

Following the record of Installation of Master and Wardens on 24 June 1791 the Minutes of Domatic Lodge have an entry of some significance:

... The Lodge was clos'd and the Brethren proceeded to meet the Grand Officers at Mile End.

Although somewhat obscure, that could have meant only one purpose meaning that the brethren joined the procession at the funeral of Laurence Dermott and thus they paid due homage to that worthy and distinguished brother.

Three days later the lodge was visited by RW Bro James Perry, Past Deputy Grand Master, and RW Bro Thomas Harper Past Senior Grand Warden, and it would seem possible that the visit arose from their attendance at the funeral. The foregoing may well add a slim thread to the little that is known of that event. The affinity with Grand Officers of the day may well have led to the appointment of one of their members, for the Minutes of Grand Lodge, held at the Crown and Anchor, Strand, on 11 December 1793, include mention that 'John Taylor of No. 234 was elected J.G.W. for the year'. He was in very good company for his fellow Grand Officers for the year included:

4th Duke of Atholl, Grand Master
James Agar, Deputy Grand Master
John Bunn, Senior Grand Warden
John Taylor, Junior Grand Warden
Rev. Edward Barry, Grand Chaplain
John Feakins, Grand Treasurer
Robert Leslie
   and   } Joint Grand Secretaries
Thomas Harper
Robert Gill, Grand Sword Bearer
Benjamin Aldhouse, Grand Pursuivant
James Swan, Grand Tyler.

Attending funerals to pay respect to departed merit had quite a degree of priority, indeed, many brethren looked to their lodges for such arrangements. It was not unknown for a lodge to purchase a site to ensure a resting place for members of the lodge who might end their days in reduced circumstances. The following is an example of how well brethren kept faith with a member who had served them so well in successive terms as Secretary, Junior and Senior Wardens, and Master, from June 1792 to June 1794:

Laurence Dermott's signature

To The R! Worshipfull William Dickey Esq! Deputy
Grand Master, the R! W. Robert Gill Esq!, the R!
W. George Bowen Esq! J.G.W. or either of them—
Greeting

I hereby Certify that our late Deceased Brother
George Owen deceased late of No. 234 at the Six
Canns Holborn upwards of ten years a member of
said Lodge clear upon the Grand Lodge Books and
having performed all his Masonick Duties in every
respect to the intire satisfaction of this said Lodge
and having died in poor and Indigent circumstances
as appears by the Certificate of the Master and Wardens of said Lodge. It is most Humbly Requested that
an Order be granted for this internment the Lodge be
Summoned to attend the Funeral of our said Deceased Brother upon Sunday next at 2 o'Clock in the
afternoon from the Six Canns Tottenham Court
Road. Given under my hand this 1st day of Aug.
1798

[Signed] Rob! Leslie G.S.
[Annotated] Granted and let the Lodges be Summoned to attend According to Regulations.
[Signed] Robert Gill S.G.W.

At the meeting of Grand Lodge held on St. John'
Day 27 December 1787 with Laurence Dermott in
the Chair, by his recommendation to the Grand
Master which was duly approved, James Perry was
installed as Deputy Grand Master in succession.
The brethren then resolved:

THAT the thanks of the Grand Lodge be given to
the R.W. Lau. Dermott, Esq., Past D.G.M., who,
after 47 years zealously and successfully devoted to
the service of the Craft, had now retired from the
Eminent Station which he held, and to whose masonic
knowledge and abilities, inflexible adherence to the
Antient Laws of the Fraternity, and impartial administration of Office, the Fraternity are so much indebted.

It is one of the later tributes paid to Dermott that
has survived.

Uniformity in Ritual and Procedure

Uniformity in ritual and procedure among Antients lodges in London was comparatively easy to
control and the system of visitation by selected
Grand Officers for that purpose was helpful in
maintenance of their standards. Lodges of Instruction rose and fell but as the eighteenth century
came to an end and attention was being focussed
by all men of goodwill towards a Union of the
two authorities, and attitudes became considerably
warmer, they were of greater importance. Domatic
'Lodge of Instructions', as it was called, came into
being on 30 October 1808 and we are fortunate
that the Minute Book has been carefully preserved. The first page has the following:

LODGE OF INSTRUCTIONS
Every Sunday Evening at the Coach & Horses High
Holborn at 6 o Clock, when each of the three Degrees
of Ancient Masonry will be given by Brothers, who
will Regular Attend for that Purpose the following
Resolutions was agreed to by the Brothers Present
this Evening the 30 Oct! 1808
Resolved That the Three Principal officers to Represent the Lodge shall be Elected on the last Sunday in
every month and after such Election & there Taking
such Situations and do not attend they shall be fined
as follows the Worshipfull Master 6d ... The Sinior
and Jun! Warden 4d Each which fines shall be placed
in the hands of B! Thomas the Present Landlord as
Treasurer and Disposed of for Candles &c. &c. for
the School of Instructions and each Sum as may be
left in his hands shall be Expended in a way the Lodge
shall think Proper at the Conclusion of the Season
which shall be on the last Sunday in March 1809.
Resolved. That on Every Occashon the Lodge of Instructions shall be subject to the By Laws and Constitution of the Regular Lodge.

The book contains Minutes of meetings from that
date through to January 19 1812 with items of
varying interest, e.g., in the latter stage Deacons
also were fined for non-attendance if they had
accepted the appointment at a previous meeting;
also, that book was used in the customary manner

16   *A page from Domatic Lodge of Instruction minute book dated 27 November 1808*

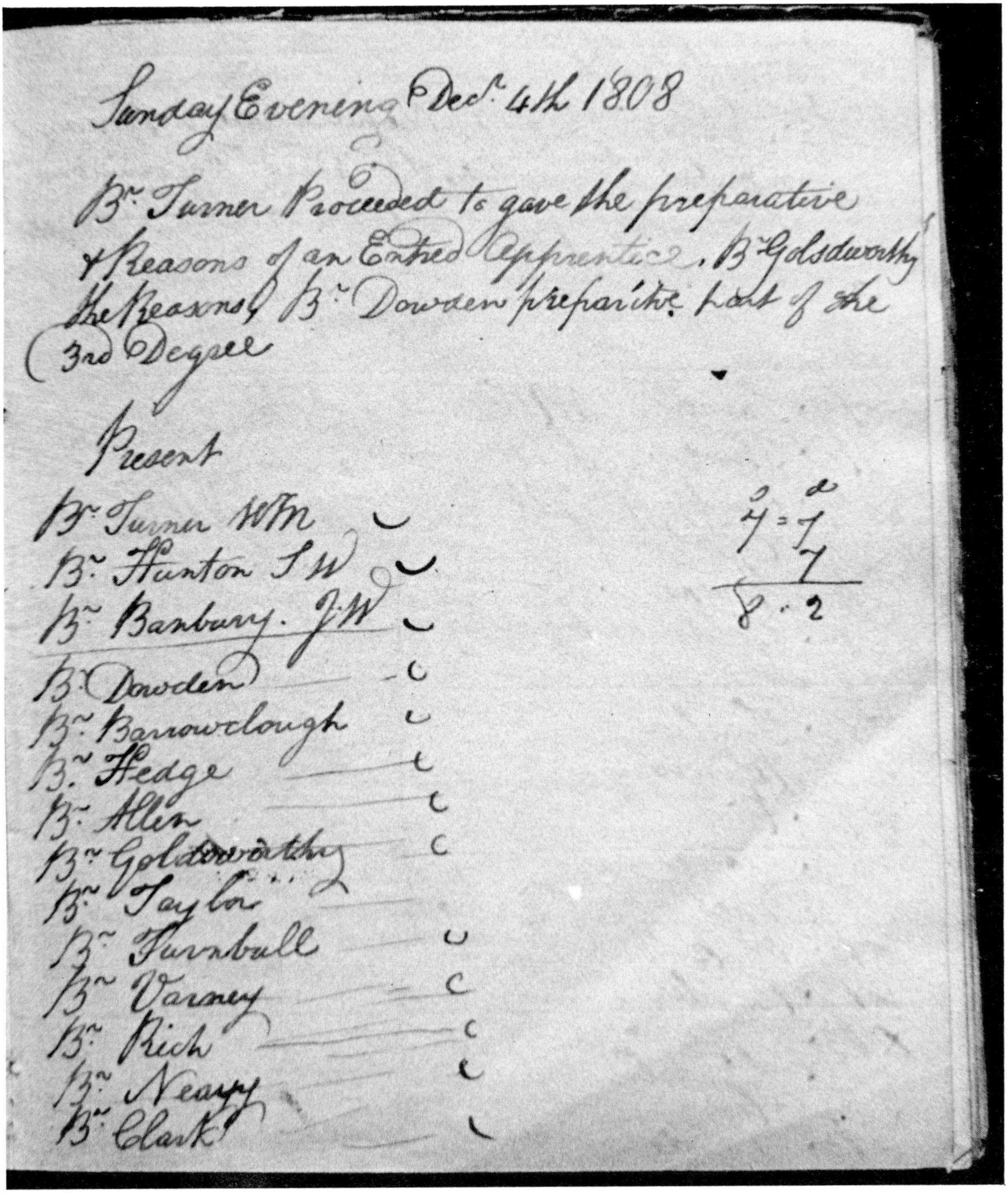

Sunday Evening Decr. 4th 1808

Br. Turner Proceeded to gave the preparative & Reasons of an Enterd Apprentice, Br Goldsworthy the Reasons Br. Dowden preparitve Last of the (3rd Degree

Present

Br. Turner WM
Br. Hunton SW
Br. Banbury. JW
B. Dowden
Br. Barrowclough
B. Hedge
Br. Allen
Br. Goldsworthy
Br. Taylor
Br. Turnbull
Br. Varney
Br. Rich
Br. Neary
Br. Clark

$$\frac{\overset{\frac{2}{4}=\frac{d}{1}}{7}}{8 \cdot 2}$$

17 *Another page from Domatic Lodge minute book this time dated 4 December 1808*

43

for accounts purposes by turning it upside down and using the last page as the first for entering income and expenditure, the income being from fines. Attendances ranged from a highest number of twenty-one to the lowest being six, but a fair average of twelve. The dues of 7d each appears to have been for the cost of refreshment as a balancing figure is shewn, annotated, 'House Bill Settled'. The main part of the record for each meeting is a list of those who were present, the payment of Dues, and a very brief reference to whatever ceremonial that was rehearsed. The following may be taken as fair samples:

Sunday Evening Dec. 4th 1808
B. Turner Proceeded to give the preparative & Reasons of an Entered Apprentice. B. Goldsworthy the Reasons & B. Dowden preparitive part of the 3rd Degree.

Oct. 22nd 1809.　Open'd in due form
Officers present　The W.M. then gave the preparative in the first degree. The Reasons by B. Banbury

[listed]

Decorations by B. Ward
2nd Degree the preparative by B. Banbury
Reasons by B. Ward
House Bill Settled.

The secretarial effort may be judged from the pages reproduced in Plate No. 16/17. Special attention is drawn to the name 'Goldsworthy' who was to make quite a stir in his opposition to adoption of the system later to be advocated by the Lodge of Reconciliation which was set up by virtue of the Union in 1813. He was an accomplished ritualist, had served the Antients Grand Lodge as one of the 'Nine Excellent Masters' whose duty it was to bring uniformity in Craft Working among Antients Lodges, and in due course was appointed as a member of the Lodge of Reconciliation. However, he was soon suspended from that body apparently for his resistance to certain decisions affecting changes in the ritual. He was of such prominence that he was later elected to the Board

of General Purposes and received the rank of Senior Grand Deacon in the United Grand Lodge.

Among the names listed on 31 December 1809 as attending Domatic Lodge of Instruction are three that are of interest: 'B. George Sinclair, B. Benjamin Sinclair, and B. Ch. Sinclair'. We recall that Charles Sinclair was one of the two brethren who did so much for Domatic in the Dispensation period and rejected when they applied to join the lodge, and one may be inclined to think that a truce had been reached and Bro Charles was now sponsoring two relatives. Soon after that meeting it was decided that lodge numbers should be inserted against those attending and whilst Bro. Charles Sinclair's name does not appear again the other two are shewn as 'B. Sinclair Jn. No. 234' and 'B. Sinclair S. No. 10'.

As one would expect, the attendance at the weekly meetings of the Lodge of Instruction consisted mainly of brethren from Domatic Lodge and most of the names are familiar in that respect for that period. After the resolution to insert lodge numbers we find that brethren had been attracted from various Antients lodges including the following: Nos. 2, 4, 5, 6, 13, 37, 104, 122, 141, 159, 205, 240, 259, 290 and 314. Obviously the quality of the work was to the standard acceptable to requirements of the 'Nine Worthies' whose eagle eyes would have been focussed on such activity. It tends to recommend the quality of performance and it is possible also that the centrally situated venue and the regularity of the meetings had a strong bearing on the mixed attendance.

In the Minutes of 6 October 1811 is an indication that punctuality was a prime consideration:

A motion was made by B. Purton seconded by B. Allan that the Secret. be free of dues if not attending dureing the Evning to fine six pence. That the W.M. be fined 6d and the Wardens 4d each, Deacons 2d each if not in the Lodge at a quarter past six o clock.

Although in the eyes of brethren from both sides a Union of the two Grand Lodges was most desirable, and Lodges of Instruction as a whole were doing excellent work in rehearsing and demonstrating 'acceptable' forms of ceremonial, there remained a hard core of brethren strongly determined that fraternization should not take place until terms and conditions of such a Union be made known. An example of that attitude is to be found in the records of Lodge of Fortitude No 6 (now Lodge of Fortitude and Old Cumberland No 12) where on 7 March 1810 it was stated:

... The Secretary was instructed to inform the Master of the Lodge of Instruction, held under the sanction of the Lodge, that the introduction of Athol Masons was totally unconstitutional, and strongly recommended to him by letter not to admit Athol Masons until the result of the anticipated Union takes place. (c/f Ivor Grantham, *Collected Prestonian Lectures*, pp. 334–35)

That attitude could not have been farther from the minds of brethren of Domatic Lodge of Instruction for, within a month of that date, their Minutes for 1 April 1810 contains a list of twenty-eight being in attendance, fifteen names bracketed with the note: 'of the Prince of Wales's Constitution Obligated as Master Mason in the Ancient Craft'. One name, however, is shewn as 'B! Mivet' and, allowing for the licence used in the spelling by individuals in that period and as it is quite an unusual name, it may well have been Bro James Mivart who was a member of the special Lodge of Promulgation set up by the Moderns Grand Lodge on 26 October 1809 for the purpose of communicating to brethren under that jurisdiction a form of ritual that would be acceptable to the Antients. No other person with a name anything like that has come to prominence in Freemasonry and a visit to the Lodge of Instruction from such a brother is in keeping with the prevailing circumstances and one may be given to think that here it was that he was obligated in the Antient form. James Mivart became Master of No 128 (now Burlington Lodge No 96), was prominent in the field of ritual and, on 27 November 1823, was one of the Founders of Emulation Lodge of Instruction (now Improvement).

The Lodge of Promulgation, whose membership included James Mivart, lasted from 26 October 1809 until 5 March 1811 and in their *Report* it was stated:

... having derived the most authentic information from the purest sources; and of having so settled and determined a proper engagement thereof as henceforth to render all the ordinary Ceremonies of the Craft, in practice simple, in effect impressive, and in all respects strictly conformable to ancient practice ... special care has been taken in every respect to prefer as concise a mode of arrangement as is consistent with a retention of essentials; scrupulously avoiding at the same time any sacrifice to brevity at the expense of the Ancient Forms they are directed to ascertain and restore. ...

That was the manner in which brethren were conducting themselves in a critical period of English Freemasonry which was then wavering on a difficult course towards a desired unity, steered by those who, although having the common purpose to join together, had for so long been travelling their separate ways. The tolerance shewn by some on opposite sides, and the enthusiasm of some to press towards unity brought problems, not the least of which was an incident that involved the Master of Domatic Lodge, the details of which are contained in official records:

Stewards Lodge 19 Sep! 1810
Bro! Thomas Gorton gave Notice in writing that he had a charge to prefer against the Lodge N⁰. 234 viz., inasmuch that they had resolved among themselves to admit Modern Masons into that Lodge without previously initiating them in the Antient form And that at their regular Lodge Night in July last Henry White a Modern Mason of Lodge 352 was permitted to Visit and had the Masters Obligation given in open Lodge by the Master in the Chair Bro! Banbury—the said Brother Banbury being in attendance with his Minute Book according to the Summons by the Grand Secretary being called upon to Answer to so serious a Charge Admitted the Charge to be right but said he Conceived he was justified in so doing as it had been Carried by the Unanimous voice of the Lodge and which he Considered they had a right to do.

The Stewards felt as much astonished at the defence as in the nature of the Offence whereupon It was resolved and Ordered That the said Lodge No. 234 had infringed upon the fundamental principles of the Ancient Craft in grossly violating the Solemn Order of the Grand Lodge of 1st June 1757. The said Lodge to be and the same is hereby suspended from its

Masonic functions and it is Ordered That the Warrant 234 be delivered into the hands of the Deputy Grand Master until it should otherwise be disposed of. . . .

Fortunately for the brethren of Domatic Lodge it was restored to them at a later stage of that meeting following appropriate action on their part which was recorded in the following terms:

The Petition and Memorial Signed by the Master Wardens and Secretary and several Past Masters of Lodge 234 in Attendance shewing that they were very sorry for the Conduct and Offence they had been guilty and undertaking to recind all and every Motions that might appear on their Books and also not to permit nor the same to be acted upon in future nor infringe in any manner any of the Orders of the R.W. Grand Lodge. The Warrant was thereupon restored and the Lodge reinstated under the Direction of the R.W. Dep. Grand Master.

Whilst the matter was thus settled by prompt diplomacy on the part of responsible brethren of the Lodge, so far as Bro Banbury was concerned it was far from finished as afterwards he stupidly condemned Thomas Harper, Deputy Grand Master, for his initial judgement. That too was to rear its head within a very short time and we take up the story again from the Minutes of the Stewards Lodge:

Stewards Lodge   21 Nov.! 1810
Complaint against Bro. Banbury for most unjustly and maliciously Calumniating the character of our Most Worshipful and respected Brother the Deputy Grand Master and in support of the charge called upon and produced Bro.! Tho.! Hunton W.M. Elect of the Lodge 234 who stated in direct Terms the Expressions used by Bro.! Banbury in a Conversation he had with him on 23rd Oct.! last tending to degrade the Character and Conduct of the Deputy Grand Master, And pretending the matter would be represented to His Grace the Duke of Atholl our Noble Grand Master; And that therefore he would not long be Continued in the Office of Deputy Grand Master.

Bro. Banbury being called upon for his defence acknowledged the purport of the Conversation and words spoken by him as stated but pretended that they were Communicated to him in Secret and under the Solemn Obligation of a Master Mason whose

Name he would not give up and must abide the Consequences be what it may. He was Ordered to withdraw.

After much deliberation on the business he was again called in and requested to Consider of his Conduct, if he had any Apology to make or anything to offer in Mitigation or defence it was incumbent on him so to do. He Answered he had Nothing further to offer, the Stewards Lodge must use their discretion, he must abide the consequences.

It was then upon Motion made & Seconded. Resolved Unanimously That the said Thom.! Banbury be and is hereby expelled and deprived of all his Masonic Rights and privileges from this day. The said Thomas Banbury being again called in the above resolution was made known to him by the R.W. Senior Grand Warden Bro.! Malcolm Gillies and he heard the same and retired in silence.

The following month Banbury presented a Petition that was supported by a number of Past Masters and the Masters of several lodges asking for re-instatement and for a re-hearing of his case but, unfortunately for him, that was unanimously rejected. Nine months later another Petition was filed which this time met with an approval that perhaps had been earned during the period of expulsion:

Grand Lodge   4 Sep.! 1811
The following Petition from Thomas Banbury late of Lodge 234 was read and Ordered to be inserted in the Minutes viz., To the R.! Worshipful the Grand Lodge of Ancient Free and Accepted Masons. The Humble Petition of Thomas Banbury late member of 234 sheweth that about September or October last he circulated a false and calumnious report of the R.! Worshipful the Deputy Grand Master for which he was very justly expelled by your R.W. the Grand Lodge.

Your Petitioner is conscious of the impropriety of his Conduct in acting towards the R.W. the Deputy Grand Master in such an Unwarrantable and unjustifiable a Manner in uttering so base an unfounded Calumny do with the Most sincere Contrition intreat the R.W. Deputy Grand Master to intercede on behalf of your Petitioner with this Grand Lodge.

And if upon serious and liberal Consideration which is the peculiar Characteristic as to be restored to his former privileges his future Conduct will be proof of the sincerity of his professions contained

18 *Peter Gilkes, eminent ritualist and preceptor*

herein and your Petitioner as in duty bound will ever pray and so forth This Petition is Recommended by Broʳ. Wᵐ. Fox, P.M. of Lodge Nº. 4, Brº. Stepⁿ. Morton, P.M. 104 Jnº. Ward, P.M. 234

It was Moved and Ordered that the Petitioner (being in waiting) be Called in and restored to his Seat in Grand Lodge as Past Master of Lodge Nº. 234. Broʳ. Banbury was then called in and after a Suitable Admonition from the R.W. Deputy Grand Master, he was restored and took his Seat in Grand Lodge this meeting.

The erring brother had been brought back into the fold but we find that he did not stay very long with Domatic Lodge as he is shewn in official Returns as 'Resigned 1812'. It is evident that he was looking for wider horizons as he laid the founda-tion for a lodge that was to attract some outstanding Freemasons, amongst whom we find Dr R.T. Crucifix who was mainly responsible for what was to become the Royal Masonic Benevolent Institution and was editor of the *Freemasons' Quarterly Review* from 1834; Peter Gilkes, the eminent ritualist and Preceptor; George Claret the controversial compiler and publisher of masonic rituals, the earliest of which is dated 1838 and bore the phrase—'comprising those taught by the late Peter Gilkes'—with whom he had been in close collaboration: it is to Claret that Freemasons of today owe the respectability of printed masonic rituals, for he pioneered in that field and was the first printer to be almost accepted as a purveyor of manuals that were not treated as masonic exposures.

Bro Banbury joined forces with others who had been members of Domatic Lodge and they combined in obtaining the Warrant of a lodge that had been Constituted in 1765, lapsed in 1768 and had remained dormant since that time. The only record of the Constitution of their new lodge is contained in the *Rough Minute Book* of the Antients Grand Lodge and is therefore worthy of comparison with what is on record for Domatic:

Grand Lodge of Emergency   13 July 1813
Present: R.W. Br?. Thomas Harper Dep?. Grand
              Master
              Malcolm Gillis S.G.W.
              Robert McCann J.G.W. (pro Tem)
              Robert Leslie G. Sec
              W. Fox P.M. No. 4 G.Swd.B. (?pro
              Tem)
Grand Lodge opened in due form. Warrant No. 136 Granted and Revived at Queen's Head, Little Pulteney S?. and the Master and Wardens thereof Installed with suitable Charge and Admonition from the R.W. Deputy Grand Master the Grand Lodge closed and adjourned thereon and the Lodge N?. 136 was opened in due form.

Temple Lodge, as it was eventually named in 1816, is now No. 101 on the Register of United Grand Lodge. It was one of the last six lodges Constituted by the Antients Grand Lodge in 1813 prior to the Union at the end of that year. That list is as follows:

Present Nos	Name	Date of Warrant
101	Temple Lodge	2 July 1813
209	Etonian Lodge of St. John	13 ,, ,,
246	Royal Union	29 ,, ,,
175	East Medina	8 Sept. ,,
54	Lodge of Hope	12 Nov. ,,
121	Mount Sinai	21 Dec. ,,

Of the eight Founders of Lodge No 136 (now Temple Lodge), seven had resigned from Domatic Lodge for whatever reasons and at various times, but they gathered together in support of Banbury in this venture; the other Founder was the landlord of the Queen's Head, Soho. A glimpse of their masonic records is of some interest:

Thomas Banbury—Breeches Maker—Initiated in 234 in 1808—WM 1810—Resigned 1812—Master of the new Lodge 136.
James Blackmore—Smith—Initiated in 234 in 1809—Resigned 1810—Senior Warden of the new Lodge.
William Blackmore—Smith—Initiated in 234 in 1809—Resigned 1812—Junior Warden of the new Lodge.
Thomas Allen—Plasterer—Joined 234 from 264 in 1810—Resigned 1812.
John Ward—Coach Painter—Initiated in 234 in 1803—WM in 1806—Shewn in Grand Lodge Register as 'Resigned 234' but no date given.
Job Davis—Messenger—Initiated in 234 in 1812—Resigned 1813.
William Martin—Coach Maker—Initiated in 234 in 1812—Resigned 1813.
William Lloyd—Victualler—No masonic details available—Not a member of 234. Landlord of Queen's Head.

Those brethren were the Founders of one of the last six lodges on the Antients Register, a quite significant feature if we bear in mind that after the Union of the two Grand Lodges no Warrants were granted or re-issued in London from 1813 until 1839.

In January 1821 there were nine members present and three visitors including Peter Gilkes who, according to the Minutes, 'Installed the Master in a most impressive manner'. That remark is of some importance as the Installation ceremony did not receive the attention of the United Grand Lodge until 1827 when a special lodge was Warranted for a short period to produce uniformity for the conduct of that ceremonial. It would appear that the attendance of Peter Gilkes anywhere attracted interest and Temple lodge was no exception for, at the Installation of Bro Mansell on 5 January 1829 although there were only eleven members of the lodge there was a total of twenty visitors. The ceremony was performed by Gilkes but that meeting was the last one attended by the Master whom he installed and the following year saw his resignation. However, Peter Gilkes occupied the Chair of Temple Lodge five times during that term of office in the absence of the Master and went on to instal the successor. For services rendered between 1821 and 1832 to Temple Lodge in particular, the brethren elected him to Honorary Membership but regrettably that distinction was short lived as Gilkes died the following year. In a biographical article in *Freemason's Quarterly Review* (1834) it states, *inter alia:*

> ... he filled successively the chair of 23, 188, 201, 211, 318, 259, and 7, several times each and died in office as Master of St. Michael's Lodge No. 255.... The difficulties Bro. Gilkes had encountered in perfecting himself in Masonry made him resolve to teach gratuitously such brethren as were disposed to attend him every day from one o'clock till the time to attend some lodge or other; he was always ready to receive them for this purpose, and even made several journeys into Lincolnshire, Cambridge, and Norfolk, refusing all remuneration further than the expenses of his visit ... He was in a manner something Johnsonian in regard to Masonry—no advantage could be taken of him in lodge—he would not allow the slightest deviation in *word*, or *manner*, or *matter* to please the most learned or the most accomplished in other subjects; we have observed him correct many men of rank and influence for deviations from the standard Masonic illustration, and who, to their credit, acknowledged the reproof with all courtesy which became their allegiance to the Craft....

In his youth he must have been an extremely powerful man, for when in his 67th year, on his return from the Blackfriars Lodge, he was attacked in Lincoln's Inn Fields by four men, three of whom he knocked down; he generally carried a cook's knife to defend himself with in case of attack; but fortunately he had left it at home on the night of the attack.

Although universally held in esteem amongst Masons, his conduct was always characterised by good sense; he never aspired beyond his station in life, and *declined the honor of an office in the Grand*

19 *The memorial tablet to Peter Gilkes in St James' Church, Piccadilly*

Lodge, because he considered that his circumstances in life were not equal to the appointment....

Peter Gilkes died on 11 December 1833 and was buried on the 19th in St. James's Churchyard, Piccadilly. The following month a Committee was formed to collect subscriptions for a monument to be erected to his memory. Stephen Barton Wilson, Past Grand Deacon, a close friend and pupil and one of the three instructors who carried on the high standard of precepting, designed and executed the memorial tablet placed in the South aisle in St. James's Church. It bears the inscription:

SACRED
To The Memory Of
Brother PETER WILLIAM GILKES, P.M.
A Zealous, Active and Distinguished Freemason,
who departed this life December 11th, 1833,
in the 69th year of his age.
This Monument was erected by several of the
Brethren of the Masonic Order to Commemorate
their high esteem of the Character and Talents
of their departed Friend.
1834

For an impression of this brother's style see Plate No. 18 which shews him wearing the gallows square form of Past Master's collar jewel, and the Royal Arch jewel of the Order on his left breast.

Before passing from the subjects of Temple Lodge and Peter Gilkes matters would be incomplete if reference were not made to another outstanding character and associate in the person of George Claret. He was in close company with Peter Gilkes as an ardent pupil, attender at Lodges of Instruction, and at the official Lodge of Reconciliation set up for the purpose of standardising Craft ritual forms, after the Union. About the year 1819 Claret left London for Gloucester, where he continued his masonic activity in no mean style. But in 1830 he returned and then resumed his association with Peter Gilkes, becoming a Joining member of Temple Lodge ('from Lodge 401' although his dues had ceased to them five years earlier). He was indefatigable in his work for and on behalf of Temple Lodge but unfortunately it all turned sour and ended on a sad note. (See 'George Claret 1783–1850, Ritual Printer' by Roy

A. Wells, *AQC* Vol 87 for a full study)

For his useful contribution to posterity in setting a pattern for acceptance of printed manuals for both Craft and Royal Arch, George Claret richly deserves his place in London Freemasonry. He suffered the slings and arrows winning his way as a masonic printer and publisher, as well as a supplier, and set down for the brethren the nearest we will ever get to the form of ritual that was approved but never officially printed. He won respectability for the printed word out of the strong condemnation of all previous attempts which were ever dismissed as masonic exposures. For some idea of his trading see Appendix E for a copy of a leaflet that he distributed in 1844. Dr E.H. Cartwright, an eminent masonic scholar, in *A Commentary of the Freemasonic Ritual* (Fenrose, 1973) wrote:

> After Gilkes's death, George Claret printed a ritual which, with a degree of probability amounting to virtial certainty, presented Gilkes's working.... it is the earliest complete record of any post-Union working we have ... Claret's ritual and its numerous subsequent editions were effectively brought to the notice of the Craft at large and, the usefulness of a printed ritual being quickly recognised, they found their way to all parts of the country. There can be no doubt that quite a number of provincial Lodges, where copies had been introduced, brought their workings into accord with the version therein presented, in many cases, pretty certainly at the cost of dropping old and perfectly legitimate variants. It was thus that Gilkes's rendering of the ritual became so widely known and adopted.... The publication, and the wide-spread use, of the successive editions of *Claret's Ritual* resulted in the disappearance of a large number of old workings and a much greater uniformity ensued.

The link between Claret, Gilkes, and the Lodge of Reconciliation, is well forged in a letter from William Henry White, Grand Secretary, sent on 6 September 1843 to the Master of Lodge 523, Kidderminster, Worcestershire (quoted by Henry Sadler in his *Notes on the Ceremony of Installation*, Kenning, 1889):

> In reply to your letter of the 5th instant enquiring whether any alterations have been made in the Cere-

monies of Initiation, &c., since the late P. Gilkes was in the Country; I beg to say (without knowing at what period that visit took place) that no alterations have been made since the G. Lo. formally approved and decided on them in the year 1816. Br. Gilkes was fully Master of all the Ceremonies, and I believe most strictly observed them.

I remain, W. Master,
Yrs fraternally,
W.H.W., G.S.

Attention to the Lodge of Reconciliation will be given in later pages but we have yet to look at the efforts made towards bringing the two Grand Lodges together, eventually achieved on 27 December 1813.

Towards the Craft Union

Although the Antients Grand Lodge came into existence to preserve 'ancient forms of Freemasonry', having charged the premier Grand Lodge with neglect of certain items of ceremonial and the introduction of innovations, there was no real animosity between the two organisations. The situation is best described as just plain non-recognition on both sides, brought about by the 'differences' some of which were outlined by Laurence Dermott in his published *Address* of 1778. However, those 'differences' did not always prevent fraternisation between friends on both sides, honour could easily be satisfied by the 're-Making' process if visits were under contemplation. It was no problem for brethren to belong to lodges from each Register, to possess a Certificate from each Grand Lodge, and not unknown for a lodge to possess Warrants from, and to pay dues to, both Grand Lodges.

Various brethren rose to the fore in their efforts to heal the breach between the Moderns and the Antients and one in particular, who came to a sad end in Freemasonry, was perhaps well before his time, for undoubtedly Captain George Smith was a somewhat controversial character. He was appointed Provincial Grand Master in and over Kent in the year 1777 by the premier Grand Lodge, and the following year as Superintendent of the County of Kent by the Grand and Royal Chapter which had been set up in 1766 by Moderns brethren to control the unrecognised Royal Arch. His sympathies with the Antients is shewn by his classification of the Royal Arch as 'the 4th Degree of Masonry' recorded in Grand Chapter *Minute Book No. 1*:

8 April 1774. B^r Capt Smith read to the C^{ns} a Dissertation on the 4th Degree of Masonry contain^g many Instructive & Ingenious Remarks & rec'd the Unanimous Thanks of the C^{ns} from the Chair.

Capt George Smith was an Inspector at the Military Academy at Woolwich and it was from there his letter was sent on 15 November 1776 to James Heseltine, the Grand Secretary, which included the following:

1. His Grace the Duke of Athol would wish to know by what authority the G.L. of England, pretends to a supremacy over the G.L. of Scotland instituted by Royal Charter granted by King James the Sixth to the family of Roslin in the year 1569 and then acknowledged to be the new head and first Lodge in Europe.
2. Why the G.L. of England has thought *propper* to alter the mode of Initiation, also the Word, *password* & Grip of the different degrees in Masonry.
3. Whether Dermott constitutes Lodges in his own Name or in the name and Authority of the Duke of Athol, and whether anything can be laid to his charge, inconsistent with the character of an honest man and a mason.
4. Whether any mode of Union could be thought of, and in such a manner, that might appear probable to both parties.

It was an early attempt to have the matter assessed at high level but all it seems to have produced was a hardening attitude in his own Grand Lodge, for the Moderns shortly afterwards passed their Resolution which, in April 1777, literally outlawed the Antients. All that the Resolution drew from Laurence Dermott was his evaluation of the state of affairs in his *Address* from which we can detect a sympathetic chord having been struck by Capt. Smith, for he, too, expressed a heartfelt desire which was worded in the last paragraph:

I shall conclude this, as I did in former editions, with

saying, that I hope I shall live to see a general conformity and universal unity between the worthy masons of all denominations.

But it was not to be in Dermott's lifetime as he died in June 1791 when the separation was even wider and that division having official blessings from both sides. Bitterness and contention had, by then, built stumbling blocks frustrating many attempts to create unity at official levels. Following further derogatory statements made against their jurisdiction, at a meeting on 2 March 1802 the Antients Grand Lodge issued an examination of the state of affairs between themselves and the Moderns which ended with:

> ... The Ancient Grand Lodge of England has thought it due to its character to make this short and decisive declaration on the unauthorized attempts that have recently been made to bring about a union with a body of persons who have not entered into the obligations by which we are bound, and who have descended to calumnies and acts of the most unjustifiable kind. They desire it therefore to be known to the masonic world, and they call upon their regular Lodges, their Past and Present Grand Officers, their Royal Arches and Masters, their Wardens and Brethren, to take notice, that they cannot, and must not, receive any person who has not received the *obligations of Masonry according to the Ancient Constitutions*, as practised by the United Grand Lodges of England, Scotland, and Ireland, and the regular branches that have sprung from their sanction—And this is our unalterable decree. By Order of the Grand Lodge.

We should now take into consideration one particular lodge on the Register of the premier Grand Lodge, then No 15 but now Globe Lodge No 23. In his comments on *Memorials of the Globe Lodge No. 23, 1723-1861*, Henry Sadler made special reference:

> ... It is indeed remarkable that the Globe, which derived its authority from the Grand Lodge of the Moderns, should have admitted to membership so many brethren who held prominent positions in the Grand Lodge of the Antients. Of the five brethren who signed the *Articles of Union* on behalf of the Antients, three were members of the Globe; they were Thomas Harper (Deputy Grand Master) the well-known

Jeweller and Silversmith, *to whom I consider belongs the chief credit for the Union*, James Agar (Past Deputy Grand Master) and Robert Leslie (Grand Secretary)....

Thomas Harper joined the Moderns Lodge No 15 (now Globe Lodge) in 1787, became Master in 1793 and its representative Grand Steward in 1796; the list of Antients who were together in that lodge is impressive:

Thomas Harper, Joined in 1787, was then	Senior Grand Warden
Robert Leslie, Joined in 1787, was then	Past Junior Grand Warden
William Comerford Clarkson, Joined in 1789, was then	Grand Treasurer
James Agar, Joined in 1790, was then	Senior Grand Warden
John Bunn, Joined in 1791, was then	Junior Grand Warden
Robert Gill, Joined in 1797, was then	Past Senior Grand Warden
Peter Gilkes, of Antients No. 4 (and others) joined in 1798	

Henry Sadler commented further by stating 'Globe Lodge contributed more than any other lodge in the Craft to bring about the Union of the two Grand Lodges in 1813'. The nature of Freemasonry in that period, however, was a continuous state of flux, with enthusiasm rising and falling. Whilst some brethren were striving for a settlement of 'differences' others, in both Grand Lodges, hardened their hearts, until in one fell swoop the curtain came down on all their efforts in 1803 when the premier Grand Lodge saw fit to expel Thomas Harper, an action which was recorded in the following terms:

> Grand Lodge. 9 February 1803
> Resolved. THAT the said Thomas Harper be expelled the Society, for countenancing and supporting a set of persons, calling themselves Ancient Masons, and holding Lodges in this Kingdom without authorization from H.R.H. the Prince of Wales, the Grand Master duly elected by this regular Grand Lodge. Resolved also. THAT this resolution be inserted in the printed accounts of the Grand Lodge, to prevent the said Thomas Harper from gaining admittance

20 *Summons for Globe Lodge No 23, formerly the Moderns Lodge No 15*

into any regular Lodge. And it was further resolved, that whenever it shall appear that any Masons, under the Constitution of this Grand Lodge shall in future attend or countenance any of the Lodges or meetings of persons calling themselves Ancient Masons, under the sanction of any persons claiming to be Grand Master of England, and not duly elected by this Grand Lodge, the Laws of the Society will be strictly enforced against them, and their names will be sent to the several Lodges under the Constitution of England.

It was an acrimonious period for many brethren, but Thomas Harper acted with the utmost diplomacy and as the years went by resentment diminished, more and more brethren under the premier Grand Lodge became acquainted with,

and adopted procedures viewed with favour by associates from Antients lodges, and although pockets of resistance survived, glaring opposition weakened until finally, in 1810, the Resolution passed seven years earlier was rescinded. The greatest damage was thus repaired and constructive work at higher level could be officially resumed.

Enthusiastic brethren at a lower level had never abandoned the desire for unity and were ever ready to seize any opportunity or prepared to explore ways and means of healing the breach, and the Master of Domatic Lodge, in the first half of 1806, was no exception. He joined forces with two brethren from Lodge 264 in an approach to HRH the Duke of Kent asking for permission to nominate him as Grand Master. The Duke of Kent, was viewed as being astride both Grand Lodges in that he was Provincial Grand Master, as the office was then known, of Gibraltar and Andalusia, an appointment by the premier Grand Lodge in 1790, and two years later held a similar office in Lower Canada on behalf of the Antients Grand Lodge. Before his departure from Canada he received a joint petition from the brethren of both jurisdictions in that country urging the consolidation of friendly relations earnestly hoping that through him it would lead to unity. We learn the story of the involvement of the Master of Domatic Lodge from the Minutes of the Grand Stewards Lodge (Antients):

Grand Stewards Lodge.   16 Apl. 1806
Bros Tuffield and Allen of Lodge 264 and Bror Ward of Lodge No. 234 had taken upon themselves to address His Royal Highness the Duke of Kent and requested His Royal Highness to accept and take upon himself the Office of Grand Master and to which address His Royal Highness had been pleased to return an Answer under the Impression that the said address had been written by the Order of or under the Sanction of the Grand Lodge.

It is possible that it was in the minds of those three brethren that the cause of the Union would be strengthened considerably; the two royal brothers holding the highest office in each Grand Lodge would hasten the project; they may have been imbued with the thought that such an action was the wishful thinking of brethren as a whole. There is no record of the reply from the Duke of Kent but the story is continued:

Grand Stewards Lodge.   21 May 1806
R.W. Thos Harper DGM in the Chair.
Upon hearing Brother Thos Tuffield, James Allen, & John Ward in respect of their Conduct in writing to and waiting upon His Royal Highness the Duke of Kent requesting his R! Highness permission to be Nominated as Grand Master without any vacancy having taken place or any Authority of or from this R.W. Grand Lodge. It was thereupon Resolved that such Conduct is highly reprehensible and Contrary to the Laws and Regulations of Masonry. Ordered that Bros Tuffield, Allen and Ward be severely reprimanded from the Chair for Unwarrantable Conduct

and that such like Conduct will in no case be permitted to pass in future.

We should not lose sight of the fact that the first positive step had come from the Antients Grand Lodge when in December 1797 it was proposed and seconded:

That a Committee be appointed by this R.W. Grand Lodge to meet one that may be appointed by the Grand Lodge of Modern Masonry and with them to effect a union.

Unfortunately it met with short shrift as another brother moved 'the previous question' and the matter was dropped, almost unanimously. But what was an inhibited desire by most brethren at a lower level was now beginning to be openly expressed.

In common with most organisations, Freemasonry has never lacked members anxious to thrust theories, ideas, and recommendations before their contemporaries and this subject was not excepted. Carefully preserved in the archives is a four-page pamphlet compiled by Thomas Motte Caton, shewn as an Honorary Member of Royal Naval Lodge (now No 59). It is entitled *Masonic Union* and was addressed 'To the whole body of English Masons'. Published in June 1803, it contains a lengthy review of the setting-up of the Antients Grand Lodge, the cleavage between the two authorities, the non-recognition exercised by each side with regard to each activity, the acrimony that had built up between them, and ends with the hope and trust that both parties 'would soon meet upon the square and part upon the level'. It expressed just what the majority of men of goodwill desired and at least was added pressure in that direction. With further pressures at work within the premier Grand Lodge, eventually with Committees from both sides meeting together, not without difficulties, exploring ways and means without loss of face, within a few years their work led to the following:

Grand Lodge.   12 April 1809
In consequence of a Recommendation of the Committee of Charity held on 7th April 1809, it was Resolved:
THAT the Grand Lodge do agree in opinion with

the Committee of Charity, that it is not necessary any longer to continue in force those Measures which were resorted to in or about the year 1739 respecting Irregular Masons, and therefore enjoin the Several Lodges to Revert to the Ancient Land Marks of the Society.

The long-lasting error of judgement on the part of the premier Grand Lodge paved the way for Bro Cranfield to propose the following in the Antients Grand Lodge, on 6 September 1809:

That a Committee be appointed from the Grand Lodge to consider of and adopt such prompt and Effectual Measures for accomplishing so desirable an Object as a Masonic Union.

It was his second attempt, as he was pressured to withdraw it when raising it on 7 June earlier that year. This time it met with what must be deemed the peak of diplomacy from Thomas Harper who was in the Chair; bearing in mind that his expulsion from the Moderns had not at that time been rescinded. Cranfield's proposal again met with resistance:

The R.W. Bro. Charles Humphreys, P.S.G.W. objected to the Motion being received as tending to annihilate the Ancient Craft.

A long debate ensued, one might be tempted to think 'arguments' would be more appropriate, ending with:

The R.W. Dep.y Grand Master in the Chair after Maturely Considering hereon and as at present advised and according with his Duty as Dep.y Grand Master conceiving it incompatible with his Situation in the absence of the Grand Master to receive such a Motion.

But, this time persistence on the part of Cranfield paid off for he raised it yet again on 6 December 1809 and, probably with much lobbying having been done on the subject, ample support was then forthcoming for the Motion which was duly accepted. A Committee was then appointed one of whom was John Ward, Past Master of Domatic Lodge No 234.

In spite of factions against their efforts but with encouragement as a counterbalance, full informa-tion was communicated to the Grand Lodges of Scotland and Ireland and the turning point was reached with the following resolution:

Grand Lodge (Antients) Crown and Anchor Tavern London
Wednesday 7 March 1810
THAT a Masonic union of the Grand Lodge under the present Grand Masters His Royal Highness the Prince of Wales, and His Grace The Duke of Atholl, on principles equal and honourable to both Grand Lodges and preserving inviolate the landmarks of the Ancient Craft would in the opinion of the Grand Lodge be expedient and advantageous to both.

The communication of that Resolution to the Grand Secretary of the Moderns, together with liason between members of both sides, had the desired effect and within a remarkably short time we read:

Grand Lodge held at Freemasons' Hall
Great Queen Street April 11th 1810
Resolved Unanimously that the Grand Lodge meets with unfeigned cordiality the desire expressed by the Grand Lodge under His Grace the Duke of Atholl for a Reunion.

Many problems arose but diplomacy at all levels prevailed. Breakdowns occurred in meetings with the two appointed Committees but strength of purpose was the winning factor. Inspired estimates of the 'differences' between the forms employed by both sides have been made by various students in that field of study, but it takes for granted that there was uniformity among working even among lodges in the same jurisdiction, and that was not always the case. Perhaps the one greatest inconsistency for both was the position of the Royal Arch. The rejection of it by the Moderns' Grand Secretary, Samuel Spencer, in 1759 was clearly stated in the phrase, 'Our Society is neither Arch, Royal Arch, or Antient ...' but members of that jurisdiction were not to be denied so in 1766 they set up an independent Grand Chapter, which itself was not recognised by their Grand Lodge, which exercised a most efficient control of the system; it laid foundations for the government that was to come into existence after the Union. Yet, the Antients Grand Lodge, formed to preserve Freemasonry 'According to the Antient Institution' developed the Royal Arch within the framework of the 'Institution' without any evidence whatsoever that it existed at the time of the formation of the premier Grand Lodge in 1717. Nevertheless they treated it as a 4th Degree and, amongst other things, Laurence Dermott described the Royal Arch as 'the root heart and marrow of Freemasonry' also 'this degree is certainly more august, sublime, and important than those which precede it, and is the summit and perfection of Ancient Masonry'.

So much work was to be done in regard to Craft matters that, for a few years, attention was focussed upon uniformity acceptable to both sides and the Royal Arch became somewhat neglected. That story will arise later, but in the meantime we turn our attention to the Lodge of Promulgation set up in London on 26 October 1809:

> For the purpose of promulgating the ancient Land Marks of the Society and instructing the Craft in all such matters and forms ...

It lasted until 5 March 1811 and in that period agreed that 'deacons, being proved on investigation to be not only Ancient, but useful and necessary officers, be recommended'; also, 'that the ceremony of Installation of Masters of Lodges is one of the true Land Marks of the Craft and ought to be observed'. We are able to have a clear idea of the purpose of that lodge when we see the Minutes for 29 December 1810 which included the following:

> The R.W.M. then took a retrospective view of the proceedings in the three degrees of the Order.... and proceeded to point out the material parts in and between the several degrees to which their attention would be requisite, in preserving the Ancient Land Marks of the Order, such as the form of the Lodge, the number and situation of the Officers, their different distinctions in the different Degrees, the restoration of the pass-words to each Degree, and the making of the pass-words between one Degree and another, instead of in the Degree....

Thus, in London, brethren had almost instant terms of reference in the event of problems arising from 'irregular' visitation, or for 're-Making' in an acceptable manner, but partisanship was widespread and an excellent example of this love-hate relationship is taken from the histories of two lodges meeting in Newcastle-upon-Tyne in that pre-Union period. Both lodges had military connections and one would have expected that alone would have induced a certain rapport but it was not so. The following items are taken from their records:

St. Nicholas Lodge No 378 (Moderns)
1806. Information was given that Bro. W. Blain had joined the Atholl Lodge contrary to his Obligation; agreed that his name be erased from *our* Books.

New Lectures introduced to prevent the introduction of that dangerous system to the Craft called 'Atholl' Masonry any communication with which is strongly deprecated by Grand Lodge. That no Brethren after having visited the 'Atholl' Lodge in this town be admitted a member of our Lodge.

Notes taken from the history of the other lodge counterbalance that attitude:

Lodge No 131 (Antients)
1810. On this night a letter was read from the Grand Secretary, Robert Leslie, that a Brother might belong to the two Masonic Societies but ought to conduct himself as not to give offence to either.

Three Brethren under the Constitution of the Prince of Wales made Ancient Masons and charged £2 each.

1812. Two Modern Masons re-made to enable them to establish a Lodge of Ancient Masons at Blanchard and a Petition to support the new Lodge signed on 28 December.

1813. Warrant 131 exchanged for No. 15 which was granted in recognition of the zeal shewn by the Lodge for promoting the Antient Craft in Northern England.

There is a happy ending, however, that arose after the Union and a series of meetings and discussions between members of those lodges, which resulted in an amalgamation. Warrant No 15 which had been earned for useful service afforded a comparatively high position on the Register of the Antients Grand Lodge, and in turn allowed for a similarly elevated posting on the Register of the United Grand Lodge. Subsequently the re-styled lodge took an appropriate title and now thrives under the name—Newcastle upon Tyne Lodge and is No 24 on the present Register.

Close on the heels of the Lodge of Promulgation various Lodges of Instruction sprang into existence to spread the knowledge of forms acceptable to the Antients, but, Domatic Lodge of Instruction, founded in 1808, was already well established and its Minute Book of that period shews the names of brethren of note from both jurisdictions in their comparatively high attendances.

The desire to cooperate was now being made apparent from the highest level, as was stated in a report from the Moderns Grand Lodge Committee of 9 February 1811:

> THAT the Grand Lodge under his Roy! Highness the Prince of Wales had resolved to return to the Ancient Land Marks of Masonry and in Order to [achieve] a perfect Union of the two Grand Lodges they will Consent to the same Obligations and Continue to abide by the Ancient Land Marks of Masonry when it should be ascertained what those Ancient Land Marks and Obligations were.

The Committees of both sides continued working behind the scenes, but frequently headed into aggravation and frustration when points which had been agreed between them were negatived by their own colleagues upon reporting their proceedings. Patience of the Moderns Committee was at the point of exhaustion on 5 June 1811 when they wrote to the effect that any further meetings could hardly take place until such time the Antients Committee could be invested with sufficient powers to enter into meaningful discussion with arrangement of the subjects necessary to the proposed Union.

By the end of that year, however, consultation was on a much firmer basis, as shewn by the Antients Grand Lodge Committee Minutes of 13 December 1811:

> Received in due form the committee of the G.L. under H.R.H. the Prince Regent. Proceeded to business and among various items the following points were mentioned:
> The question was distinctly put to the Committee of the Grand Lodge under the Prince Regent whether in expressing their readiness to adopt the Ancient forms

it was to be understood that the practise of the Grand Lodges of Scotland and Ireland, of America, and of the greatest part of the Continent, which in perfect Union with the practise of the Grand Lodge of England under the Duke of Atholl was to be the one adopted and acted upon by the United Grand Lodge so as to give Complete Unity to the Masonic World. To this it was Answered that undoubtedly it was their wish to put an end to all diversity and to establish the one true system. But it should be essential that the true system should be ascertained. They had in fact for some time exerted themselves to Act by the Ancient forms; they had formed a Lodge of Promulgation; and they had the assistance of several Ancient Masons but in short they were ready to Concur in any plan for investigation and ascertaining the genuine Course, and when demonstrated to walk in it....

If the members of the Lodge of Promulgation were successful in determining exactly what were the masonic Landmarks, they failed to catalogue them for posterity and that subject has never been less than contentious. Numerous lists have been compiled since that date, each with a total number of items ranging from five to fifty; the figure, of course, hinges solely upon individual viewpoint and to each compiler there is only one 'correct' list!

In May 1813, HRH the Prince of Wales was succeeded as Grand Master of the Moderns by his brother HRH the Duke of Sussex, Augustus Frederick. In the same year the Duke of Athol resigned as Grand Master of the Antients Grand Lodge in favour of HRH Edward, Duke of Kent. The *Articles of Union* were agreed, drawn up and duly signed by the royal brothers at Kensington Palace in November in readiness for the great event, and one of the other signatories was Thomas Harper, Deputy Grand Master. In accordance with item five, the two Grand Masters appointed each 'nine worthy and expert Master Masons, or Past Masters to form a Lodge to be entitled the Lodge of Reconciliation' which, amongst other things was to secure:

> ... the most perfect unity of obligations, of discipline, of working the lodges, of making, passing and raising, instructing and clothing Brothers; so that one pure unsullied system, according to the genuine landmarks,

laws, and traditions of the Craft shall be maintained, upheld, and practised, throughout the Masonic World, from the day and date of the said Union until time shall be no more....

In 1813, that final year of the separated brethren, the Antients Grand Lodge had Constituted ten new lodges including No 136, later to be named Temple Lodge (now No 101), which was founded by former members of Domatic Lodge headed by the somewhat controversial Thomas Banbury. The final lodge Constituted by the Antients was on 21 December only six days before the historic Union on the Festival of St. John the Evangelist; it is on the present Register as Mount Sinai No 121 meeting at Penzance, Cornwall. The exact number of lodges on the Registers of both Grand Lodges is difficult to define as some which had failed to make regular Returns were erased a few years later, a process that took many years to clarify. The figure of 647 as a total for both is one that is perhaps as near as one could reasonably expect, bearing in mind the general state of affairs at that time and of the less attention to accounting and recording than is paid at the present time. The total is comprised from 389 Lodges from the Moderns Register and 258 from the Antients, and the total for London from that figure is generally accepted as 118.

Domatic Lodge made its final Return to the Grand Lodge of the Antients on 1 December 1813 and submitted a list of 40 names including one Joining Member and one Initiate, with a remittance of £4.0.0. It was signed by Elisha Sinclair as Master, Richard Lane, SW, John Purton, JW, and Thomas Kay, Secretary. Elisha Sinclair had served the full year as Master shewing that the term of office had changed from one St John's Day to the next, that Installation was now on St John the Evangelist Festival on 27 December each year. It would be almost a fairy-tale ending if Elisha Sinclair was a blood relative of Charles Sinclair who was so prominent in the Dispensation period, but, unfortunately we do not have such detail; nevertheless, his name can be added to those whose first names are recorded as 'Charles', 'George', 'Benjamin', and now 'Elisha'. One might be tempted to say that the name seemed to run through the records like a thread woven into a canvass and that 'Sinclair' was a name with which to conjure, from the first to the last!

A surfeit of material is on record regarding the ceremonial of the Union, but, to capture the spirit of the perfect harmony which was the desire of all, it is of interest to turn to a report from the same Province in which Thomas Dunckerley had so easily brought two lodges on opposite sides together some years earlier. It is sad that Dunckerley did not live to see such work brought to fruition to the greater degree as he died in May 1794. His effort in that connection was in Southampton when it allowed brethren from both jurisdictions to join together in procession, but this report comes from the neighbouring town of Portsmouth, quoted from the history of Phoenix Lodge (now No 257):

> St. John the Evangelist's Day, the 27th December, 1813 at Portsmouth.... The members of the several Lodges here left their seats on either side of the Church, which they had up to this moment occupied—the *Ancient* Masons on the right and the *Modern* Masons on the left—and joining together in the main aisle, proceeded to the seats reserved for them in the Chancel, where they mingled together as a *United body*, the organ playing a joyful tune.

The report expresses concisely the simple, but effective, ceremonial which, in the best of all settings asked the Almighty for blessings upon the future efforts of all brethren of goodwill; it set the scene for what must have been happening in many other Provinces imbued with similar good intent.

Precedence in the numbering of Lodges for the new Register was determined by ballot and, in that, fortune favoured the Antients. Their Lodge No 1 became No 1 on the Register of the United Grand Lodge of England, whilst No 2 fell to the Lodge of Antiquity. It produced a somewhat anomalous situation as many of the lodges in the senior positions had been founded years before the Antients Grand Lodge into existence in 1751 and as an example of that we take the Antients No 1, which did not come into being until 1756 then to occupy a vacant position left for the special purpose, whereas the founding of Lodge of Antiquity was lost 'in the mists of time' and therefore known as one of the 'Time Immemorial' lodges. The re-numbering sequence alternated between lodges from each side and, in consequence, Domatic Lodge No 234 became No 293 on the 1814 Register. Following the erasure of many lodges on both sides that had become dormant or moribund, a closing-up on the Register took place in 1832 and Domatic then became No 206, and on the last re-numbering which was in 1863 it became No 177 by which it is almost as well-known as by its name. The Moderns Grand Lodge in April 1792 ordered that the Grand Stewards Lodge be placed at the head of their list of lodges without number, a position that was continued at the Union. Incorporation with its counterpart increased the number of represented lodges from twelve to eighteen but, with a subsequent re-instatement, that number became nineteen.

The Troubled Lodge of Reconciliation

Appointed by authority of the *Act of Union*, the Lodge of Reconciliation received a Warrant dated 7 December 1813 which is the only Warrant to bear the signatures of two Royal Grand Masters. Its terms of reference have already been stated and it carried out that work until 1816 when it ended its activity by demonstrating various ceremonial that had been agreed upon, at a Special Grand Lodge held on Monday 20 May of that year. Nine brethren from each side had been appointed to act under that authority, with both Grand Secretaries in joint capacity. The nine who were appointed by the Duke of Kent, on behalf of the Antients, were:

R.F. Mestayer, Grand Master's Lodge No 1 (retained the number).
Thomas Harper Jnr. Grand Master's Lodge No 1 (retained the number).
J.H. Goldsworthy, No 2 (now Lodge of Fidelity No 3)
William Fox, No 4 (now Royal York Lodge of Perseverance No 7)
James Ronalds, No 16 (now Robert Burns Lodge No 25)

William Oliver, No 77 (now Royal Jubilee Lodge No 72)
Michael Corcoran, No 194 (now Middlesex Lodge No 143)
Richard Bayley, No 240 (was the lodge at Lord Cochrane—erased)
James McCann, No 244 (now Lodge of Tranquility No 185
with
Edwards Harper, Grand Master's Lodge No 1, Grand Secretary.
Bros. Thomas and Edwards Harper shewn above were sons of Thomas Harper, Deputy Grand Master, appointed to that office in 1801.

Progress at first was somewhat slow, obviously it was not an easy matter to produce a speedy uniformity among such experts, many brethren travelling from Provinces to witness events became frustrated by the limited portions of ritual which were demonstrated; added to that was the dissatisfaction of some brethren regarding the manner in which the duties of the lodge were being carried out. For various reasons, appointed brethren resigned but not only were they immediately replaced, additional brethren were appointed from the ranks of Grand Officers and Provinces, amongst whom was William Williams, Provincial Grand Master for Dorset.

In his report on 3 November 1814 to the Duke of Sussex, the Rev Samuel Hemming, Master of the Lodge, stated that seven vacancies had arisen and described one of them as follows:

... and from the improper conduct of Bro. Goldsworthy, not only from non-attendance but also in allowing his Name to appear in print as the signature of a letter, arraigning the Conduct and mode of instruction adopted by this Lodge.

Earlier, Bro Goldsworthy had been among those attending the Domatic Lodge of Instruction and his name is shewn in the attendance register. But he was now the prime mover among members of six lodges with resentment over the 'innovations attempted to be introduced by the Lodge of Reconciliation'. The six concerned were:

No 2   Lodge at Crown Tavern, Clerkenwell
        Green (now Lodge of Fidelity No 3)

No 159   Prince of Brunswick Lodge, Mitre Tavern, Ely Place (erased 1830)

No 231   Lodge at the George, Brook Street, Holborn (now Phoenix Lodge No 173)

No 234   Domatic Lodge, Hercules Pillars, Great Queen Street (now No 177)

No 277   Prince Edward's Lodge, Admiral Benbow Tavern, Golden Sq. (erased 1827)

No 314   Lodge at Sadler's Arms, Piccadilly (now United Strength No 228)

The outcome of Goldsworthy's efforts was a Memorial prepared in Phoenix Lodge to be presented to the Duke of Sussex, complaining of the innovations, etc; all six lodges were associated with it. The immediate action of the Grand Master was to refer it to the Lodge of Reconciliation for an examination of those concerned and a report then to be made to him. Following their close attention to that task, the Rev Samuel Hemming, as Master of the Lodge, sent a comprehensive Report to the Grand Master dated 3 December 1814 with the following comments:

> The Lodge further remarks, that in some instances the Masters did not state the objections as arising from themselves, but from the Body of their respective Lodges, and that the mischief seems to have been most industriously fomented and propagated by the Lodge No. 3; and in particular by Bro. Goldsworthy a Past Master of that Lodge.
>
> Upon the whole, we are of opinion that the objections we have thus far heard are confined to a small number of Lodges in London ... In consideration of the conduct of Brother Goldsworthy this Lodge have informed him that he cannot any longer be considered a Member of it, and that the M.W. Grand Master has been pleased to appoint another in his stead.

The examination of other brethren was continued on a smaller scale and whatever objections came to light were smoothed over and those concerned mollified, but with one marked exception, those from Phoenix Lodge No 231. Those brethren had already agreed 'That no Visiting Member be admitted into this Lodge unless he has taken the Obligation of the three Degrees of *Ancient* Freemasonry as heretofore practised in the Ancient

Craft'. They had also adopted a few other resolutions demonstrating their intransigence:

> 7 Nov. 1814. THAT a Memorial be presented to H.R.H. the Duke of Sussex complaining of the Innovations attempted to be introduced by the Lodge of Reconciliation.
> 20 Nov. 1814. THAT the Lodge do subscribe One Guinea towards the expenses of the Committee appointed to devise measures for opposing the Innovations. ...
> 5 Dec. 1814. THAT the Lodge do withold the Quarterly Dues till after the Quarterly Meeting of the Grand Lodge.
> 6 Feb. 1815. RESOLVED that the Lodge will not adopt or propagate the System introduced by the Lodge of Reconciliation.

Having been unable to secure the co-operation of those brethren, two members of the Lodge of Reconciliation attended the meeting of Phoenix Lodge called for 6 March 1815, Bro Bayley and RW Bro William Williams, Provincial Grand Master over Dorset. The Minutes contain this account:

> Brothers Bailey and Williams (both members of the L. of Reconciliation and the latter Prov. G.M. for Dorset) attended to be admitted into the Lodge, but not having taken the Obligation in the three Degrees of Ancient Masonry it was Resolved that they should not be admitted.
>
> The W.M. produced a Summons he had receiv'd from the Grand Secretaries to attend the Board of General Purposes (on 22nd Feb.) on the subject of the Resolution passed at the last Lodge—THAT the Lodge would not receive or practise the System of Masonry adopted by the Lodge of Reconciliation and informed the Lodge that he had attended with his Wardens accordingly, and mentioned the result of what passed.
>
> Read a letter from the Grand Secretaries addressed to the W.M., Summoning him and his Wardens to attend the Board on Wed.ᵞ next on the Resolution passed last Lodge Night and to bring the Warrant or Constitution and Minute Book of the Lodge. It was Moved and Seconded that the Warrant and Minute Book be not taken out of the Lodge to the Board of General Purposes or the Lodge of Reconciliation or any other Board or Lodge whatsoever. Carried Unanimously.

One month later the Master informed the Lodge he had attended the Board of General Purposes, in company with three brethren from the Lodge, following which, the members then Resolved:

1st. That the Resolution passed in this Lodge on 6th February last, a copy of which was sent to the Grand Secretary, is strictly in unison with the Constitution and Principles of Ancient Masonry.

2ndly. That from the report made by the W.M. assisted by Bros. Coates, Warne, and Badger, who attended the B. of G.P. in consequence of the above Resolution of 6 February last, Agreeable to Summons, it appears to us that without a manly and determined Opposition on the part of the Ancient Lodges the Noble and renowned fabric of Ancient Masonry will be greatly destroyed.

3rdly. That we will not assist in, or countenance the Subversion of Ancient Masonry, which the Measures of the L of R. are strongly calculated to produce, countenanced and supported as those Measures are by the different Boards appointed by the Grand Master, and do therefore feel ourselves imperatively compelled to decline holding any intercourse or correspondence with the United Grand Lodge until the Articles of the Union are fulfilled.

4th. That those Members of the L. of R. appointed by H.R.H. the Duke of Kent on the part of the Ancient Craft who have consented to and propagate the Measures adopted by the Grand Lodge, we consider to have sacrificed their Public Duty as Masons and countenanced Measures contrary to their Obligations and the Principles of Ancient Masonry, and therefore we declare those Members unworthy of our confidence, and in consequence that they shall not be permitted to visit this Lodge.

5th. That we will co-operate with any Ancient Lodge, who may resolve to defend and preserve true Ancient Masonry.

In support of that last item, at their meeting held on 9 April 1815 the brethren passed the following Resolution:

THAT Brothers of other Lodges who may think proper to withdraw themselves from the Lodges they respectively belong to, on account of the Objections to the New System shall be permitted to Lodge their Certificates in this Lodge on paying the sum of 5s each.

The following month, at an Emergency Meeting held on Sunday, 5 May, the brethren decided upon a Communication to be sent to the Board of General Purposes. It was their attempt to heal the breach and had this to propose:

... the present unfortunate Dispute may be amicably adjusted and brought to a speedy and happy conclusion and the Articles of Union carried into full effect, this Lodge will undertake to recommend a certain Number of Masters or P.M. not exceeding Nine to be nominated on the part of the Ancient Craft to meet an equal Number to be appointed from the other Fraternity (but no Member of the Lodge of Reconciliation to be Nominated) to consider and compare the two Systems as practised before the Union in order that one Mode of M.P.R. and Lecturing may be established out of the two without the introduction of any new Matter or Language....

It did not gain the support they hoped and the matter rested there.

Officially the only means for communicating the ritual and procedures agreed upon was by demonstration meetings held by the Lodge of Reconciliation. No written matter was issued or condoned, indeed Laurence Thompson, one of the members of it came under censure regarding that offence. It was reported as follows:

On a Motion regularly made and seconded THAT Bro. Thompson having offended against a known Masonic Rule in printing certain letters and marks tending to convey information on the subject of Masonic Instruction should for this offence be reprimanded in such terms as the W. Master of the Lodge of Reconciliation might think proper.'

Bro Thompson admitted the error of his ways and solemnly promised to collect every copy and place them in the custody of the Lodge of Reconciliation—'to be destroyed according to their discretion'. This incident has been examined in detail by C.F.W. Dyer in 'Laurence Thompson's Unauthorized Print', *AQC* 84, pp 116–140.

Writing on the tenor of events of that period, albeit a somewhat backward glance, George Claret in his *Masonic Gleanings*, published in 1844, wrote:

We discovered that some of them had been busily engaged in an endeavour to do away with the ceremonies we had been practicing and teaching nearly three years. The late Br. W. Williams Prov. G. Master for Dorsetshire, who took a very active part, and was often a visiter [sic] at their Lodges paticularly [sic] at No. 3 then held at the Crown Tavern, Clerkenwell Green, he was also on great intimacy with his R.H. the Duke of Sussex, the Grand Master, it appeared that some of the brethren to whom I have before alluded who could not learn the present ceremonies, (as a last effort) sought to induce the Grand Master with the influence of Br. Williams, to alter that which had been settled so long before by the Lodge of Reconciliation. Those of us who were anxious to retain them, after consulting together came to the determination to memorialize the Grand Master, for which purpose, a committee was formed, meetings held in different parts of London, and in a short time we obtained nearly 700 signatures to the memorial, combining all the Masonic talent in London, it was presented by Br. Chinn, Stokoe, Steward, and Claret accompanied by Br. Isaac Lindo, Grand Officer [S.G.W.] on January 29th 1816. And we have reason to know that the memorial had the effect intended as the same ceremonies have been continued.

The Memorial, a full transcript of which is reproduced in *Appendix C*, was presented to the Grand Master at 2 pm on Sunday 29 January 1816 at Kensington Palace at an audience granted for that purpose. The document contained an important request:

> ... that your Royal Highness will be pleased to declare your Sanction to the System of Freemasonry practised taught and promulgated by the Lodge of Reconciliation prior to the first of December 1815.

The faded resistance is shewn by an item in Grand Lodge Proceedings 6 September 1815, a few months earlier than the Memorial:

> A Motion was made by Bro. Goldsworthy, P.M. of No. 3 and Seconded by Bro. Godwin of No. 82, that the thanks of the United Grand Lodge be most dutifully presented to H.R.H. the Duke of Sussex, M.W.G.M., for his zealous, unremitting and fraternal care in watching over the interests of the Craft, in maintaining its ancient Landmarks and preserving inviolate its true principles and tenets. And all the

brethren testified their unanimous and unqualified concurrence by the accustomed honours.

The prime mover of the earlier resistance had now been won over. Also, although William Williams attended only five meetings of the Lodge of Reconciliation, out of a total of thirty, his valued services in the field of diplomacy during that period received due notice in the resolution passed in Grand Lodge on 6 March 1816:

> On a Motion duly made and seconded, it was RESOLVED UNANIMOUSLY: That the Thanks of this Grand Lodge be given to the R.W. Brother William Williams, Prov. G.M. for the County of Dorset, for the distinguished Services which he has rendered to Masonry by his unceasing Exertions, in promoting the best Interest and Welfare of our Ancient Fraternity. Who, possessing the purest Principles of Brotherly Affection; with a Mind highly cultivated and enriched by Masonic Acquirements; with active Zeal and unexampled Labour, to conciliate the Members of the Order, has afforded most essential Service to the Craft; more especially in the various Arrangements consequent on the happy Re-Union of the Two Societies.

The official approval, however, never went beyond the stage of demonstration which occurred at a special meeting of Grand Lodge on 20 May 1816 when members of the Lodge of Reconciliation opened a lodge in the First, Second, and Third Degrees respectively and demonstrated the ceremonies of Initiation, Passing, and Raising. The report is contained in the Minutes of 5 June 1816:

> The Minutes of the Grand Lodge on 20th May last were read, when the Ceremonies and Practices recommended by the Lodge of Reconciliation were exhibited and explained; and alterations on two points, in the Third Degree, having been resolved upon, the several ceremonies, &c., recommended were approved and confirmed.

The last mention of their work was on 2 September 1816 when:

> ... the W. Master, Officers, and Brethren were awarded the thanks of the Grand Lodge for their unremitting Zeal and Exertion in the cause of Freemasonry.

The following is a list of brethren associated with Domatic whose names appeared in the record of the thirty meetings of the Lodge of Reconciliation from 7 December 1813 to 3 May 1816:

Broadfoot, P. No. 300A, 244A, (now 217 & 185)	20 attendances	
(appointed as a member following the exclusion of Goldsworthy)		
Goldsworthy, J.H. No. 2A (now 3)	4	,,
(appointed as a member but later excluded for acting in opposition)		
Gilkes, P. No. 14M (now 23)	10	,,
Mivart, J. No. 8M, 128M, 205M (now 16,96,157)	6	,,
Dowden, A. No. 234A (now 177)	1	,,
Lane, R. ,, ,,	2	,,
Purton J. ,, ,,	1	,,
Prince, E. ,, ,,	1	,,
Banbury T. formerly of Domatic but became founder of No. 136A (now 101)	2	,,
Blackmore, J. No. 136A ,,	2	,,
Ward, J. ,, ,,	1	,,
Thomas, D. ,, ,,	1	,,
Martin, W. ,, ,,	2	,,
Allen, T. ,, ,,	1	,,
Davies, J. ,, ,,	1	,,
Matthews, W. No. 258A (now 192)	3	,,
Merry R. ,, ,,	3	,,
Palmer, J. ,, ,,	1	,,
Sotheran, T. ,, ,,	5	,,

At each meeting of the Lodge of Reconciliation a controlled number of lodges were summoned to be represented but, for various reasons, only a percentage of those notified attended. Brethren in the Provinces were beset by problems in cost of travel and accommodation and the futility of travelling great distances sometimes for so little information. Instruction was slower to reach them but it eventually percolated through qualified brethren invited to visit for that purpose. For a few years isolated incidents arose involving individual rebels who refused to conform and another upsurge occurred in 1827 in connection with the Rites and Ceremonies of Installation which were promulgated by demonstration in yet another especially Warranted Lodge in London. That, also, produced a uniformity to receive official approval from the wide diversity of practice that had been performed, or in some cases not performed at all.

The objections to revision in ritual and ceremonial was not confined to members from the former Antients jurisdiction, indeed a classic example from a Moderns lodge has been written up in the history of *Old Dundee Lodge No 18* by Arthur Heiron, (Kenning, 1921, pp 122-23). The lodge was then meeting at 'Dundee Arms' tavern at Wapping which was then a thriving port on the river Thames in London. Under the sub-heading 'Objections to the New Ritual' the author commented:

Although our R.W.M. John Walton acted as a member of the Lodge of Promulgation [1809] and recommended his Brethren to accept loyally the alterations in the Ritual agreed upon as a fair compromise between the claims of the 'Moderns' and the 'Antients' yet there were many Masons (both Modern and Antient) who obstinately refused to coincide with these views. The chief opponent in Old Dundee was Br. Clarke Stanley P.M. He was a builder and carpenter, residing at 'Samson's Gardens' Wapping, and had been a loyal supporter of the lodge for twenty-five years; having been 'Made a Mason' by us on 24th June, 1790, and acted as Secretary in 1794 and was W.M. in 1798 and 1807. He had been brought up imbued with a love of our ancient customs, and strongly disapproved of the New Ritual, including the appointment of Deacons [1810] and the installation of Br. John Pickett [1814]. He kept away from the Lodge for two years, and desired to resign, but objected to pay his arrears of quarterage, his complaint being 'That he had not been comfortable when he attended the Lodge on account of the alteration in the Lodge'; eventually he and ten other Members resigned rather than agree to the new regulations. On 8 March 1810 he had refused to be re-Obligated even though at the previous meeting of the Lodge 43 members of Old Dundee Lodge had been 'newly Obligated'. It seems that other brethren did not approve of the New Ritual and, as a result of withholding their dues it is recorded on 14 April 1814—'The Names of 32 Brethren were ordered to be Erased from the Lodge Books, being Defaulters in Quarterage'.

The troubles from the Lodge of Reconciliation had been additional to those created by the Lodge of Promulgation, but, as ever, time proved to be an effective healer.

Lodges of Instruction

Some of the members of the Lodge of Reconciliation became quite effective missionaries of the new system by precepting in various Lodges of Instruction in London, and by taking long journeys to convey those details to brethren in the Provinces. In 1844 George Claret published his *Masonic Gleanings*, and writing on the state of affairs existing between the Lodge of Promulgation (1809-1811) and the Lodge of Reconciliation (1813-1816) he stated:

Masonry at the time I am now speaking, viz., 1811,

the period of my Initiation into the order was in many Lodges at a very low ebb, compared to what it is in the present day, but being at that time young, and seeing the very slovenly manner in which several of the officers of our lodge performed their duties, I determined to try if it were not possible to learn somewhat more of the science than they appeared to possess, for which purpose I attended our various Lodges of Instruction, and at that time I have been Master of seven in a week, [that is] on every lodge night except saturday, but on sunday afternoon and evening as at that time there were more lodges of Instruction than there are now. . . .

It is important to bear in mind that Claret attended the Lodge of Reconciliation on six occasions and his signature in the attendance Register has been reproduced. Twice he acted as Candidate for the Raising ceremony and obviously he mixed freely with the experts involved at that time. In company with Peter Gilkes he attended Burlington Lodge of Instruction which, although meeting spasmodically at that time was to make its mark a few years later. Claret went on the record:

I opened the first lodge of instruction, at the west end of the town, [I was] one of the founders of the Western Reconciliation Lodge of Instruction, assisted in the formation of one at the Horn Tavern, Doctors Commons. Thus, it will be seen that as regards genuine modern Freemasonry, I owe precedence to no one.

Claret's obsession with ritual and procedure from the Lodge of Reconciliation, 'genuine modern Freemasonry' as he described it, was to last all his life. He was in London until 1818, then he left to take up residence in Cheltenham where he pursued his interest in the dissemination of masonic practice, although rather controversially it must be said. Eventually he returned to live in London and in 1830 joined forces yet again with Peter Gilkes, this time in Temple Lodge (now No 101).

Judging from accounts of squabbles in that period it is clear that 'genuine modern Freemasonry' was subjected to much interpretation demonstrated by individual experts. The first noteworthy teaching authority for the approved forms arose on 19 December 1817 when Stability Lodge

George Claret's signature

No 381 (now 217) gave sanction for a Lodge of Instruction to be formed. It was the nearest follow-up to the Lodge of Reconciliation and, of the seventeen brethren present at the first meeting and therefore deemed to be the founders, three were members of that former official body:- Bros Philip Broadfoot, James McCann, and Thomas Satterley. They were strengthened by another acclaimed expert, Peter Thomson a member of Lion and Lamb Lodge, holders of that second Warrant that had been purchased from Domatic brethren; in the succeeding years Thomson and his colleagues were to give considerable support to Stability Lodge of Instruction. Indeed, twenty years later, in an account of his activity, published in *Freemasons Quarterly Review* (1837, p 223) he is quoted as having stated publicly that 'he had been scrupulously attentive to instruct the Brethren in accordance to the plan laid down by the Lodge of Reconciliation after the Union.' He died in 1851 and at the meeting of the Stability Lodge of Instruction on 9 March of that year Bro John Havers stated:

> I claim for the memory of Peter Thomson and the active teachers of his time a large share of merit in our present position. When all was disarranged, when all was unsettled, when every difficulty beset the young aspirant after Masonic knowledge, then Godwin and Gilkes, and Broadfoot and Thomson, then White and Goldsworthy, Laurence Thompson and Satterley, were the Masons who manfully and zealously attempted (and succeeded in the attempt) to procure uniformity in Masonry and to disseminate the genuine principles of our Order.

Peter Gilkes tended to disapprove of certain aspects of the teaching in Stability and we find him in company with James Mivart when the latter was Master of Burlington Lodge and Preceptor of its Lodge of Instruction—just at the time when the name 'Br. Mivet' was listed in Domatic Lodge of Instruction Minute Book among those—'of the Prince of Wales's Constitution as been Obligated as Master Masons in the Ancient Craft'. Gilkes teamed up with Goldsworthy who, despite the seemingly stern rebukes which came his way, never really lost his high standing, as well as Bro Godwin. Jointly they laid charges against Broadfoot and Satterly for teaching items of ritual contrary to both Antient custom and the Act of Union. Upon investigation the charges were not upheld by the Board of General Purposes but the occasion tended to shew that 'genuine modern Freemasonry' had been affected by an element of self-righteousness, plus more than a little professionalism.

The stage was set for another teaching authority to arise, not so much in opposition but certainly more in accord with the views of Peter Gilkes and his colleagues. A little of that story is worth recounting in order to shew the intricate windings of things masonic in that era.

The former Antient Lodge No 4 had many members of rank and masonic prominence amongst its membership and among them were Charles Bearblock (Grand Secretary 1779-83), William Dagnia (JGW 1793), William Fox (member of Reconciliation), and Peter Gilkes. Following the Union, upon the re-numbering, that Lodge became No 7 but the members were rather dilatory in selecting a name for the lodge and communicating that to Grand Lodge. Eventually, in response to a peremptory demand, they stated that they wished to be known as Stability Lodge, but the request could not be granted as the name was already in use. The Minutes for October 1817 have the following:

> ... in consequence of finding in the list another Lodge of our former intended name, Bro. Bohn proposed that they select [sic] to be called St. Martins.

Apparently the proposal was not confirmed and the matter was left in abeyance, yet again. But in 1821 an order was received from Grand Lodge to communicate a name for the lodge forthwith and then the members agreed that they should be known as Lodge of Hope. One member was commissioned to call upon the Grand Secretary to acquaint him of their choice and to ask for their *Book of Constitutions* to be brought up to date, thus admitting that official directives had been ignored over the years. The reason for compliance this time, and the desire to conform for the future, is probably stated in the final sentence of the Minutes for that meeting: 'Bro. Gilks visited the Lodge'. He kept in touch with them, paying two visits that year, four the following year, and five in 1823 when another important decision was made. It may well be said that Peter Gilkes attendances set a hall-mark on their proceedings as he was often acting as Master to confer a degree, or to give a Craft lecture. Eventually he became a subscribing member and was immediately elected as Master (1828). But before we attend to the details of that important decision it is necessary to look back in time in the records of a Moderns lodge which was Constituted in 1776 at the Kings Arms, Kew Green, which, in accordance with custom, was known by the name of its meeting-place; it was No 322 on the List. In 1779 it took the name Lodge of Perseverance, but fourteen years later, as most of its members were non-commissioned officers in the Coldstream Regiment of Foot Guards whose Colonel was HRH the Duke of York, they took the name 'Royal York Lodge of Perseverance'. At the Union it was re-numbered 409.

Military precision seems to have been reflected in masonic behaviour and the lodge has a record of more than one centre for instructional purposes; their Minutes of 7 February 1800 have:

> RESOLVED. That in consequence of the frequent attention which Bro. Patterson has paid to this Lodge in particular as well as *our schools of Instruction* in general, that the members of this Lodge do present him with a medal as a grateful acknowledgement of his meritorious service.

In 1818 one of its 'schools' adopted the name United Lodge of Perseverance, the word 'United' being in common usage at that time as a demonstration of fraternal goodwill. When Lodges of Instruction were required to have official sanction from a sponsoring Lodge, that one was adopted by British Lodge No 8 which was the mother lodge of Peter Gilkes. The other 'schools' lost their identity, probably because the attendances were drawn from other lodges whose members had been encouraged by such enthusiasts as Bros J. Mivart, J.H. Wilson, and E. Whittington, except one which was sustained by those three, duly supported by Peter Gilkes. Sanction for that one was obtained on 27 November 1832 from the Lodge of Hope which:

> Agreed to sanction a Lodge of Instruction entitled the Lodge of Emulation at present held at the Red Lion, Old Cavendish Street, Meetings every Friday.

Thus, Emulation Lodge of Instruction, which had been meeting in an organised manner since 2 October 1823 obtained a proper sanction. (For a definitive work on that subject see *Emulation, A Ritual to Remember*, C.F.W. Dyer, London, 1973). For economic reasons Lodge of Hope No 7 could not survive on its own and on 12 March 1832 merged with Royal York Lodge of Perseverance No 409. It retained its seniority as No 7 on the Register and the founding date of 1751 of that lodge from the Antients, but adopted the name of the Moderns lodge which was founded in 1776.

Shortly after the ending of the Lodge of Reconciliation we find the names of those outstanding experts, Philip Broadfoot and Peter Gilkes appearing in the Minutes of Domatic Lodge and it must be noted in somewhat intriguing circumstances.

21 *Philip Broadfoot, Preceptor*

On 21 December 1816 Broadfoot attended and took the Chair to Initiate George Morgan. He attended again on 18 January 1817 and not only Passed Morgan but gave three Sections of the Entered Apprentice Lecture presumably for the benefit of that brother. Quite what was special about Bro Morgan we do not know but it is, to say the least, significant that on March 15 Peter Gilkes attended Domatic Lodge and, according to the Minutes, 'rose Bro George Morgan to the Sublime Degree of a Master Mason'. The connection with those famous masonic teachers probably influenced the brethren in Domatic to revive their interest in the practise of ritual for, in the Minutes of 16 October 1820 we find:

> That a Lodge of Instruction under the Warrant of this Lodge be formed and meet once a week at the Lodge quarters.

Formerly the lodge had been meeting at Hercules Pillars, Great Queen Street, but by then it had moved to The George, Brook Street, Holborn.

Such practising, rehearsing, and teaching bodies rarely stood the test of time and were apt, because of the varied attendances, to become peripatetic, and whilst Minutes of their meetings were sometimes taken they were seldom, if ever, preserved for posterity. The changing membership caused the initiative to pass from one to another and the identity disappears. On the Motion of Joseph Smith, who was then Immediate Past Master in Domatic Lodge, it was agreed in that lodge on 12 January 1846 to sanction the holding of a Lodge of Instruction at the Falcon Tavern, Fetter Lane, and the resolution stated that a circular was to be prepared and sent to all members. That spell of

instruction thrived because we find it listed in *Freemasons Quarterly Review* in 1855 under the appropriate heading, as 'Domatic No. 206, Falcon Tavern' with one other, 'R. Burns No. 25, St Martins Lane'. According to the attendance listed in a report in *FQR* 1858 (p 412), the only member from Domatic supporting that meeting was Bro T.A. Adams. It is noteworthy that in a report in the *Freemason Magazine* (2 Feb 1867) Domatic Lodge was described as 'One of the largest Lodges in London in point of numbers.'

22 *Peter Thompson, Preceptor*

Part Two

The Royal Arch

The Earliest references to the Royal Arch in the records of the Antients occur in the year 1752. In March of that year it was recorded that complaints had been made against two brethren who had been examined by Laurence Dermott because they were reported to have:

> ... Initiated many persons for the mean consideration of a leg of Mutton for dinner or supper to the disgrace of the Ancient Craft ... that upon examining some brothers they pretended to have made Royal Archmen the parties had not the least Idea of that secret ... and they had not the least Idea or Knowledge of Royal Arch Masonry.

In September it was recorded that a lecture was given by Laurence Dermott '... and every part of Real Freemasonry was traced and explained except the Royal Arch'. However, we have to wait until 2 March 1757 for the first positive mention:

> Order'd the Masters of the Royal Arch shall also be Summon'd to meet in Order to regulate things relative to that most valuable branch of the Craft.

The Antients Grand Lodge kept an overall authority of the Royal Arch and throughout their existence, until 1813, completely controlled the administration as we see by the following references from their Minutes:

> Grand Lodge Minutes 1 December 1784
> Read and Confirm'd the Minutes of the last Royal Arch Chapter and the Choice of Excellent Masters for Superintending.

Similar entries occur which shew an even wider range of their control:

> Read the Minutes of Royal Arch Committee and afterwards those of the Stewards Lodge of December, January, and February and the same passed Unanimously.

Even when the words 'Grand Chapter' had been included in the title the Minutes still came before Grand Lodge for approval

> Read the Minutes of the last Grand Chapter of the Royal Arch and same passed Unanimously.

Thus we see that the Royal Arch was officially treated as an extension of the Craft and intended for those who had attained mastership of a lodge under that jurisdiction; although the one exception to that was allowed to accommodate any brother about to go abroad.

> Grand Chapter. 4 Dec. 1771
> At a General Grand Chapter held on the above date it was Resolved, THAT no person for the future shall be made a Royal Arch Mason but the legal Representative of the Lodge [i.e., the Master], except a brother that is going abroad who hath been twelve months a Registered Mason.

Such was the nature of the Royal Arch and its relationship to the Craft according to the Antients, but it was, without question, the biggest point of contention between the two Grand Lodges; although not necessarily between brethren. It is proper now to review the situation under the Grand Chapter of the Moderns, bearing in mind that they were not a Recognised body in the eyes of the premier Grand Lodge of 1717. In the *Charter of Compact*, by which the Grand Chapter was set up at the Turk's Head, Gerrard Street, Soho, in the year 1766, relative items were stated thus.

> Sixthly, that none but discreet and experienced Master Mason shall receive exaltation to this Sublime degree, in this or in any other Chapter that may hereafter be duly constituted.
>
> Eighthly, that none calling themselves Royal Arch Masons shall be deemed any other than Masters in Operative Masonry, nor shall be received into any regular Chapter of the Royal Arch, or be permitted to reap or enjoy any of the Benefits, Dignities or Ensigns of that most Exalted Degree, save and except those who have received, or shall or may hereafter receive Exaltation in this Grand and Royal Chapter, or in some Chapter to be Chartered and Constituted by us or our Successors, Most Excellent Grand Officers aforesaid.

The Royal Arch degree was not general to all Antients lodges but often worked by qualified brethren known to each who would gather together from various lodges for the ceremony of Exaltation or Installation, such proceedings being held under the Warrant of one of the lodges, or a Chapter which may have been Chartered for such purpose. Companions who were 'Made' in that manner were included in the Returns or Reports to the Grand Chapter Committee.

The following item from the *Daily Advertiser*, dated 11 January 1754 is one example of how a Chapter meeting was called in that early period:

> All Brothers who were made in the E.G. and R.C. commonly call'd the Royal Arch, are desired to attend on Sunday night, at Five in the evening, at Brother John Henry's the Crown and Anchor, in King Street, Seven Dials, in order for a Grand Installation, and to chuse the P.T.H.J Z.L. and J.A. as Grand, and to proclaim the worthy S.O.J.N.R.S. with the two P.L.R.S. By Order of the P.T.H.J.Z.L. and J.A.
>
> W.L. Secretary
>
> Note: Removed from the Fountain in Monmouth Street.

The abbreviations contained in that Notice may be read as follows: 'E.G. and R.C.' to stand for 'Excellent Grand and Royal Chapter'; 'P.T.H.J.' = 'Prophet Haggai' (the letters J and I

being interchangeable); 'Z.L.' = 'Zerubbabel'; 'J.A.' = 'Jeshua'; 'S.O.J.N.R.S.' = 'Sojourners'; 'P.L.R.S.' = 'Pillars' (the two Scribes being described as 'Pillars' supporting the Arch which was represented by the three Principals); 'W.L.' = William Lilly, Grand Pursuivant in the Antients Grand Lodge 1752–56.

The proper qualification for admission to the Royal Arch was that of having been installed as Master of a Craft lodge and served that office for six months from one St. John's Festival to the next, that is from St. John the Baptist Day, June 24, to St. John the Evangelist Day, December 27, or *vice versa*, and that routine was well observed by the Antients in the early period.

We have an excellent illustration of how the Moderns were influenced in that respect in a ritual which was brought to notice by J.R. Dashwood, a former Secretary of Quatuor Coronati Lodge, (AQC Vol 71, pp 106–7). The ritual concerned stems from the Exaltation of 'several foreign Gentlemen' at an Emergency meeting of Grand Chapter in London on 28 October 1783. It is annotated 'Ritual for Royal Arch Chapter in possession of the Royal Norwegian Arch-Lodge 'Dovre' at Christiania'. The original is now in the Danish Grand Lodge library at Copenhagen. Dashwood stated that it was almost certainly supplied by the Moderns Grand Chapter in London and that it could probably be dated *circa* 1784. The qualification for a Candidate is stated in that ritual as:

> He who shall be initiated into the Royal Arch must have been a Master of the Chair, or else occupied that Office by Dispensation; he shall have passed the 4th degree of Craft Masonry.

It is quite significant to read the expression '4th degree' in source material emanating from the Moderns, for that itself placed it beyond Recognition for the premier Grand Lodge who limited Freemasonry to three Craft degrees.

Not all Past Masters entered the Royal Arch, for their various reasons, and in order to sustain this 'Fourth Degree', and to afford an opportunity for junior brethren, it became a common practice for brethren to be installed as Master of the lodge, to be entrusted as such, then to resign immediately from that position and the Master to resume. Indeed, many brethren might be so treated on an Installation Night and thus become 'Virtual Masters' but not having presided as Master for the requisite period. On 4 December 1771, a strong stand on that behaviour was taken by Laurence Dermott, an account of which is recorded in the Minutes of the Antients Grand Lodge:

The R! Worship! Deputy Grand Master informed the Grand Lodge of the proceedings of the *Royal Arch* meeting, Viz., on the 2nd October and 6th of November last and expatiated a long time on the scandalous method pursued by most of the Lodges (on S! John's Days) in passing a Number of Brethren through the Chair on purpose to obtain the sacred Mystery's of the *Royal Arch*, and proved in a concise manner that those proceedings were unjustifiable; therefore Moved for a Regulation to be made in order to Suppress them for the future. The Deputy was answered by several Brethren, that there were many Members of Lodges who from their Proffessions in Life (the Sea for Example) that could never regularly attain that part of Masonry, tho' very able and deserving Men, and humbly Moved that might be Considered in the New Regulations. The Grand Lodge in General thought such a Clause necessary and therefore the Question being put for the Regulation, it was unanimously Resolved: THAT no person for the future shall be made a *Royal Arch Mason* but the legal Representative of the Lodge [i.e. W. Master], except a Brother (that is going abroad) who hath been twelve months a Register'd Mason; and must have the Unanimous Voice of his Lodge to receive such qualification—and in order to render this Regulation more Expedient it is further Order'd that all Certificates granted to Brethren from their Respective Lodges shall have Inserted the Day the Brother or Brethren joined or was made in said Lodge and that this Regulation take place on S! Johns Day the 27th Dec. 1771.

On the subject of the regular occupation of the Master's Chair, as a preliminary qualification, we cannot do better than refer to the comment made by Laurence Dermott in his earlier publication, in 1756, of the Regulations under the title *Ahiman Rezon*. Following the inclusion of *Ahabath Olam*—'A Prayer repeated in the Royal Arch Lodge at Jerusalem'—Dermott went on to state:

Having inserted this Prayer, and mentioned that Part of Masonry commonly called the Royal Arch (which I firmly believe to be the Root, Heart, and Marrow of Free-Masonry) I cannot forbear giving a hint of a certain evil Designer, who has made a Trade thereof for some Time past, and has drawn in a Number of worthy, honest Men, and made them believe that he and his Assistants truly taught them all and every Part of the above-named Branch of Masonry, which they soon communicated to the worthy Brethren of their acquaintance ... till the whole field comes to be but one Heap of Miscarriages. This is the Case of all those who think themselves Royal Arch Masons, without passing the Chair in regular Form, according to the ancient Custom of the Craft: To this I will add the Opinion of our Worshipful Brother Doctor Fifield D'Assigny, printed in the Year 1744— 'Some of the Fraternity (says he) have expressed an Uneasiness at this Matter being kept a Secret from them (since they have already passed the usual Degrees of Probation) I cannot help being of Opinion, that they have no Right to any such Benefit until they make a proper Application, and are received with due Formality: And as it an organised Body of Men who have passed the Chair, and given undeniable Proofs of their Skill in Architecture, it cannot be treated with too much Reverence; and more especially since the Characters of the present Members of that particular Lodge are untainted, and their Behaviour judicious and unexceptionable: So that there cannot be the least Hinge to hang a Doubt on, but that they are most excellent Masons.'

The Respect I have for the very Name of Free-Mason, is sufficient to make me conceal the Name of the Person here pointed at; and, instead of exposing him, or stigmatizing him with a Name he justly deserves, I earnestly wish that God may guide him back, out of his present labyrinth of Darkness, to the true Light of Masonry; which is Truth, Charity, and Justice. . . . .

Despite the *Regulations*, and the recommendations, it remained commonplace for brethren under each Fraternity to Exalt those who could provide a Certificate from their lodge confirming that they had 'Passed the Chair' and had been entrusted. The situation was such that the *Regulations* were being honoured in the breach but it was at least tidied up by the Antients Grand

Lodge on 5 November 1783 when they passed the following Resolution to ensure that the Principals Chairs were not occupied by virtual Masters:

> RESOLVED. THAT Masters and Pastm^{rs} (bona fide) only ought to be admitted Master of the Royal Arch....

That was the state of affairs in the Royal Arch under the Antients jurisdiction by the time Domatic Lodge came on the scene. The first reference to 'Passing the Chair', although not in those exact terms, occurred on 27 December 1786 in the first year:

> Open'd at 7 o clock When proceeded to raise B^r Cook to the Masters Chair for the ensuing half year also B^r Wilcox Sr Warden, B^r Chadwick J^r Warden, B^r Parker Secretary, B^r Cellers Treasurer, B^r Abbott Sr Deacon, B^r Crouch J^r Dacon Likewise to *past B^r Broad the Chair*. Visited by B^r Chapman of 192, B^r Harpin of St John, B^r Banks of ditto Clos'd at half past 8 in good harmony.

Broad was thus made a 'virtual' Master, doubtless for the purpose of Exaltation in the Royal Arch on production of the appropriate Certificate. Unfortunately we know not where for there is no record of Royal Arch activity in lodge Minutes; in accordance with a directive on that subject. From other records we learn that Broad attained mastership of Lodge No 192 one year later and in that manner became an 'actual' master which would allow him to occupy the Principals' Chairs in a Chapter, but, of that, there is no apparent record.

Challenges to the practice of 'passing the Chair' were not isolated and the following example is taken from the records of Lodge No 6, bearing in mind that several Grand Officers were members of that lodge:

11 November 1788
It was ordered by the W. Master and the *Majority* [author's italics] of the Lodge No. 6 to summons the Master and Wardens of No. 225 for a trespass committed by them in passing a member of Lodge No. 6 through the Chair in order to obtain a seat in the H.R.A contrary to Constitution.

A few years later an item in Domatic records reveals a change in attitude regarding that:

30 December 1794
A Motion was made by B^r Cook for B^r Joseph Miller and B^r Staveley to pass the chair, agreeably to a Resolution passed last Quarterly Communication at the Grand Lodge that all Brothers having been made Masons one year, and not having opportunity to fulfil the offices, shall, if found worthy by the Master and other presiding officers, be passed the chair to enable them to receive the degree of the Royal Arch.

The Moderns Grand Chapter, of 1766, at first treated the admission of brethren with less restriction inasmuch as their *Regulations* allowed them— 'To admit, pass and exalt ... all such experienced and discreet Master Masons as they shall find worthy'. But it is evident that Antients procedure for the Candidate to have attained the Chair of a Craft lodge as a prerequisite must have made an impression; an alteration in their *Laws* appeared in those which were passed in the Grand and Royal Chapter in 1778:

> ... must have passed the three probationary degrees of Craft Masonry; been regularly appointed and presided as Master, to be justly entitled to, and have received the Past Master's token and pass-word ...

Whilst that was designed to restrict entry to the Royal Arch only to those who had actually served as Master of a lodge, that *Regulation* was too stringent. Four years later the *Laws* were amended and the words '*been regularly appointed*', as well as '*to be justly entitled to and have received the Past Masters' token and pass-word*' were deleted.

In the preamble to a manuscript Royal Arch ritual written by William Earle, *circa* 1793, a Companion well qualified to comment upon events of his time, for amongst other offices he had been Secretary of the Moderns Grand Stewards Lodge in 1787 and in 1790, we find his description thus:

> Royal Arch Masonry was originally Considered as a Mark of Distinction. A reward of merit and was extended to such worthy Brother only who had presided over a Lodge the whole time for which they were elected Master, but this restriction rendering it difficult to assemble a number competent to hold a Chap-

ter of the Order it was ordained that it should be lawfull to admit and exalt master masons who are skilfull in the three probationary degrees of Symbolic Craft Masonry (being of good repute) to this sublime degree by being previously installed Master of the Lodge and Pass'd to the Degree of Master of Arts and Sciences.

The subterfuge of brethren being 'Passed the Chair' was a practice that was widely adopted in Chapters, whether under Antients or Moderns jurisdiction, and the *Regulations* that stood from time to time were conveniently ignored. The content of the ceremony varied considerably; for the Antients it would take place in a Craft lodge on Installation night, but for the Moderns because of the rigid non-recognition of the Royal Arch by their Grand Lodge, the ceremony had to be performed in a Chapter with the members then forming what was called 'a previous lodge'. When that ceremony had been performed the Exaltation would take place, in the Chapter opened for that purpose.

Perhaps the most positive statement on the subject was contained in the preamble of *The Constitution of Free-Masonry or Ahiman Rezon* (Revised from the original of the late Laurence Dermott, Esq, by Thomas Harper, DGM) printed by T. Harper Jnr and published in 1807; probably to co-incide with efforts then being made to promote the Union of the two Grand Lodges. Here is the title and introduction to that section of the book:

LAWS AND REGULATIONS
for the
Instruction and Government
of
THE HOLY ROYAL ARCH CHAPTERS
under the sanction of
The Grand Lodge of England
according to the Old Constitutions.
His Grace the Duke of Atholl, Grand Master.
Revised, amended, and approved in General Grand Chapter
at the Crown and Anchor Tavern, Strand, London,
1 April 1807.

ANCIENT MASONRY consists of four Degrees— the three first of which are that of Apprentice, the Fellow Craft, and the sublime degree of Master; and a Brother, being well versed in these degrees, and otherwise qualified, as hereafter will be expressed, is eligible to be admitted to the fourth degree, the Holy Royal Arch.

This degree is certainly most august, sublime, and important than those which precede it, and is the summit and perfection of Ancient Masonry. It impresses on our minds a more firm belief of the existence of a Supreme Deity, without beginning of days, or end of years, and justly reminds us of the respect and veneration due to that Holy Name. Until within these few years, this degree was not conferred upon any, but those who had been a considerable time enrolled in the Fraternity; and could, beside, give the most unequivocal proofs of their skill and proficiency in the Craft.

It must of consequence, be allowed, that every regular and warranted Lodge possesses the power of forming and holding Meetings in each of these several degrees, the last of which, from its pre-eminence, is denominated, among Masons, a Chapter. That this supreme degree may be conducted with that regularity, order and solemnity, becoming the sublime intention with which it has from time immemorial been held, as an essential and component part of Ancient Masonry, and that which is the perfection and end of the beautiful system ...

23 *Frontispiece to* Ahiman Rezon, *1787 edition*

The following *Regulation* from the book shews the firm stand adopted regarding admitance:

iv. That no person shall be admitted to this Supreme Degree, but he who hath regularly and faithfully attained the three progressive degrees, and hath passed the Chair, nor until he hath been registered in the Grand Lodge books, as a Master-Mason, for twelve months at least prior to his application for that purpose; ...

After the Union of the two Grand Chapters in 1817, the agreed-upon *Regulations* which were passed in Grand Chapter on 8 May 1822, had the above, but with the deletion of 'hath passed the Chair'. But, old habits and customs are not lightly dismissed and there are abundant records available shewing that 'Passing the Chair' ceremonial continued in many areas and was being practised as late as the year 1870. (See B.E. Jones on that subject *AQC* Vol 70). In the Antients Grand Lodge on 4 December 1811, doubtless as a move towards uniformity, the end of half-yearly terms of office was approved in these terms:

> That from and after St. Johns Day next no Brother shall be eligible to be elected Master of any Lodge unless he shall have acted for Twelve Months in the same Lodge as Warden and that he shall not be entitled to the privileges of a Past Master until he shall have served one whole year in the Chair of his Lodge.

It was one of the few concessions that was made to the other Fraternity.

Royal Arch Certificates

The first mention of a 'recommendary Certificate' to pass the Royal Arch', directly involving brethren of Domatic Lodge comes from those who formed their second lodge, No 258. The Certificate was granted on 11 February 1790 to Sir Watkin Lewes and there is little doubt that it would have followed the form and wording of the period in the following style:

> To the Grand Chapter of Excellent Master Masons WHEREAS our trusty and well beloved Brother [Sir Watkin Lewes] a Geometric Master Mason and Member of our Lodge has solicited us to recommend him as a Master Mason every way qualified so far as we are Judges of the necessary qualifications for passing the Holy Royal Arch we do Certify that the said trusty and well beloved Brother [Sir Watkin Lewes] has obtained the unanimous consent of our Lodge NO. [258] for the recommendation and signing this Certificate.
> Given under our hands this ... Day of ... 17 ...
> Secretary   Master
>   S. Warden
>   J. Warden

Unfortunately it is not on record where his Exaltation took place.

Let us now return to those two stalwarts who were so involved in the Dispensation period of Domatic Lodge but were rejected as Joining Members when they applied, Charles Fenwick and Charles Sinclair. Their names were included in the official *Register of Excellent Masters*, the compilation of which was approved in the Antients Grand Lodge on 5 November 1783. In that List they were shewn as 'Regular Royal Archmen'. Some impression of their activity in that period in the Royal Arch can be formed from an account in the *History of Mount Moriah Lodge No 34* which was formerly Antients Lodge No 31. It shews them to have been experts in this field:

> 27 June 1785. Lodge No 31 met in the Arch upon an Emergency and by appointment of the Ex. Br.s Sinclair of No. 8 and Fenwick of No. 194 (Grand Chiefs) opened at 8 o clock ... Br. Hardie and Lanceman acted as Scribes, then conferred the Supreme Degree of the Royal Arch upon B.r J.no Philips in the presence of B.r Davies and Bowyer and B.r Westley of No. 6 B.r Auldhouse of No. 63 ...

The expression 'Grand Chiefs' was commonly applied to those who occupied the Principals Chairs and does not of necessity mean that those so described were Grand Officers. The following month we find them both recorded in 'Royal Arch Lodge No. 128 meeting on 27 July 1785' shewn as '1st Grand Chief' and '2nd Grand Chief' respectively. However, in 1791, Charles Sinclair did become a Grand Officer in an active capacity, and in excellent company as the attendance list for April portrays:

> Gen.l Grand Royal Arch Chapter, Crown & Anchor, Strand
> Wed.y 6 Ap. 1791
>   Grand Chiefs
> The R.W. Excell.t Bro. James Agar. Tho.s Harper. J. Feakins
>   Scribes
>   Robert Leslie   Chas. Sinclair
> With Excellent Bro.s of the different Warranted Lodges.

James Agar was Deputy Grand Master, Thomas Harper was then Past Senior Grand Warden, John Feakins Past Senior Grand Warden was then Grand Treasurer, Robert Leslie Past J.G.W was Grand Secretary.

In order to bring Domatic brethren into this picture we have to look at Minutes of the last two meetings prior to the Constitution as Lodge No 234 on the Antients Register. Two names then emerge through whom we are enabled to see just how widespread masonic activity was for some

24 *A Royal Arch Certificate dated 1792*

brethren. In company with others on 30 January 1786, Hugh Knight took all three degrees at the one meeting and, before the Closing John Knight was proposed 'to be made next meeting'. At the next meeting John Knight also took all three degrees. The two brothers made some progress in the lodge, for example in the second half of 1787 John was appointed Junior Deacon and re-appointed for the first half of the next year. Hugh acted as Tyler in 1787 and was apponted Senior Deacon for the first half of 1788, but neither made any further advance in Domatic Lodge. Whether that was due to any difference of opinion or a clash of personalities is not recorded, but in October 1789 John Knight is shewn in the Minutes as a visitor and is described as 'W.M. No. 13'. Also, it is sad to record that he chose that occasion for a confrontation with John Wood, the first Master of Domatic Lodge:

> Bʳ Knight caused a Disturbance during Lodge hours and accusing Bʳ John Wood of not being a Mason. He likewise Proceded in ill Language Against Bʳ John Perkins and said He was Likewise a snake against Him. Bro. Knight was Desir'd to Withdraw to Settle These Controversys With Bʳ Wood, But after With-drawing Refused so to Do, as Witnessed by several Brᵒʳˢ Whereupon The Worshipfull Master and Officers of the Lodge with the Rest of the Brᵒʳˢ Present Desir'd the Lodge to Be Closed against Bʳ John Knight for His Misconduct and Ill Behaviour during Lodge Hours.

Harmony must have been restored between those concerned, as two months later, in December, he is listed again as a visitor and there is no comment.

The next month we bring the two Brothers Knight together again, this time in company with Charles Sinclair, not in Domatic Lodge but on two occasions in Lodge No 13 (now Neptune Lodge No 22):

> Lodge No. 13 Kings Arms Deptford. 4 Janʸ 1790 Opened in due form at 5 o clock when it was unan. agreed by all members present that a Royal Arch Chapter be held here on Sunday the 17ᵗʰ January when Bʳ John Knight, Bʳ Michael Murray and Bʳ Edmund Gundry is to be initiated . . .

Lodge No. 13 Kings Arms Deptford. 17 Janʸ 1790 Master in the Chair all Officers present when a Royal Arch Lodge was held and Bʳ John Knight, Bʳ Hugh Knight, Bʳ Michael Murray and Bʳ Edmund Gundry was Initiated into that Sublime Degree aforesaid. Opened at 1 o clock 6 closed at 9 in good harmony.

> Bʳ C. Sinclair ⎫
> Bʳ Cooke   ⎬ Grand Chiefs
> Bʳ Boyne   ⎭

The first reference to the Royal Arch in Domatic Lodge appears in the Minutes of 13 October 1793 when Coyte and Grundy (the name is mispelt in the above Minutes as 'Gundry') both Past Masters of 234, and Crow and Wight who were members of the lodge but Past Masters of No 258, the lodge emanating from the additional Warrant held by Domatic, 'drew their recommendary certificates for the Royal Arch'. It is significant that was the founding year allowed for Domatic Chapter, a matter that will arise later.

It is now of interest to note that John Perkins, mentioned above as having 'ill language' from John Knight, had a somewhat mixed year of effort in 1792. In the months of May, August, and September he petitioned the Grand Stewards Lodge for charitable relief and on each occasion it was dismissed as 'unworthy' but on 21 November he did receive £2. 2. 0. 'for Drawing for the Grand Lodge Royal Arch Certificate', and that might well have been a design for a printing plate for their official issue.

The earliest Royal Arch Certificate in the official archives is dated 8 May 1792 and the de-sign was in continuous use until the latest one dated in 1816. There is nothing to guide us as to who was responsible for the design but it is quite possible that it was done by John Perkins and that amount of £2. 2. 0 being a somewhat delayed pay-ment for work done by him earlier in the year. His persistent applications for relief might well have been avoided if an earlier settlement had been made; but that, of course, is pure speculation.

Excellent Masters or 'Nine Worthies'

With regard to the maintenance of uniformity of ritual and ceremonial, and to ensure supervision of Craft procedure in general, certain brethren were chosen by the Antients Grand Lodge for that very purpose. However, it should be noted that the choice remained with the Grand Chapter, obviously in conjunction with other Grand Officers from time to time.

Resolutions made in the Antients 'General Grand Chapter' or 'Grand Lodge of Royal Arch Masons' on 4 December 1771 and 3 January 1772, according to how they were defined, were not only confirmed at the meeting of Grand Chapter on 5 November 1783 but were expanded by another nine Resolutions which, in effect, were *The Laws and Regulations* operative for the Royal Arch when Domatic Lodge came into existence. The three 'Chiefs' presiding at the meeting were Laurence Dermott, described as 'Deputy Grand Master of Masons', James Read, Senior Grand Warden, and 'The Worshipful John McCormick, past Master of the Lodge No 6'. The earlier Resolutions were read aloud, adopted, and then nine further items added. The following extracts are relevant:

5 Novr 1783
THAT this Chapter do perfectly coincide with the foregoing Resolutions. And that Masters and Pastm^s (Bona fide) only ought to be admitted Masters of the Royal Arch . . .

2^d RESOLVED That for the better preservation of the Supreme Degree of Free Masonry (aforesaid) the names of all the Regular Royal Archmen shall be Recorded (gratis) in a particular Book prepared for that purpose And to be called SEPER ENHOLAH RABIIM i.e., The Register of Excellent Masters; So that the names and merit of the several Masters may be brought into one point of View; and examined when Occasion shall require.

3^d RESOLVED That the Members of the General Chapter so Recorded (and none other) shall meet (not less than) twice every year (or oftener if any six of them require it) such meetings to be for their General improvement and Rectitude.

4th RESOLVED That as it is Universally Acknowledged, That the Regular Masters of the Royal Arch (only) are in possession of the Supreme Degree of Freemasonry: THE GENERAL GRAND CHAPTER shall once in every year (for the future) when duly Congregated in conjunction with the Right Worshipful Grand Officers for the time being, Make choice of a Certain Number of the Most Excellent Masters amongst themselves, Which Number shall not exceed Nine persons, whose names and addresses shall be Return'd and Recommended to the General Grand Lodge. To Examine the Abilities of all and every of the person or persons (of the Ancient Lodges) who shall take upon him or them. To Perform any of the secret Ceremonies Relative to the Royal Arch, the Installation of Grand Officers or Processions &c &c &c. And upon finding any such person or persons Master or Lecturer &c defective or unworthy, To report him or them to the Grand Master or his Deputy for the time being; So that such defective performer may be suppress'd and forbid to use his Craft until he or they shall be found more Capable. And in Case of non-Compliance To be forever Excluded.

6th RESOLVED That the Excellent Masters Chosen, & Appointed as aforesaid shall (in Conjunction with the Grand Officers for the time being) Use their utmost endeavours to Study, Learn, Rehearse and practise, the several Ancient Ceremonies &c &c &c &c performed in the Craft; particularly the Mysteries of the Holy Royal Arch, the Installation of Grand Officers, in General, and Processions &c &c In order that the Ancient Landmarks may be faithfully preserved, and handed down pure and undefiled to Our posterity for ever.

7th RESOLVED That in Order to render those Regulations more Expedient and Effectual; no person (though a Regular Master or Pastmaster) shall be made a Royal Arch Mason (within thirty miles of London) without the Assistance or Concurrence of Six of the Masters whose Names are upon the Royal Arch Record. Nor shall the name of any Mason be recorded amongst the Excellent Masters Without the Order of a General Chapter or a Certificate sign'd by three (or more) of the Masters chosen (for that year) for Regulating the Craft as aforesaid.

Another Resolution called for a list of names to be printed and issued annually, but, if that was carried out nothing of that nature has survived.

There cannot be much doubt that the selection of Excellent Masters was made strictly in accordance with those *Regulations* as frequent relative entries appear in the Minutes of Grand Lodge and incidents regarding official visitations are recorded. The target of efficiency and uniformity as a pattern for Antients ceremonial, at least in London, was jealously guarded and controlled and was even sought after by the desire of those who were placed at a distance. An example of that was quoted in *Lodges of Instruction* by Ivor Grantham in his Prestonian Lecture for 1950:

> ... the authority of at least one of the Nine Worthies was recognized in the west country as late as 1811, in which year on St. John's Day in Harvest at a meeting of the Royal Cambrian Lodge No 135 at Newport, Monmouthshire:
>
> > It was recommended by Bro. Benj. Plummer, that our Bro. Ronalds, P. Nine Worthy of the Grand Lodge, do attend this lodge to give Instruction and for which this lodge engages to defray his expenses from London and back, and to pay him two guineas per week, as long as he remains with this lodge. The sense of the lodge was taken on this question and it appeard to be unanimous.
>
> *(The Collected Prestonian Lectures, p 337)*

Grantham also commented: 'other contemporary allusions to the Nine Worthies may well exist amongst private lodge records, but no other instance was noted during the preparation of this lecture'.

Among the thirty-seven names listed on Folio 1 of the *Register of Members of the Royal Arch (Antients)*, as it was styled, we find 'Charles Sinclair, P.M. 8' with the year 1780 alongside, and 'Charles Fenwick, P.M. 194' with the year 1782. Sinclair was appointed as an 'Excellent Master' for the year 1792 and at that date the process of the selection was re-stated:

Grand Lodge &c. 7 March 1792
RESOLVED AND ORDERED—THAT a general uniformity of the practice and ceremonies of the Ancient Craft, may be preserved and handed down unchanged to posterity. The Lodges in London and Westminster shall be required to recommend a Brother from each Lodge who must be a Master or Past Master and otherwise well skilled in the Craft, to be put in nomination at the Grand Chapter, in October of each year, to be elected of the Nine Excellent Masters; who are allowed to visit Lodges: and should occasion require, they are to report thereon to the Grand Chapter, or the R.W. Deputy Grand Master, who will act as he shall deem necessary.

The first Minute Book of Domatic Lodge, however, has an entry relative to this subject but has proved rather baffling. For the first two years the Minutes are written on a right-hand facing page with the left, or reverse side, blank—with one exception. Overleaf from the record of the first meeting by Dispensation, indeed what is *now* the first page of the book, the following, in complete isolation, has been written:

Samuel Livi } 221
John Murphy }
Lewis Barnet one of the Nine Wortheys
Br Cox W. Master of 31
Br Newman of 55

No reason whatsoever was stated for that list and at no time do any of those names appear attending a meeting of the lodge. The first two are shewn as members of '221' which is the number of the lodge then meeting at the Horse and Leaping Bar Tavern, Whitechapel. In 1819 that lodge took the name Lodge of Judah but unfortunately went into decline and was erased from the Register on 3 March 1830. Lewis Barnet is a name that appears twice in the official Index of names, shewn first as '231', an Antients lodge constituted 26 September 1785 at Southwark and is now Phoenix Lodge No 173, and then shewn as '253' a lodge Constituted 21 April 1789 at the Globe, Hatton Garden, and is now Lodge of Joppa (named in 1816) No 188. It is probable that he was a member of both lodges. The item 'Br. Cox W. Master of 31' may help to date the entry as, the records of that lodge shew two brethren of that name, 'Bro. John Cox Senr. W.M. 1799' and 'Bro. John Cox, W.M. 1804' thus the earliest dating for the annotation in Domatic Minute Book is 1799 which is a period outside the range of that book. The last name, 'Br. Newman of 55', leads us to the lodge Constituted on 2 August 1756 the brethren of which later purchased Warant No 3 (dated 6 June 1759), was named St. Georges Lodge but on 6 December 1843 united with Corner Stone Lodge and is now known under the joint name 'St. Georges and Corner Stone' No 5; a lodge having the privilege of nominating a Grand Steward for the year. Lodge No 31 met at the Ship and Anchor, Gun Dock, Wapping. In 1817 it was named as Mount Moriah and is still on the Register as No 34 with a founding date of 1754.

The distinction and honour of an appointment as one of the Nine Excellent Masters for the year 1796 came to Domatic and was recorded by them as follows:

Domatic Lodge 29 Sep! 1795
A letter was read from the Grand Lodge requesting a return of the Royal Arch Brothers and a person to stand as Candidate for an Excellent Brother to assist the Grand Officers in visiting the Lodges to see the Ancient Craft duly performed.

Bro Wight, the Secretary was then chosen by them for consideration by the General Grand Chapter, and was accordingly appointed 'one of Nine Excellent Masters for preserving the Craft free from innovation', as it was expressed. In addition to serving for 1796 he was re-appointed for the following year and thus had the distinction of two successive tours of duty. Even though Wight did not serve Domatic Lodge as Master, but had served as such in No 258 whilst that additional Warrant was in their hands, he was then presented with a Past Masters jewel, 'at the expense of the Lodge', presumably to mark their pride and pleasure; it was not an automatic presentation to an out-going Master as is the custom in most lodges nowadays.

A few years later the following item appeared in the Minutes of the (Antients) Stewards Lodge:

18 November 1801. A Motif was made and Seconded that the Nine Excellent Masters for the time being should have a Medal emblematic of their office which should be given up when they were out of Office for their Successors which was agreed to Subject to the Opinion of the Grand Lodge.

That recommendation was carried into practice and a distinctive jewel was struck, the obverse of which shewing a brother using a crowbar to remove the keystone of the central of three arches, the reverse having a number of masonic symbols. In this connection, further entries in the Stewards Lodge records are also of interest (plate 13):

21 July 1802. Grand Lodge Regalia Nine Worthies Paid for Nine Silver Medals chased on both sides with Emblems of Masonry & Morocco Case to each @ 52/6 ... £23.12.6. Hanging for Ditto made with broad blue Ribbon and swivel to each £3.7.6.

16 December 1807. Account presented to Bro. E. Harper for Silver Chains for the Nine Worthies Jewels—12 Warrants—etc. £22.17.0.

It should be noted that in the later *Articles of Union* between the two Grand Lodges the same method of supervision was adopted:

V. ... the two Grand Masters shall appoint each nine worthy and expert Master Masons, or Past Masters, of their respective Fraternities, with Warrant and instructions to meet together ...

Nine Excellent Masters, or Nine Worthies, thus became eighteen for the Lodge of Reconciliation with the two Grand Secretaries in attendance. The brethren appointed by the Duke of Kent to represent the Antients Grand Lodge were:

R.F Mestayer	No	1	now Grand Master's Lodge	No	1
T. Harper Jnr.	,,	1	,, ,, ,, ,,	,,	1
J.H. Goldsworthy	,,	2	,, Lodge of Fidelity	,,	3
W. Fox	,,	4	,, Royal York Lodge of Perseverance	,,	7
J. Ronalds	,,	16	,, Robert Burns Lodge	,,	25
W. Oliver	,,	77	,, Royal Jubilee Lodge	,,	72
M. Corcoran	,,	194	,, Middlesex Lodge	,,	143
R. Bayley	,,	240	,, erased in 1836		
J. McCann	,,	244	,, Tranquility Lodge	,,	185

Those appointed by the Duke of Sussex Were:

Rev. S. Hemming	No	384	now Lodge of Harmony	No	255
W. Meyrick	,,	1	,, Lodge of Antiquity	,,	2
W. Shadbolt	,,	21	,, Old Kings Arms Lodge	,,	28
S. Jones	,,	1	,, Lodge of Antiquity	,,	2
L. Thompson	,,	54	,, Lodge of Felicity	,,	58
J. Jones	,,	66	,, erased		
J.H. Sarratt	,,	118	,, Moira Lodge	,,	92
T. Bell	,,	180	,, Caledonian Lodge	,,	134
J. Joyce	,,	435	,, Bank of England Lodge	,,	263

Thus the experience of some who were engaged in the Lodge of Promulgation was called into valuable use once more.

Towards Another Union—1817

In order to appreciate the somewhat anomalous position of the Royal Arch in the latter half of the eighteenth century, we have to recall that the Antients treated it as a progressive step, literally as a fourth degree. At first it was supervised by a Committee of those who were qualified and registered as such on a proper Register, but that was later styled 'The General Grand Chapter'; always their deliberations were under the government of the Antients Grand Lodge. The Moderns had consistently refused to acknowledge anything beyond the three Craft degrees, although it is quite possible that a form of the Royal Arch may have been performed in Masters' Lodges. Brethren under the premier Grand Lodge were not to be denied and did participate, even to the extent of raising a Grand Chapter themselves in 1766, but it was unrecognized and entirely separate from their own Grand Lodge. In 1769, just three years after its formation, and to make the facility available on a wider scale, that Grand Chapter issued Charters for the formation of other Chapters. We owe much to their organisation, sound administration, and recording of considerable detail of activity.

Non-recognition of the Royal Arch by the Moderns Grand Lodge was repeatedly made clear by successive Grand Secretaries. In 1768 Thomas French wrote:

> ... the Royall Arch masonry comes by no means under our inspection. You are desired never to insert the transactions thereof in your regular Lodge Book nor to carry on the business of that degree on your stated Lodge nights. ...

In 1774 James Heseltine, his successor, wrote:

> ... With respect to the information you have rec'd, as to the Grand Lodge of England's having Degrees and Mysteries superiour to the three Degrees already communicated to you may rest assured it has not the least foundation in truth. I may now give you my word of honour as a Mason that the Grand Lodge of England has not any other *acknowledged* Degrees. It is true that many of the Fraternity here belong to a Degree

in Masonry say'd to be superiour to the other three, call'd the Royal Arch. I have the honour to be a member of this Degree and its principles and proceedings are truly praiseworthy—but it is unknown in Grand Lodge, and all Emblems or Badges of distinction in that Degree are prohibited from being worn in G.L. . . .

In 1792, the next Grand Secretary, William White, wrote:

> That this Lodge do agree with its Committee that the Grand Lodge of England has nothing to do with the proceedings of the Society of Royal Arch Masons. . . .

(A documentary Paper—'The premier Grand Lodge and the delayed Recognition of the Royal Arch'—was compiled by the author and appeared in *AQC* Vol 82, pp 74-100, the *Transactions* of Quatuor Coronati Lodge No 2076.)

In the last decade of the eighteenth century, whilst the attention of most brethren was focussed upon the desired Craft Union, which was eventually achieved in 1813, the Royal Arch laboured under considerable difficulties which were certainly aggravated by some Companions under the Moderns Grand Chapter. In condemnation of their efforts an official statement was made on 10 May 1793, which included the following:

> In the place of attempting to create a Schism in the Order and conceiving themselves qualified to compact one with another to take the future management of the Royal Arch Masonry into their hands, they would ... have complied first with those Resolutions which were passed when they were present ... The framers of that Memorial have assiduously misrepresented the conduct of the Grand Lodge of Craft masons upon a complaint made by a late Companion against the Officers of the Grand and Royal Chapter. The Grand Lodge very properly observed on that occasion that it had nothing to do with a Matter originating in another independent Society competent to judge of and determine on its own affairs. ...

Royal Arch Companions fell into two main groups, those who had received the Past Masters' token and word, either by right, having served the office as Master, or having received them expressly for the purpose of Exaltation in the Royal Arch. Brethren of the first group were to be found in the membership of both Antients and Moderns jurisdictions, but among the Moderns were those described as 'experienced and discreet Master Masons' not all of whom had even been on the Register for the required twelve months probation. It was thus a conglomerate of qualifications among the membership in general and contained many seeds for dissension not only among the Moderns companions themselves but between the two authorities. Not all companions were in possession of the required token and word as Masters of Arts and Sciences.

That situation led to the Modern Grand Chapter bringing the matter under consideration and their Minutes of 28 March 1792 have the following:

> PROPOSED to adopt some test word of communication for all regular Companions of the Royal Arch.

Unfortunately we do not have a record of what was considered or adopted, such matters would not appear, but there is no subsequent reaction on record. It may well have been then that the biblical reference from Hosea was considered, but manuscript rituals or writings of that period have no guidance on the subject. However, in principle, history was being repeated as the premier Grand Lodge had transposed certain words in the Craft 'in or about the year 1739' to create a means of identifying their own brethren. Although in 1809 that situation was corrected by reverting 'to the old Landmarks', as it was stated, the adjustment was not made on the Continent, and ritual exposures of the mid-eighteenth century shew that the change was taken there as an export from the Moderns.

Sir Peter Parker, Deputy Grand Master (Moderns) 1787–1811, was also active in Royal Arch administration serving as First Grand Principal, or 'Grand Master Z' as it was often styled, for the years 1792–93. We get some idea of the earnest desire among Companions for the Royal Arch to become acceptable by the Moderns Grand Lodge from the following dedication in the publication

Free-Masonry, A Word to the Wise (Thomas Wilkinson, Dublin, 1796) and this, not being previously quoted by students in this field, is now shewn in full:

To the Honourable Sir Peter Parker, Bart., Admiral of the Blue Squadron of His Majesty's Navy. Supreme Grand Master of the Grand and Royal Chapter of the Royal Arch of Jerusalem and Deputy Grand Master of the Antient and Honourable Society of Free and Accepted Masons.

Sir,

As I have ever considered dedications merely as a form of compliments, the subsequent Sheets were intended to have made their appearance without any ceremony of this nature, but the attempt in agitation to impeach the integrity you have displayed, in coming forward at a time, when innovation appeared on the most essential Degree of Masonry, impels me, thus publicly, to declare the high sense that I, in conjunction with every member of the Society, have of the obligations we owe to you.

Persevere, Sir, in establishing the union which cements the Grand Lodge of England with the grand and Royal Chapter of the Royal Arch of Jerusalem; be assured that the calumny of the unworthy and disaffected, will never reach the eminence to which your rectitude has elevated you.

Proceed, Sir, and convince the Brethren, that your principles in Masonry invariably correspond; and that your conduct will ever be such as to defy the venom of irregularity, and the malice of disappointment.

I am, Sir,
With due deference and respect,
Your most Obedient and
Humble Servant,
The Editor.

Nov. the 20th 1796.

Admiral Sir Peter Parker was President of the Grand Chapter Council (Moderns) for the years 1784–90 and 1796. There can be little doubt that he influenced the situation quite favourably, but as he died in the year 1812, it is sad to think that he did not survive to see any of the fruits of his labours in that connection.

In that period, and into the nineteenth century, Companions in the Provinces under that jurisdiction were being sadly neglected by the administrators in London. Answers to letters and requests were seemingly ignored or belated, but when we compare the strength of the Province of Lancashire with that of London, just to take one example, 38 Chapters for Lancashire and 17 for London, it will be appreciated what valiant efforts were being made by those who were set at such a distance. They were much on their own in many respects but their support for the Royal Arch shewed just how much it meant in their masonic lives.

It is possible that the state of neglect in the administration of affairs of Grand Chapter had been the cause of some Companions to think that if it was taken under the aegis of the grand Lodge it would then be better served and presented to others in better light. Letters were being left unanswered, receipts for fees for registration were not forthcoming, requests for advice met with little response, indeed the state of ineffectiveness may be estimated from a comment in a letter from one prominent Grand Officer to another sent on 23 March 1793:

> ... The Attendance of the Companions but especially the Grand Officers having been so seldom and at so late an hour that little or no business of consequence could be translated (if ever a chapter was formed) with the regularity and solemnity appertaining to the government of a Royal Arch Chapter of Jerusalem. It is therefore absolutely necessary that every Companion in Office should either attend his duty in person or nominate a proper Companion to officiate in his situation. If this is not attended to for the future, the Grand and Royal Chapter must unavoidably dissolve. ...

That letter was from F.A. Winzer, Grand Scribe N 1792, Principal Sojourner 1795, Third Grand Principal 1796, to John Allen, Grand Treasurer 1794–1806, Inspector General 1778–96, etc.

A rescue operation may well have been triggered by his action but it was some years before any real improvement was noticeable. In 1801 a special Committee was set up to give attention to the financial state and to determine which Chapters had failed to meet their obligations and later to erase from the Register those which had become moribund. In 1803 the Earl of Moira was installed as First Grand Principal, Earl Mountnorris as Second Grand Principal, and Waller Rodwell Wright as Third Grand Principal. Under the leadership of such important Freemasons it may be taken that Grand Chapter gained considerably, but, despite the constant communication that was taking place between the Earl of Moira and Thomas Harper trying to create grounds for a Union in the Craft, the Royal Arch was proving to be quite an obstacle. Patience and assiduity still had to be exercised and an unbelievable tolerance was called for at that level.

Eventually, at a Special Convocation of the Grand Chapter (Moderns), held on 30 November 1813, it was announced:

> ... H.R.H. the Duke of Sussex had entered into preliminary Articles with the Grand Lodge now under the Duke of Kent for an Union of the two Grand Lodges under one Grand Master. THAT by those Articles the Royal Arch was acknowledged as the perfection of the Masters Degree. ...

Official recognition at long last! The next hurdle was how to present the Royal Arch, which was under an entirely separate administration for the Moderns by the Grand Chapter which had been set up in 1766, in such a manner that it would not be a bar in any way to the Craft Union. At that same meeting two Resolutions were passed and it is well to keep both in proper perspective. The first dealt with the relationship that was to be taken by the Grand Chapter with their grand Lodge on the subject of a union:

> ... RESOLVED unanimously that as the Grand Lodge of England has through the M.W. Grand Master communicated its determination to acknowledge the Royal Arch this Grand Chapter does consider an Union of this order with the Grand Lodge highly proper and desirable.

It was a first step; a joint demonstration from the Grand Chapter and the Grand Lodge to show to the Antients a willingness to identify the Royal

Arch with the Craft. However, we should carefully note that it was to be 'an Union' which was 'highly proper and desirable' an identity was to be preserved; it was not going to be a merger in which initiative would be lost. The point is clearly seen in the second Resolution which was a logical follow-on:

> ... RESOLVED that H.R.H. the Duke of Sussex, M.E.Z. be invested with full and unlimited Powers to negotiate and conclude an Union on behalf of this Supreme Grand Chapter with the Grand Lodges under their Royal Highnesses the Dukes of Sussex and Kent in such a way as may appear to H.R.H. most conclusive to the General interest of Masonry.

Thus, the Moderns grand Chapter, before the Craft Union of 1813, gave 'full and unlimited powers' to their First Principal 'to conclude an Union' with *both* Grand Lodges, whilst there were two in existence, for soon there would be just one. Time was short, however, and whilst all parties seemed to honour the principles contained in those Resolutions, nothing tangible in regard to the Royal Arch resulted. The Union of the two grand Lodges took place on 27 December (St. John's Day) 1813 and the United Grand Lodge of England came into being, but with the Moderns Grand Chapter apparently left out on a limb, as it were.

In the *Articles of Union* the acknowledgement of the Royal Arch was stated in the following terms:

> 11. It is declared and pronounced that pure and Ancient Masonry consists of three degrees and no more, viz., those of the Entered Apprentice, the Fellow Craft, and the Master Mason, including the Supreme Order of the Holy Royal Arch. But this Article is not intended to prevent any Lodge or Chapter from holding a meeting in any of the degrees of the Orders of Chivalry, according to the Constitutions of the said Orders.

It was a compromise but it left a problem. The Antients Grand Chapter had been an integral part of their Grand Lodge but lost its identity when the governing body merged with the moderns Grand Lodge, whereas the Moderns Grand Chap-

ter, possessing a separate power exercising authority over Chapters to whom Charters had been granted, remained as a separate entity. Some idea of the sort of problems that arose can be estimated from the following extract of a letter dated 15 October 1816 sent to London from St. Johns Lodge, No 670, in the Province of Lancashire:

> To Edw. Harper Esq., Joint Grand Secretary
> Freemasons Hall, London
> Dear Sir,
>   One part of our Brethren that are Arch-Masons were made under the Modern system of an Arch-Warrant, the other under the Ancient system have been Arched and the Craft. Now the former looks upon the latter as not legall; we wish to have youre advice on the subject how we ought to procede, as many of our Brethren are desirous to take it; and some of them have taken it at the neighbouring Lodges, we wish to know if we shall be justified in Makeing Arch-Masons on the Ancient System; or if we could have a Dispensation from the Grand; untill such times as we can have an Arch-Warrant, if Warrants are to be granted for that Degree. ...

Such was the fluid state of affairs around the country, genuine pleas for advice some of which were difficult to resolve as consultation on such matters had not even begun. The Craft Union had been a major turn of events and still demanded concentrated effort from all concerned with their attention focussed upon settling 'differences', in its widest interpretation, in ritual and procedure, and then upon the promotion of acceptable forms. The questions relating to the Royal Arch were referred to those who had been concerned previously in its administration, and the weakened Grand Chapter of the Moderns remained as a form of authority giving an appearance of regularity for companions from both sides.

The strongest influence in the Royal Arch came from the membership of the Chapter of St. John as it had prominent Grand Officers from both former jurisdictions, including Thomas Harper who bridged the two. Records of this period are sparce regarding this situation but it is evident that a constructive effort was necessary to bring affairs under proper control and this was initiated in

1817. The following compilation of the essential facts will convey an accurate picture of the re-shaping:

Grand Chapter. 18 March 1817
A report was made from the other Gr. Ch. that they had unanimously resolved that an Union of the two Gr. Ch. was desirable. ...

From the Minutes of the joint meeting of the two Grand Chapters, held on the same day for the purpose of forming such Union, we have:

The Members of the two former Grand Chapters having been summoned to meet this day they assembled in separate apartments; and the Chapter having been opened the members proceeded to a Third Chamber where His Royal Highness the Duke of Sussex M.E.Z. was waiting to receive them; the United Grand Chapter was then formed as follows:—
[then appears a list of twenty names of which only four were from the former Antients Grand Chapter]

together with The Three Principals of the several Chapters in the London District.
The M.E.Z. then acquainted the Companions that he had convened this meeting for the purpose of forming a Junction of the two Grand Chapters and that certain Laws and Regulations might be enacted for the future Regulation of the Order. ...

A worthy tribute was paid to Thomas Harper upon whom the Duke of Sussex conferred the rank of Past Second Grand Principal, the one and only time it has ever been used, to mark the sterling work, diligence and patience, as well as the forbearance he had displayed throughout the protracted negotiations to achieve amity and for companions in both jurisdictions to be united.

Six months later the regularity of the Union in the Royal Arch, and its new administration, was duly acknowledged by the United Grand Lodge of England which was recorded in the following extract from their Minutes:

The Grand Lodge having been informed that the two Grand Chapters of the Order of the Royal Arch, existing prior to the Union of the Craft, had formed a junction ...

RESOLVED unanimously, THAT the Grand Lodge will at all times, be disposed to acknowledge the Peoceedings of the Grand Chapter, and so long as their arrangements do not interfere with the Regulations of the Grand Lodge, and are in conformity with the Act of Union, they will be ready to recognise, facilitate, and uphold same. ...

A new Register was necessary and the authorities first had to check regarding the effectiveness of Chapters remaining on the Roll; the Returns were examined and work to bring orderliness to the situation began in earnest. Among the *Laws and Regulations* passed and printed in 1817 was the following:

That all Chapters of Royal Arch Masons which existed and were registered in the books of either of the two Fraternities of Antient Free Masons, and which met at stated periods, prior to the 27th December, 1813, shall be considered and are hereby acknowledged as regular existing Chapters, and shall, on application, within six months, to this United Grand Chapter, receive free from every expenses, a Charter of Constitution to be attached to their Craft Warrant. That such regular Chapters as have existed prior to the said 27th December, 1813, without being attached to any regular Lodge, shall unite themselves to some Lodge.

The application which was sent by the companions of Domatic Chapter has the following particulars and was dated 8 March 1818:

We ... (names listed) The Deomatick Chapter of Holy Royal Arch are desirous of continuing attached to the said Lodge ... to meet on the Second Sunday in every month.

(Signed)	Robert Gill	Z.
	J.A. Farthing	H
	John Purton	J
	Thomas Key	E
	Enoch Prince	N
	Richd Pratt	
	Wm Scaplehorn	
	W. Frampton	

Official acknowledgement appears in the records and is noted as:

> 293 to be attached to the Domatic Lodge 293 & to be called Domatic Chapter held at Hercules Pillars, Great Queen St. on the 2nd Sunday.
>
> 29 Octr 1818

Robert Gill who signed as First Principal of the Chapter had been a prominent and active worker on behalf of the Craft Union but his efforts in the 1790's had brought only disappointment. A Senior Grand Warden of the Antients Grand Lodge 1798-1801 he had been in very good company. Indeed, in 1798 he was one of the Founders and Governors of what is now the Royal Masonic Institution for Boys but was then styled 'The Masonic Charity for Cloathing and Educating the Sons of Indigent Free Masons according to the old Institutions'; The Governors were listed as:

MW Bro The Duke of Atholl, Grand Master
RW Bro Thomas Harper,
    Deputy Grand Master
RW Bro Robert Gill, Senior Grand Warden
RW Bro William Burwood,
    Junior Grand Warden
RW Bro Robert Leslie, Treasurer to the Charity
    Bro Benjamin Aldhouse, Secretary to the
    Charity.

It is also worthy to note that Robert Gill not only signed the Petition as First Principal of Domatic Chapter on the 8 March but the following day signed another, also as First Principal on behalf of what is now Mount Sinai Chapter No 19, but then to be attached to Lodge of Concord No 56. Both Charters of Confirmation, for that is what they were then called, were issued and dated for 29 October 1818. Lodge of Concord was erased in 1860 and Mount Sinai Chapter successfully petitioned to become attached to Royal Athelstane lodge No 19. It is also of interest to note that before the Royal Arch Union of 1817, Robert Gill had occupied each of the three Grand Principals' Chairs in the Antients General Grand Chapter and that Royal Arch Certificates of that period

bear his signature as the occupants of one of those Offices.

Whilst the Charter of Attachment for Domatic Chapter is dated 29 October 1818, it was not handed to them until 14 March 1819 and that date was mistakenly taken by the Companions fifty years later when they held a celebratory 'Jubilee Meeting' on 25 March 1869 to mark the 50th Anniversary. The noted historian and then librarian at Freemasons' Hall, Henry Sadler, later produced evidence of behalf of the Chapter to substantiate regular meetings of the Companions as early as 1793; the Centenary was celebrated 100 years from that date. Henry Sadler was a constant visitor to Domatic Chapter and became a Joining member on 26 January 1893, shewn in the records as 'from No. 169'; he was then Grand Tyler and Grand Janitor.

Cases have come to light where a few Chapters in the country had a foot in both camps and, in order to enjoy the best of both worlds, held Warrants/Charters from both jurisdictions before the Union. A Chapter was formed within the membership of an Antients lodge but then application was made for a Charter from the Moderns Grand Chapter and were thereby entered upon their Register. At the Union anomalous situations required attention and some essential pruning had to be done. The close association of the Royal Arch with the Craft was constantly before the Antients and was a major pursuit; there is little doubt that their pressure caused the wording in the new *Royal Arch Regulations* (1817) that each Chapter, when newly Registered, would receive 'a Charter of Constitution *to be attached to their Craft Warrant*'. Even in the Charters that are issued at the present time that intention is still perpetuated in the wording '*to be held with and attached to the Warrant of the Lodge*'. It was a custom born more to be honoured in the breach than in the observance and it is quite unpractical, as the Warrant of the lodge and the Charter of the chapter would be in possession of different persons; it would be extremely rare for both to be in the charge of one person at any one time, although not impossible. The original wording must have been yet another

25 *Henry Sadler, Grand Tyler 1879–1909*

point of compromise but remains as an example of effective diplomacy.

The number of Chapters on the Registers of each Grand Chapter at the date of the Union in 1817 has ever been in contention; they were not listed in the Minutes where the only mention made was the attendance of 'Principals of the several Chapters in the London District'. Certainly Domatic Chapter would have been well represented if not by all three Principals, but by Robert Gill who filled a major role. *Royal Arch Regulations* published in 1823, six years after the Union, listed seventeen Chapters for London but that list has been faulted by various historians; particulars of the Chapters that have survived to the present day are shewn in *Appendix E*. The close association of Craft and Royal Arch has been a somewhat neglected subject but, in recent years, has received official attention and two examples will shew guidance towards its preservation. On 9 September 1981 an item was included in the Report of the Board of General Purposes placed before Grand Lodge:

Wearing of Royal Arch Jewels

Rule 241 of the Book of Constitutions prohibits the wearing of jewels, etc, unless they appertain to those degrees specified in the preliminary declaration to the Book of Constitutions, namely, those of Entered Apprentic, the Fellow Craft, and the Master Mason, including the Supreme Order of the Holy Royal Arch, and have been approved or allowed by the Grand Master.

In view of the wording of the preliminary declaration, the Board feels that it should be made clear that there is no objection to qualified Brethren wearing the jewel of the order of the Royal Arch with Craft clothing and that *they should be encouraged to do so.* [author's italics]

Loss of identity between sponsoring lodge and its Chapter has also come under scrutiny and a timely mention of that was made in a similar Report to Grand Lodge on 9 June 1982:

Before a Charter is granted for a new Royal Arch Chapter, a recommendation must be signed in open Lodge by the Master and Wardens of a Lodge to which it is to be attached. The Chapter will generally look to the Lodge as the main source of candidates for exaltation; it is accordingly desirable for the Lodge to remain closely in touch with the Chapter and familiar with its situation. Any Lodge which has lost touch with Chapter attached to it is encouraged to re-establish friendly links.

The negligence of brethren from a sponsoring lodge, countered by the enthusiasm of those from one or another lodge elsewhere has sometimes been the cause of an undesirable division, albeit local and insular to the brethren concerned, is a repair that can be made with very little effort.

Uniformity in the Royal Arch

It has been made clear in the foregoing that the Antients Grand Lodge kept an eagle eye on masonic procedure and behaviour, having undertaken a self-imposed guardianship of ancient forms. Before the Craft Union, when the attention of brethren of both jurisdictions was focussed upon a mutual acceptability of Craft procedure, the Royal Arch was also borne in mind and on 1 April 1807 the revised *Laws and Regulations* were approved by the Antients Grand Chapter. They included the following:

That a general uniformity and the practice and ceremonies of Ancient Masonry may be preserved and handed down, unchanged to posterity—the Grand Chapter shall elect annually in October, nine skilful Royal Arch Masons, who must be Past Masters, and approved of by the Grand Lodge, and shall be allowed to visit the Lodges; and if occasion should require, they are to report thereon to this Grand Chapter, or to the R.W. Deputy Grand Master who will act as may be deemed necessary.

In effect it re-stated what had been agreed upon in 1783, but the accent was firmly placed on the Royal Arch.

Ritual monitors and manuals did not, in general, make any great impact until the dawn of the nineteenth century and for the Royal Arch there were earlier attempts to produce aide-menoire only in manuscript, but of those very few have survived. The following is an example of the attitude taken towards such a practice:

William Hodgson was reported to the Grand Sec. W.M. White in a letter dated 3 March 1791 asking that he be 'censured for violating his oath as a Mason in that he possessed and used a manual of the three degrees in masonry as well as one also for the 4th degree of the R.A. which he got for the purpose of teaching an intended Lodge and Chapter at Leeds, and that he procured from the Provincial Lodge at York or some one or more of its members ... (*AQC* 73, p 69. F.R. Worts, Chapter of Unity No 72)

The latter half of the eighteenth century was a fertile period for 'other degrees' and novelties, most of which were manufactured on the Continent. It is quite feasible that fancied items from them were grafted upon local Workings in both Craft and Royal Arch by the various 'experts', and an element of blurring in practice was inevitable. Research upon the limited material available for the Royal Arch has brought a common conclusion that there was very little difference in ceremonial worked by Chapters under both Antients and Moderns control, ever bearing in mind that the Turk's Head in Gerrard Street, Soho, in which the first (Moderns) Grand Chapter arose was a meeting-place for Companions from both sides. There was no need for 're-Making' for Companions in the Royal Arch to visit or to join a Chapter on the other side, it was sufficient only for an obligation to be taken; an example of that is taken from the Minutes of the Chapter of St. James dated 12 January 1809:

> Comp. Hippolyto Joseph da Costa of No. 1, new Inn, who had already been exalted to the degree of a Royal Arch Mason under the sanction of the Society generally called Ancient Masons, was this evening obligated as a R.A. Mason & paid the Reg^n Fee of 5s. 0d.

On the subject of ritual format, seeing that at the erection of their Grand Lodge the Antients membership was predominantly Irish and that they based certain *Regulations* on those from the Grand Lodge of Ireland, it will be appropriate to refer to what was written by R.F. Parkinson in his Paper 'Ireland and the Royal Arch Degree' (*AQC* 79, pp 181–193):

It seems probable that the 'J' [Josiah, repair of the Temple] legend was worked by the Dublin ritualists of the 1780's. Various legends have been adopted to convey the teachings of the Royal Arch degree. D'Assigny hints that there were two competing versions in Dublin in his day [1744]. Certainly it is safe to assume that Dermott received the 'Z' version [discovery in the Vault] ... but the competing one may well have been the 'J' [the present-day theme]. Both legends were current in Ireland until 1864, some Chapters practising one version and some the other; in that year our Supreme Grand Chapter [i.e. Ireland] adopted the Ritual now in use, after a strong Commission had considered the matter for ten years. (p. 187)

The present Irish ritual was finally adopted by Grand Chapter [Ireland] in 1864. The Degree of Virtual Past Master was abolished; those of Excellent and Super Excellent combined as the first part of the ceremony, the Passage of the Living Arch and of the Veils. Based on incidents in the life of Moses, the great Law Giver, it may be deemed a period of probation, after which the Candidates are permitted to take part in the preparatory work for the Repair of the Temple, during which the Recovery of the Volume of the Sacred Law, with other articles of value and importance is made. (p 188)

Companions in London were well endowed with opportunities for instruction and in some cases members on both sides mixed quite freely in Royal Arch pursuit. Possibly the pattern was set by the Chapter of St. James but others were also quite active, an example of which is quoted from Royal Cumberland Chapter No 18 [Moderns] in which, on 20 March 1788, it was proposed 'That a Chapter of Instruction be held between each Chapter Night'. Unfortunately, whilst it was well attended and worked from 1783–1801, it then declined to such an extent that it sold the Charter, and 'paraphernalia', to some Companions in Coventry where it operated from 1801 to its end *circa* 1827. It was eventually erased from the Register in 1861.

Publicity for the Royal Arch was also available via *The Morning Advertiser* which printed items such as the following, taken from the copy dated 8 December 1794:

ROYAL ARCH MASONRY

A Grand and Royal Chapter of this Sublime Degree is held on the second Thursday in every month, at the Kings Arms Tavern, Old Compton Street, Soho; and a Chapter of Instruction is likewise held on every intermediate Thursday at seven-o-clock precisely.

However, the Chapter of St. James was, without question, the most important on the Register of the Grand and Royal Chapter (Moderns) in that its membership provided a 'voice' to set the pattern, having a nucleus of senior Grand Officers. It was recorded in the Minutes of its meeting on 9 April 1801:

The M.E.Z. was pleased to report that on the last Thursday in each month during the Convocation of the Chapter, a Meeting would be held at the Hercules Pillars, Bro. Fox's in Great Queen Street, for the purpose of giving Instructions to the members of the Chapter who were severally entitled to receive the same; any Companions desirous of becoming a Member, may on intimating such intention to the M.E.Z., or Companion Foulston the Secretary. The regulations for the guidance of this Chapter of Instruction are, that each Companion must be proposed and balloted for, and on admission pay 2. 6d. which sum is for the purpose of paying the Janitor who attends each meeting night of the Chapter.

It is noteworthy that Domatic Chapter is known to have held a meeting in 1789, perhaps others that were not recorded, at the Hercules Pillars but by 1801 the lodge had moved its venue to the Coach and Horses, High Holborn, literally just around the corner.

E Comp Waller Rodwell Wright, Second Grand Principal of the Moderns Grand Chapter and a member of the Chapter of St. James, stated officially in 1810:

... I have only to add that we consider the main secrets of the Royal Arch as those of the true Master Mason, to which we must pass from the substituted ones by filling the Chair of a Lodge consisting of three Past Masters at least by their election and appointment, which preparatory Lodge any Royal Arch Chapter may hold under its Charter for that purpose only.

The Chapter of St. James possesses a manuscript giving details of the ceremonial for that purpose and was continued in use until 1835; it made clear that the ceremony did not entitle the Candidate to wear the badge of a Worshipful Master, nor to rank as a Past Master in the Craft.

One of the first acts of the Grand Chapter that came into being at the Union in 1817 was to ensure that Principals of Chapters in London were to be qualified and in regular occupation of their offices. In consequence they passed the following:

RESOLVED that a Committee be now appointed according to the recommendations of the Committee for the purpose of installing the Principals of Chapters in the London District.

RESOLVED that the said Committee do consist of the three Most Excellent Principals of the Grand Chapter and the seven Companions undernamed, they being regularly installed Principal Z, viz:

Comp. H.I. Da Costa
Comp. Robert Gill
Comp. I.C. Burchard
Comp. W.H. White
Comp. I.I. Moore
Comp. I. Thompson
Comp. W.D. Cammius

We have already met some of those names and it must be recalled that Robert Gill was a member of Domatic Chapter.

The desire for 'regularity' became apparent and pleas for guidance and assistance came from various parts of the country. Indeed, one example is worth quoting from the Chapter of Friendship now No 257, at Portsmouth, the members of which wrote asking 'for a Dispensation to instal the Principals in London as there are not enough qualified to perform the solemn Rite'. Other problems rose to the surface in different areas, and whilst gallant efforts were made to maintain some sort of control in administration, it left much to be desired owing to the preoccupation with uniformity efforts in Craft ritual and procedure. For a period the Royal Arch affairs fell into a state of comparative neglect with a 'make do and mend' attitude. The first constructive action came from a proposal in Grand Chapter on 1 May 1833 when

26 *George Aarons, Preceptor*

Companion Arthur L. Thiselton, a member of Domatic Chapter as well as others, moved:

> THAT a Committee be appointed to take into consideration the various Ceremonies for Installation of Principals as well as the various other Ceremonies of the Order. . . .

A Committee under the chairmanship of the Rev George Adam Browne was set up, five of the nine appointed were members of the Chapter of St. James. An excellent study of the subject under the title 'George Adam Browne' was compiled by Harry Mendoza in a Paper given to Quatuor Coronati Lodge and appears in *AQC* 88, pp 32–49. Unfortunately, owing to economy measures at that time, comments on the Paper which were actually quite useful additions were not included.

During the period of the deliberations of that Committee attention was directed to a particular facet of the ritual which, although in conformity with the legend from which it has been adapted, was anomalous in the period in which it was used. The matter was raised by George Aarons, a completely competent ritualist who had been initiated in 1819 in Lodge of Israel (now No 205) and was a pupil of Peter Gilkes. He was Exalted in United Chapter of Prudence in 1820 which was the same Chapter of which George Claret described himself as 'Past H of No 12'; thus he was in company with the experts. Aaron lost his sight in later life but he continued his precepting in both Craft and Royal Arch at his house in King Street, Covent Garden. We do not have specific details of his statement or letter but we have the purport from a copy of another letter dated 17 July 1834 now in the archives, and from that a fair estimate of his subject can be gauged:—

> ... As the Arch ceremony is under consideration of the Committee of the Grand Chapter ... Comp. Aarons ... should attend and explain his ideas ... a particular belief in religion which should be entirely got rid of as the Arch should be open to persons of every species of religious belief acknowledging a Deity.

The New Testament, as described in the legend recorded in *Orbis Miraculum*, and translated by Rev Samuel Lee in 1659 from a fourth century source, was no longer in keeping with such an Old Testament setting.

The work of that Committee resulted in reconstruction of Royal Arch ritual and ceremonial, and the eventual report that it made met with 'the entire concurrence and approval of His Royal Highness the Duke of Sussex'. At the Special Convocation of Grand Chapter on 21 November 1834 unanimous approval of the various ceremonies, which by then had been well demonstrated, was signified by all those present. A Special Chapter of Promulgation 'to establish a conformity of practice and working throughout the Order' was Warranted on 6 May 1835, its membership extended to twenty-seven which included Arthur L. Thiselton. But how dull life would be without a rebel or two! A few of them have been found so far and now this Chapter of Promulgation was to provoke a revival of one, no less than Companion Goldsworthy! As MEZ elect of Fidelity Chapter No 3, he announced his intention 'to conduct the discipline of the Chapter according to the former Athol system ...' The members of the Chapter sought guidance and, on 4 November 1835, Grand Chapter made the following announcement:

> Some misconceptions having arisen as to what are the Ceremonies of our Order it is hereby resolved and declared that the Ceremonies adopted and promulgated by Especial Grand chapter on the 21st and 25th November 1834 are the Ceremonies of our order which it is the duty of every Chapter to accept and obey.

An abortive attempt for non-confirmation of that

Minute was made, also a Motion for 'compliance to be a voluntary measure' failed to gain support.

Visitations from the appointed Nine Worthies and other experts who rose to the fore in that period were in great demand and Chapters of Instruction became a necessity; the written word was still condemned. It was about this time that George Aarons suggested to a Tyler that he might write out in full the ceremonial of the Royal Arch; his incitement was duly reported to Grand Chapter and for that offence he was excluded. Eventually he was re-instated in a most distinguished manner for he was re-clothed with apron and sash by the Grand Master himself. (See *Records of Mount Sinai Chapter No 19*, p 58, J.E.N. Walker.)

We must now pay further tribute to George Claret who undoubtedly suffered masonic 'slings and arrows' in his efforts as a ritual printer. He was the product of the age of standardisation and uniformity of ritual in both Craft and Royal Arch, having been initiated in 1812 in the Moderns Lodge of Ionic and Prudence (now Royal Alpha Lodge No 16). In December 1813, just prior to the Union he was exalted in United Chapter of Prudence.

Unlike William Finch, a purveyor of masonic rituals which were sent to all parts of the country and much used, whose work was condemned as 'Exposure' material, it happened to a much less degree as far as Claret was concerned. Claret was involved in or was associated with the Lodge of Reconciliation, the Burlington Lodge of Instruction, and many brethren of outstanding ability not the least of whom was Peter Gilkes. The Craft ritual published by Claret in 1838 has the following statement printed on the title page: 'of whom also may be had the following Royal Arch Masonry. Opening & Closing. Passing the Vails. Prayers. Exortations & the R.A. Lecture.' That Royal Arch material he was then supplying in manuscript but it is important to bear in mind that it was only three years earlier Supreme Grand Chapter had given the form its official approval following the demonstration given by the Chapter of Promulgation. It would appear that the general demand for the Royal Arch ritual did not justify the cost of printing as a manual so it was not until 1845 that a printed version appeared under the title of *The Ceremonies of the Holy Royal Arch*. It went into many editions and as the years went by was pirated by other printers. It should be noted that Domatic Chapter of Instruction, which was to outlive all others from that period and continues to teach through to the present time, came into existence only five years later. The masonic and business career of George Claret has been documented by the author in *AQC* 87, pp. 1–20 under the title 'George Claret (1783–1850) Ritual Printer'.

Royal Arch in the Nineteenth Century

The importance of the first half of the nineteenth century in Freemasonry in general cannot be over-emphasised for it was in that period the attention of the brethren in London was concentrated upon attainment of acceptable forms of ritual, procedure, regalia, and furnishings, and to achieve uniformity as far as was reasonably possible. Thus we turn to Domatic Chapter to see what can be gathered from their records and there could not be a better starting-place than the Inventory recorded ten years after the completion of the Chapter of Promulgation. The details were written into the Minute Book covering the period 1845–71 as follows:

INVENTORY of the Regalia and furniture belonging to the Domatic Chapter taken the 23rd May 1844

Large Chest with two locks and keys
1 Deal Box containing 3 Silk Principals Robes and 5 White Surplices
1 Deal Box containing 3 Sojourners Caps
1 Deal Candle box
2 Tin Cases containing 2 Principals Coronets 1 Brass Mitre and Breastplate 2 Scribes Caps
Pedestal—Brass Triangle and frame—Case for same 3 Sojourners Collars and Jewels
1 Treasurers Collar and Jewel
6 Candlesticks
3 Hassocks
Bible Square and Compasses
Shovel Pick Axe and Crow
Sword and Trowel
Transparency

1 Minute Book	from 18 November 1804 to 20 December 1812
1 —do—	from 17 January 1813 to 30 November 1826
1 —do—	from 27 March 1827 to 28 November 1844
1 —do—	from 23 January 1845 to

Signature Book—Bye Laws
2 Principals Collars and 3 Silver Gilt Jewels
Set of letters for the Pedestal complete
12 Banners of the various Tribes painted on Tin plates with box containing the same lock and key
Box with twelve Wands for same
Scribes Mahogany Desk
Scriptural Extracts
Pair of Slippers

An interesting comparison between that list and one taken today would find quite a few items discontinued, yet, when compared with items in overseas jurisdictions where they still appear shews a common link with pre-Union furnishing. It is to be regretted that the Minute Books prior to 1845 have not survived and a pencil note on the first end-paper of that book states that they were missing even in 1861:

The previous Minute Book appears to be lost—after the death of Comp. Child, his Widow was applied to for it but stated that she had never seen it. H.G.B.

Stephen Child, who died in November 1860, was a Past Master of Domatic Lodge and PZ as well as Scribe E of the Chapter. A letter of condolence to his widow was copied into the Minutes by Henry Gustavus Buss, PZ, who was appointed Scribe E, in succession and was responsible for that note. Buss was an employee on the staff of the Grand Secretary and how much he was valued in that position is shewn by the following mention in the Minutes of Grand Lodge for 23 June 1859:

... the President of the Board next moved: 'That the Salary of Brother Buss, the second clerk, be increased to £150 a year such increase to take effect from 1 January last'—and he added, 'He should not be doing his duty unless he paid that Brother the tribute due to him. No Society ever had more zealous and useful officer than Brother Buss.' ...

Brother H.G. Buss was appointed Assistant Grand Secretary in 1877 by Grand Lodge and the following year was honoured in Grand Chapter with the rank of Grand Standard Bearer. In 1880 he was appointed Assistant Grand Scribe E, a newly created office, which position he held for four years.

Domatic Chapter still possesses a leather-bound book, gold-blocked with the title *Domatic Chapter of H.R.A. Treasurer's Accounts*. It spans the period from 27 May 1827 to 22 March 1932, one hundred and five years of accountancy, with each year's income and expenditure audited and signed by contemporary senior officers of the Chapter. Certain items from it are worth noting such as the different heading which occurs after the first two year's accounts. Whereas the heading is twice shewn as 'Domatic Chapter of H.R.A. Masons', from 1829 to 1836 it is changed to 'Domatic Chapter of United Strength'. This, however, was not so much a change in the name of the Chapter but was occasioned by the change of Treasurer who might have been following what was quite a fashion of the period by including the word 'United' which was being commonly adopted in the titles of quite a number of Lodges and Chapters purely as a display of loyalty and support for the Union. But, in this instance, such was not the case because reference to the Return of 7 May 1829 from Domatic Chapter (then No 293) to Supreme Grand Chapter has a list of names as Joining Members, between the period 27 March 1827 to 14 April 1829, with the annotation '399 Lodge U. Strength'. It was one of the 'rebel' lodges among the Antients which had opposed certain recommendations and adoptions made by the Lodge of Reconciliation and stood apart for some eighteen months, co-operating only after their principal points of contention had been conceded. they adopted the name Lodge of United Strength in 1817 and now appear on the Register as No 228; their meeting-places in that period were:

Shakespeare's Head, Covent Garden	...	1825
New Exchange Coffee House, Strand	...	1826
Furnival's Inn coffee House, Holborn	...	1828
Salisbury Tavern, Bear Street,		
Leicester Square	...	1829

From 1832, when the closing-up and re-numbering of Lodges on the Register of the United Grand Lodge took place, Domatic Lodge, and of course its Chapter, became No 206 and all records then bear that number. The Treasurer's book contains many entries relating to postage, samples of which are:

29 Oct. 1835	Postages	... ...	1.	2
14 Apl. 1836	Postage of letter returned	...		2
28 „ „	Postage of letter	... ...		2
30 Jun. „	Postage of letter from Comp.			
	Hamer	... ...		2
23 Jan. 1840	Returned letter (J. Hamer)	...		2
9 Apl. „	Prepaid Letters	... ...	6.	0

Before 1840 such entries would have been disbursements to carriers or agents and payment for undelivered or 'returned' letters would still have had to be made to them. But the entry for 9 April 1840 is of special interest as that would have been for issue of summonses to the members and is one month before the introduction of the adhesive 'Penny Black' which was to appear on 6 May. The originator, Rowland Hill, had proposed a postal reform in 1837 but it was not until May 1840 that the results came into being. The postal state for Domatic Chapter was somewhat fluid as we find an entry for 24 March 1842 shewing that they had abandoned the postal service—'To Janitor & delivering Summonses ... 5. 0'. It became one of the duties of the Janitor, but it is quite possible that he would have found it unprofitable to deliver in person to any member living at a distance and may have resorted to the mail for an odd one or two. According to the records the postal service was brought back into use in November 1857.

On 25 September 1829 the Janitor is identified in the item—'Comp. Canham for 2 Collars £1. 0. 0.' This would have been the very well-known figure in London Freemasonry, associated with many leading lodges and in company with many influential brethren and widely known as 'Canham the Tyler'. As Junior Warden he represented Universal Lodge (now No 181) on three occasions at meetings of the Lodge of Reconciliation in 1816. He became a member of several lodges and Chapters as his

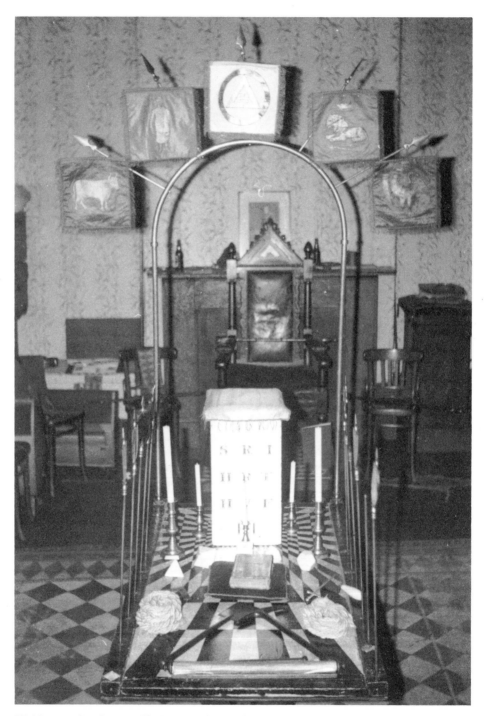

27 *Miniature furnishings used by Domatic Chapter of Instruction No 177*

services were much sought after; he was also prominent in the 'higher' degrees and fully active until his death in 1837. He had been a strong supporter of the Aged Masons' Asylum, and was a liveryman in the City of London.

Another item of interest appears against the date '11 Dec. 1829—To Comp. Thiselton for Painting Pedestal 7s. 6d.' This is the same Companion. Thiselton we have already met regarding the setting up of the Chapter of Promulgation, but he was certainly the right person to paint the pedestal as he was occupied as a scene painter at Drury Lane and had produced Tracing Boards for some lodges. He was initiated in Bedford Lodge (now No 157)—a Moderns lodge that also had the distinction of being an 'Operatives Lodge' a matter to which we will return later—and was Exalted in United Mount Sinai Chapter (another misuse of the word 'United' for its title did not have that expression which was in use only for a few years) and he joined Domatic Chapter 14 April 1829. He was a very active Freemason serving on various official Committees and eventually appointed to the Board of General Purposes. A member of many lodges and Chapters, he became a close friend of Peter Gilkes and was one of the pall-bearers at his funeral. That eminent brother bequeathed his Royal Arch jewel to Thiselton and when a Committee was formed to consider a Monument to Gilkes, Thiselton served as its Secretary. A memorial tablet was duly erected in St. James's church in Piccadilly.

Items of expenditure in that period are interesting and include frequent mention of 'washing Surplices' the amount of 7. 0d being usually paid to the Janitor who, presumably, attended to that. As indeed were repairs to such items as 'shovel ... 1. 0d'; 'Candle Box ... 1. 0d'; 'Z's Robe ... 7. 0d'; but on 25 September 1829 'For Brass work &c for Pedestal', at the same time that Thiselton was paid for painting that article, might well have been a new purchase and not a repair. A non-uniformity had existed in regard to the Pedestal which is shewn by the Minutes of the Grand and Royal Chapter (Moderns) in 30 November 1802 when it ordained: 'That the side of the Pedestal be repaired & the letters transposed etc.' It is regrettable that we have

no guidance regarding the transposing, but in a report on the Grand Chapter Pedestal, in 1837 after the work of the Chapter of Promulgation, the recommendation made then was:

> That names, words and letters should be in Hebrew characters—names of the 3 G.M's should be on the front of the plinth and the triple tau in the centre on the front of the shaft of the pedestal, and all indented. Subordinate Chapters to adopt Hebrew characters or at least Roman as heretofore and not Latin. This to follow the arrangement agreed to by those who revised the ceremonies.

Because the miniature pedestal used by Domatic Chapter of Instruction, almost from inception, has Latin, it is logical to expect that it followed the pattern in use in the parent and sanctioning Chapter. An entry in the Treasurer's Account Book, against the date 16 April 1845, has 'Trowel 1. 9d, Letters 1. 3d'. The letters may have been just a replacement for some that had been 'lost'—a situation that is not unknown even today. In a masonic suppliers' catalogue of the period (Richard Spencer, 314 High Holborn) a complete set of letters are described as 'Roman and Hebrew letters for the top (18 in number), loose, of burnished brass, the set £0. 16. 6'.

For some years Domatic Chapter had been meeting at the Unicorn Tavern, Jermyn Street, St. James's where, it would seem that the Chapter furnishings were owned by the proprietors. At the Chapter meeting on 13 January 1846 a decision was taken to move to the Falcon Tavern, Fetter Lane, Fleet Street, and this was to herald a new era for the name Domatic. Over the next few years sufficient items appear in the accounts to shew either initial furnishing or a high standard of maintenance of equipment as these extracts will shew:

13 Jan	1846	Banners	2.	2.	0
22 ,,	,,	Plates for Banners		7.	6
,, ,,	,,	Box for same		7.	6
26 Sept	1848	Floorcloth		15.	9
,, ,,	,,	Expenses —do—		4.	9
3 Oct	,,	Porterage		2.	0
26 ,,	,,	Bennison on a/c painting Floorcloth	2.	0.	0

22 Feb	1849	Bennison balance ...	...	1.	10.	0
26 Oct	1848	Gilding Sceptres ...	...	1.	0.	0
26 Apl	1849	Silk for 5 Banners ...	...		12.	6
,, ,,	,,	Expenses Painter ...	...		3.	0
24 May	,,	Painter on a/c of Banners ...	1.	0.	0
25 Oct	,,	Bennison balance painting Banners ...	...	1.	12.	0
,, ,,	,,	Lace for Robe of J.	...		5.	0
28 Feb	1850	10 Tassels, Cord & Fringe for Banners	...	...	18.	8
1 Oct	1853	Robes and cleaning Fur	...	2.	10.	0
22 Jan	1863	Ballot Box ...	...	...	16.	0

Charles Ireland, landlord of the Falcon Tavern and a member of Albion Lodge, No 9, was Exalted in Domatic Chapter on 28 May 1846. He was of such character and attracted such masonic patronage that his premises came to be known as 'The Masonic Hall, Fetter Lane'. Indeed in the Minute Book, Domatic Chapter meetings were shewn to have been held thus from June 1858 to January 1861 but that assumed name was discontinued the moment Henry Buss was elected as Scribe E of the Chapter; he was, after all, 'second clerk' to the Grand Secretary at Freemasons' Hall, and would frown upon any such unapproved title.

Of the items listed above from the Treasurer's accounts it would be constructive to comment upon the 'Floorcloth' supplied and painted by Bennison in 1848. Such an item is not shewn in the Inventory of 1844, probably because it was the property of Unicorn Tavern; the same may also be said of 'Banners', that being an item dealt with so promptly on removal to the Falcon.

The Floorcloth for the Royal Arch might well be deemed a successor to the early artistic 'floor-drawings' executed by the Tyler and varied according to the degree to be performed; that work gradually faded from use when an 'all purpose' style floorcloth, painted on a canvas, rolled up when out of use but suitable for any degree as it bore appropriate symbols for all, became popular. The one for the Royal Arch was of specialist nature and is shewn to advantage in Spencer's catalogue named *Freemasonry its outward and Visible Signs*. On the facing page it is well described thus:

The Plan opposite shows the arrangement of a Chapter, approved by the Duke of Sussex whilst Grand Z. The description and quality of each item will be found in the price list which follows hereon.
The Floor-cloth. The site for the Pedestal is placed nearer to the Principals' throne than is shown in the plan, and the chequered pavement points to it from all sides in diminishing perspective, giving an idea of greater distance, 10 ft × 6 ft price £4. 4s; or 10 ft × 5 ft £3. 3s. The proportion borne by the length to the breadth of the room, should determine these dimensions.

The high standard of recommendation from that quarter may be measured by the fact that a Comp Richard Spencer was appointed Grand Director of Ceremonies in Supreme Grand Chapter in 1817 immediately following the Union of the two Grand Chapters. The one who is mentioned in the following extract from *The Freemasons* Vol 2 No 41, 18 Dec 1869 is possibly a son with that name who was maintaining similar standards and authenticity:

Bro. R. Spencer begs to inform the Craft he has purchased the copyright of the Royal Arch and Craft Tracing Boards; also the new and improved Tracing Boards designed by Bro. John Harris. The Tracing Boards (the small size) were patronized by the late M.W. Grand Master H.R.H. the Duke of Sussex, who, as a special favour allowed them to be dedicated to him.

Of the *Scripture Readings*, a copy is shewn to have been purchased by Domatic Chapter on 23 October 1845 as 'Scriptural Extracts ... 5s 0d.' it was described in the contemporary catalogue of Spencer 'As directed by the Grand Chapter to be read during the ritual of Exaltation ... price 4s. 0d sewed, 5s. 0d half-bound, 7s. 0d Whole bound, the latter with lock case 10s. 0d.' It has remained comparatively unchanged, a standard publication.

Although Minutes of Domatic Chapter prior to 1845 have not survived, from various items that appear in the *Treasurer's Account Book* dating from 1829 and the subsequent entries in the Minutes that are available we are able to measure something of the ceremonial that was practised before, during, and following the work of the Chapter of Promulgation. 'Paid for Slippers ... 7s. 6d' in 1835 tends

Masonic Depôt; 23ᵈ Great Queen Street, London.

28 *The Chapter layout as printed
in Spencer's catalogue 1884*

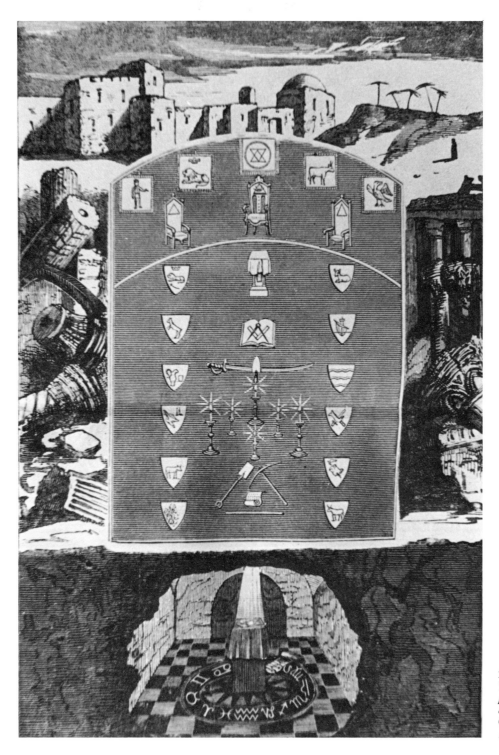

29 *Royal Arch
Tracing Board
printed in the 1884
edition of the*
Oxford *Royal Arch
Ritual*

to shew that the Candidate was 'prepared' for the ceremony of Exaltation. In the Minutes the Candidates are usually described as—'being present and properly prepared and entrusted, was introduced and Exalted to the Supreme degree of R.A.M.' There is sufficient there to make up a mental picture, and, in the years 1845–46 when there seems to have been lack of Candidates, rehearsals to make up a programme included such entries as—'The M.E.Z. gave an explanation of the pedestal' and 'The Historical, Symbolical and Traditional Lectures were given', even 'The Ceremony of Exaltation was gone through Comp. Jacobs acting as Candidate', and, 'There being no particular business before the Chapter part of the ceremony of Exaltation was worked by way of instruction'. That happened to be one end of the scale, but it was well counterbalanced by peaks on other occasions and, bearing in mind that Candidates were proposed at one meeting, balloted for at the next and, if present were then Exalted, if not, that could take place at a subsequent meeting. Here is the intake for seven consecutive meetings:

January	1863	Exalted	1	Proposed	17
March		,,	11	,,	14
April		,,	5	,,	4
October		,,	1	,,	2
November		,,	1	,,	5
January	1864	,,	4	,,	10
March		,,	5	,,	nil

The sequence for Installation of the Principals and investiture of Officers, following the meeting of their individual election, where sometimes up to three Companions were proposed for any one office and the casting vote of the MEZ necessary, is shewn by the following:

24 April 1845.
The Chapter was then consecrated as a Supreme Conclave of Installed P.Z's for the purpose of Installation of Officers for the ensuing year when the following Companions were severally introduced presented and obligated and inducted to their several Chairs:—

Companion Blount	Z.
,, Sherrard	H
,, Child	J

The Conclave was then closed and the Chapter re-

sumed when the following Companions were invested in their several offices:

Companion	Quivillart P.Z.	Treasurer
,,	Seton P.Z.	E
,,	Wythe	N
,,	Smith	P.S.
who appointed		
,,	Masters	1st A.S.
,,	Eagling	2nd A.S.

A P.Z. Jewel was agreed to be presented to the I.P.Z.

It is of interest to note that the Principal Sojourner appointed and invested his two Assistants, after his own investiture, right through to 1886 when the amended *Royal Arch Regulations* of that year included those two Officers with all others 'to be elected annually'. Later the appointment of the junior Officers 'to be left in the hands of the Principals elect' was permitted provided that an appropriate proposal to that effect was passed by the Chapter in general.

The word 'inducted' seems to have served the process of 'installed' and cannot be taken to mean the short form in use when appropriate, but the historian is ever suffering at the hands, or the prose and limited ability, of an earlier Scribe or Secretary who is obviously completely unaware how valueless he makes his own work. Compare that record with this one written into the Minutes of the meeting held on 22 March 1883:

… The Companions who were not P.Z. having retired A Conclave of Installed Principals was declared open. Comp. Frederick Harrison, M.E.Z. Elect, being a Past First Principal was duly placed in the First Chair of the Chapter. A Conclave of Second Principals was declared open. Comp. James McLean, H. Elect, was duly installed in the Second Chair by E. Comp. J.T. Briggs. A Conclave of Third Principals was then declared open, Comp. William Porter Webb was placed in the Chair of J., being already an Installed Third Principal. The Conclave was closed and the Companions were readmitted and the M.E.Z. invested the following officers: …

The question of sequence was the cause of unpleasantness that came between the Companions of Domatic Chapter and William Henry White the Grand Scribe E. The matter arose from an application for a Dispensation that was made in February 1845, but the story commences in the Minutes with the following, dated 23 January 1845:

> Companion Seton P.Z. brought to the notice of the M.E.Z. a Memorial which had been prepared soliciting the M.E. Grand Z. to grant this Chapter a Dispensation to enable Companion Sherrard the present J. to be installed as Z. without filling the office of H. for twelve months. After some discussion the same was deferred until the next meeting the M.E.Z. having promised to consult the Grand Scribe E. thereon.

The next meeting of the Chapter was held on 27 February and on that subject the Minutes state:

> Companion Seton P.Z. brought to the notice of the Chapter the memorial to the M.E.Z. which he brought forward at the last Meeting Night and which was directed to stand over till this Convocation when the same having been modified was on the motion of Companion Child seconded by Companion Johnson directed to be engrossed and forwarded to the Grand Scribe.

At the next meeting the following is in the Minutes:

> Companion Seton, Scribe E., reported that the Memorial which had been forwarded to the M.E.G.Z. agreeable to the Minutes of 27th February had been refused the sanction of the M.E.G.Z. . . . This being the night for Election of Principals and Officers, Ballots were severely taken as undermentioned. . . .

and, because of their failure to obtain a Dispensation for him to be installed as M.E.Z., Comp. Sherrard was elected H.

The sense of grievance, in this case quite unjustified, remained with those Companions and five years later Comps. Seton, Sherrard and others who had been in attendance during that period thought fit to place their resentment on record:

> A letter was read received from Comp.ⁿ Rowland Gardiner Alston Soliciting a Subscription from this Chapter towards a Testimonial to Brother W.H. White the G. Sec.ʸ It was moved by Comp.ⁿ Sherrard seconded by Comp.ⁿ Masters that in consequence of the want of courtesy on the part of Brother White towards this Chapter in respect of a Memorial addressed to the M.E.G.Z. the Earl of Zetland, the Scribe E. frame a letter (to be submitted to the next

Chapter) informing Brother Alston the reason of this chapter not complying with his request.

Rowland Gardiner Alston, Member of Parliament, Senior Grand Warden in 1835, Third Grand Principal 1845–54, did not receive a subscription from Domatic chapter, nor even a reply as the Minutes of the following meeting on 28 February 1850 state:

> The Chapter was opened in due form with prayer. The Minutes of the last Chapter were read (with the exception of the letter Scribe E. had been desired to prepare for the purpose of the same being sent to Brother R.G. Alston in reply to his application for a subscription towards a Testimonial to Brother W.H. White G. Sec.ʸ which application it was deemed advisable should not be further noticed) the Minutes were confirmed.

The discretion which was thus exercised rather calls to mind an anonymous stanza:

> Dost think in a moment of anger,
> 'Tis well with thy seniors to fight?
> They prosper, who burn in the morning,
> The letters they wrote overnight!

No entry can be found in the Minute Book, nor any in the *Treasurer's Accounts* of any donation having been made to the Testimonial.

To return for a moment to the list of items of Chapter furnishings mentioned above, mention of one Companion in the chapter will not only assist in bringing some entries into perspective but will shew the dedication that grows within. At the meeting on 22 February 1849 appears the following:

> Comp. Masters moved that the five Principal Banners be procured immediately, seconded by Comp. Child, P.Z. and carried unan.

It would appear that all the Banners previously used had belonged to the landlord of the former venue. The Principal Banners, painted on silk by Comp Bennison, tasseled, corded, and fringed made their appearance in due course. The tribal Banners were painted on tin plates and mounted on twelve 'wands'; those which had been 'claimed' in the Inventory of 1844 could not have belonged to Domatic so a replacement had to be organised for those. Masters presented six wands on 27 February, another six and a box to contain all on 27 November 1845 and thus that matter was rectified. Whilst he occupied the office of Third Principal of the Chapter Masters presented a new Velvet Robe as a replacement and possibly the item of 'Lace for Robe of J' was to ensure that the new one was a copy in style for the one it replaced.

It is also in 1849 we have an example of what might well be deemed a Royal Arch Clearance Certificate:

> Comp.[n] Langford stated that he was about to sail for Australia and requested a private Chapter Certificate which by direction of the M.E.Z. was granted in the following form:—"Domatic Chapter No. 206 held at the Falcon Tavern, Fetter Lane, in the City of London—WE hereby Certify that our Comp.[n] George William Langford was regularly Exalted in this Chapter and has paid up all dues and demands to this present date 25th October 1849 Witness our hands—William Blount Z. Caleb Wythe H. George Augustus Masters J. William Seton E."

The greater proportion of Candidates and Joining Members for Domatic Chapter came from lodges other than the sanctioning lodge, in fact an examination of Returns to Grand Chapter for the years 1873 to 1896 reveal that of 117 new members in that period eighty came from other lodges and only thirty-seven from Domatic Lodge. The mixed membership certainly provided wider horizons but tended to wean loyalties from the parent lodge. The Chapter built up a very high status and commanded a following of experts, a number of whom were appointed to Grand Rank during the nineteenth century and following. Before dealing briefly with that subject it would be appropriate firstly to mention Robert Wentworth Little, of Royal Albert Lodge (now No 907) who was Exalted in Domatic Chapter on 22 January 1863 and was to become involved, albeit somewhat unwisely, in the wider field of Freemasonry in London, but the story starts with the removal of Domatic Lodge from the Falcon Tavern in 1864.

Spurious Freemasonry at Falcon Tavern

In 1864 Henry Thompson, Master of Domatic Lodge, had a difference with Charles Ireland, landlord of the Falcon Tavern, or 'Fetter Lane, Masonic Hall' as it was often called. The exact nature of the clash was not recorded but it was sufficient for Thompson to call for two Emergency meetings to sort things out and consider what action was to be taken. It resulted in the lodge changing its venue to Anderton's Hotel, Fleet Street, which was literally just around the corner, and the immediate resignation from the lodge by Ireland.

The story is taken up in the Minutes of Domatic chapter for the meeting of 27 October 1864:

> The M.E.Z. stated that in consequence of many complaints by Companions, and of observations which had been conveyed to him respecting the cause of the removal of the Domatic Lodge from this House, he (the M.E.Z.) had thought it better that the matter should be brought before the Chapter and in order to prevent any Comp.[n] being taken by surprise he had caused the insertion in the Summons calling this Convocation of the Notice—'To consider the propriety of removing the Chapter'—it was therefore open for any Comp.[n] to move in the matter.
> Comp.[n] Buss enquired if any Comp.[n] who was a member of the Lodge would explain the reason of the removal of the Domatic Lodge. Comp.[n] J. Smith, P.Z. & Treas.[r] stated that in his opinion the Lodge matters had no bearing on the chapter affairs, but that it was a question whether or not the Chapter should remove, and hold its meetings at the same House as the Lodge, and after some further observations from other Comp.[ns] and no Motion being made, the subject was not proceeded with.

The Chapter was not prepared to associate itself with a lodge problem, but the time was yet to come when, for a totally different reason the Chapter was to remove from the Falcon Tavern also to Anderton's Hotel, and the Minutes of 25 October 1866 have that account which was also followed by the resignation from Charles Ireland:

> Some discussion arose as to the propriety of moving this Chapter in consequence of a Spurious Lodge of so-called Freemasons of the Order of 'Memphis' or

'Philadelphes' holding its meetings in this House. Comp.ⁿ Smith, P.Z. & Treasurer moved, 'That this Chapter be forthwith removed from the Falcon Tavern, Fetter Lane, and that its future meetings be held, pro tem, at Anderton's Hotel, Fleet Street, in consequence of a spurious lodge of Freemasons meeting at the Falcon Tavern'. Comp. George Wilson seconded the Motion. The Motion was supported by Comp.ⁿˢ Cottebrune, P.Z., R.W. Little, S.N., Burmeister, Buss P.Z. & S.E., all of whom strongly urged the necessity of removing at once as it was highly improper, if not impracticable that the Chapter should continue to meet at the Falcon Tavern where a spurious Lodge of Freemasons was admitted to be held, and the S.E. read the circular letter of the Grand Secretary of the 24th October 1859, calling the particular attention of the Craft to · that body calling itself 'The Reformed Masonic Order of Memphis or Rite of the Grand Lodge of Philadelphes'.

The Motion was put by the M.E.Z. and was carried nem. con. The M.E.Z. then stated that he would call the next meeting of the Chapter at Anderton's Hotel in accordance with the foregoing resolution.

The Rite of Memphis was constructed in Paris *circa* 1839. In the main, however, that was a revival of an extinct system with expansion of material that was both borrowed and invented producing at least ninety-one degrees. It lived a somewhat chequered existence until 1862 when it obtained Recognition from the Grand Orient of France which limited activity to only the three Craft degrees. The use of high sounding titles of those who achieved rank in its various 'high degrees' was not permitted and their work ceased. On the subject of 'Recognition' it must be said that any lodge meeting within the regular territory of a Grand Lodge and not applying for a Warrant from that authority would be deemed irregular, and most certainly one working unrecognised degrees would be barred.

One such lodge, meeting at the King of Prussia, in Stratford, an east London suburb, caused the Grand Secretary to send out a directive on behalf of Grand Lodge to all lodge Secretaries in the year 1859, and that is the circular referred to in the Minutes above. Particular emphasis was made that '... brethren can hold no communication with irregular lodges without incurring the penalty of expulsion from the Order ...' But Charles Ireland, the landlord of the Falcon Tavern and a member of

Domatic Chapter had created an impossible situation by allowing meetings of the Order of Memphis to be held in his premises and the Chapter had no alternative to remove forthwith, with Robert Wentworth Little among those who 'strongly urged the necessity of removing at once as it was highly improper.' That was in October 1866 but, three years later we find him not only 'P.Z. of 975' but MEZ of Domatic Chapter, editor of *The Freemason* magazine the first copy of which he produced in March 1869, but employed as second clerk and cashier on the Grand Secretary's staff at Freemasons' Hall. It seemed that he had unlimited capacity and unbounded enthusiasm and was capable of wearing several hats, but in this case, aprons. Among his many masonic activities he included the Rite of Memphis which had been the subject of veto ten years earlier. It caused some searching questions to be raised in Grand Lodge in 1871, one of which was so framed:— 'That if Grand Lodge itself did not countenance certain quasi-masonic degrees, including the Rite of Memphis, how could it be considered consistent that a subaltern in the Grand Secretary's office could take a lead in unrecognized degrees?'. Another alleged that the clerks in the office 'on their own account formulate, tabulate, and send abroad other degrees, and they make the office the place from which they emanate.' A report in the *Freemasons' Magazine* for 5 August 1871 (p 112) shews that Grand Chapter also had this matter under review as the following notice of motion which had been given by Matthew Cooke, who had been exalted in Domatic Chapter on 25 November 1958 but was then PZ of No 534, was one of their features:

THAT whilst this Grand Chapter recognizes the private right of every Companion to belong to any extraneous Masonic organisation he may choose, it as firmly forbids now, and at any future time all Companions while engaged as salaried officials under this Grand Chapter to mix with such bodies as the Ancient and Accepted Scottish Rite, the Rites of Misraim and Memphis, the spurious Orders of Rome and Constantine, the schismatic body styling itself the Grand Mark Lodge of England, or any other exterior Masonic organisation whatever (even that of the order of Knights Templar which alone is recognized) under the pain of immediate dismissal from employment by the Grand Chapter.

Diplomacy, by its very nature, is seldom seen at work but although it may be shrouded it is none the less effective. In November 1872, just one year later, R.W. Little was appointed Secretary of the Royal Masonic Institution for Girls and his departure from Freemasons' Hall thus removed what must have become quite an embarrassment for the authorities.

Grand Pursuivants and Others

How fruitful were the efforts, and fertile the ground that was tended by members of Domatic Chapter is shewn by their appointments to various ranks in Grand Lodge and Grand Chapter from the mid-nineteenth century onwards, and their Grand Officer associates were often to be found in company. One example of that was the occasion of the Exaltation of Robert Wentworth Little in January 1863 when the one visitor to the chapter was William Farnfield, Assistant Grand Secretary (1854–66), who was succeeded in that office by Henry Gustavus Buss. It is probable that Farnfield was the guest of Joseph Smith, a former Grand Director of Ceremonies in Grand Chapter but then Past Grand Pursuivant in Grand Lodge, Treasurer of Domatic Chapter. The offices of Assistant Grand Pursuivant, and Grand Pursuivant seem to have been cornered for members of Domatic Chapter for quite a few years as the following table will shew:

30 Past Master's breast jewel presented to W Bro Joseph Smith who was Master of Domatic Lodge in 1845 and 1847

Asst: G Purs.		G Purs.	Grand Chapter & other appts:
	Joseph Smith	1856–59	G.D.C. 1856–7
1859*	Thomas A. Adams	1860–61	G. Stwd 1861 for Lodge 23.
1862–3	Thomas G. Dickie	1864	
1869	James Brett	1870	G.D.C. 1871
1870	John Coutts	1871	
1872	C.A. Cottebrune	1873	A.G.D.C. 1893
1873	Thomas Cubitt	1874	

* the first appointed to this new office.

In a similar manner, and for a total of 53 years, the dual office of Grand Tyler and Grand Janitor was held by only two Companions both of whom were active members of Domatic Chapter; Charles Bryant Payne held the appointment from 1875–79 and on his death in that year was followed by Henry Sadler 1879–1909. As a professional Freemason Henry Sadler had a most distinguished career in that he served under four Grand Masters and an equal number of Grand Secretaries, and whilst serving in those offices took part in 600 Consecrations as well as assisting in many other important masonic events. When he relinquished the office in 1909 he was appointed Librarian and Curator of the Museum at Freemasons' Hall and honoured with the rank of Past Assistant Grand Director of Ceremonies. His masonic scholarship and authorship was fully recognised in his election to full membership of Quatuor Coronati Lodge No 2076, the premier lodge of masonic research; regrettably he died during his mastership of that world-famous lodge in 1911. It was mostly due to the efforts of Henry Sadler that Domatic subsequently was granted a founding date of 1793 for the Chapter and were able to celebrate the Centenary on a more appropriate date. The Jubilee of 50 years was actually celebrated to date from 14 March 1819 which was the date the Companions received the Charter of Confirmation issued on 20 October 1818.

The Jubilee coincided with the Installation of Robert Wentworth Little as MEZ and the meeting opened with Charles B. Payne as MEZ, R.W. Little as H, James Brett as J:

> ... the following Companions were severally introduced and installed into their respective offices by Comp. Brett, P.Z.
> Companion R.W.Little (P.Z. 875)   Z ⎫
>   ,,   J.Coutts (H   382) H ⎬ inducted
>   ,,   W.J.Gilbert   J ⎭
> ... The Conclave was then closed and in the resumption of the Chapter the following companions were invested in their respective offices:— H.G. Buss, P.Z. as S.E., George Wilson as S.N., Thos. Cubitt as P. Soj., Jos. Smith, P.Z. as Treasurer, Comp. Cubitt the Principal Sojourner then appointed Comp. J.R. Foulger 1Asst. Soj., & Comp. J.W. Barrett 2nd Asst. Soj. [*Note in the Minute Book*] After the Banquet a P.Z. Jewel was

presented to Companion C.B. Payne in acknowledgement of his Services as M.E.Z. during the past year.

The award of a PZ jewel was not an automatic gesture by the Chapter but was treated as a mark of distinction and merit. The PM jewel for Joseph Smith is now in the Museum at Freemasons' Hall.

After the general business of the Chapter had been cleared, Little delivered an Address on the origin and progress of the chapter. It was fully reported in *The Freemason* (No 4) dated 3 April 1869 of which he was then the Editor, and a clipping from the magazine was affixed to the Minutes. Amongst the many things touched upon, Comp Little stated that the Chapter had arrived at the completion of fifty years of honourable labour in the cause of Royal Arch Masonry and they had met to celebrate their 'Jubilee'. He referred to the Charter of Confirmation which was dated 29 October 1818 and handed over to them 'at the first Convocation 14 March 1819 or fifty years ago'. He then made reference to those of distinction who had become members of the Chapter and mentioned Stephen Barton Wilson (27 April 1832)—John Savage (14 November 1837) who had joined from Royal York No 7—Francis Evans 'of the eminent firm in Coventry Street'—William Oman, Master of St. Katherine's Docks—and paid fitting tribute to other members of the chapter. Of C.A. Cottebrune, Little said:

> He is a noted and worthy name in Freemasonry. he is a strenuous supporter of the cause and, like most of the other Past Principals, a founder of several lodges and chapters.

Of Joseph Smith, the Treasurer, he commented:

> ... he is of inestimable value, one who studies the well-being of the chapter in every particular, a treasurer who understands the happy distinction between liberality and profusion, and between economy and parsimony. As an energetic member of the various Boards and Committees connected with Freemasonry. Comp. Smith's career is patent to every member of the Craft.

The highest tribute, however, was paid to James Brett who was exalted in the chapter on 25 March 1858 whilst occupying the office of Master of Domatic Lodge, then No 206. Of James Brett he said:

I feel that I cannot do justice to the many services which he has rendered to Freemasonry in general, and more especially to Domatic Chapter. His reputation as a teacher of the ceremonies of this supreme degree is, I may safely allege, second to none, and his name must ever be associated with Royal Arch Masonry.

Something of the work of James Brett will bear reference in the later section dealing with the Chapter of Instruction.

The establishing of the year 1793 for the founding of Domatic chapter, eight years after the lodge commenced by Dispensation, was due to the combined efforts of A.A. Pendlebury (Asst GSE 1887–95) and Henry Sadler, Grand Janitor. It was discovered that a meeting of Domatic Chapter had been held at the Hercules Pillars in Great Queen Street in 1789 but that was viewed only as 'an occasional meeting' as continuity could not be proved from that date. However, from various official records, sufficient evidence was forthcoming to shew that meetings from 1793 had been constant and that became the year duly approved by the authorities and granted by them.

The actual Centenary celebration was held on 23 March 1893 and thus Domatic Chapter became the sixth London Chapter to celebrate one hundred years existence. Great compliment was paid to Harry Nelson Price the IPZ, who had occupied the Chair as Master of the Lodge when it received the Centenary Warrant (dated 8 February 1886) a few years earlier, when he was invited to occupy the First Principal's Chair to preside over the Festival Banquet. It was at that meeting the Chapter adopted the Centenary Jewel as its motif and the use has been maintained. On that evening Henry Sadler, who had been a constant visitor to the meetings was elected as a Joining Member. Thirty-eight members and sixty-one visitors attended to see the presentation of the Centenary Warrant by W.W.B. Beach, MP, Third Grand Principal, who was accompanied by Thomas Fenn, Past President of the Committee of General Purposes, Edward Letchworth, Grand Scribe E, Alfred Pendlebury Asst GSE, and James L. Thomas, PGSwdB.

It is of interest to note that 'The Chapter was opened in due form by the Principals and then the Companions were admitted'. It was a revival of the eighteenth century custom and is first noticeable in the Minutes commencing with the meeting held on 28 November 1878 and it continues throughout the remainder of that Minute Book which ended on 24 March 1898. Four Candidates, having been the subject of a Ballot 'were entrusted, properly prepared, admitted and duly Exalted to the Supreme Degree of Royal Arch Masonry.' Separate Conclaves for the Installation of the Principals elect followed, the MEZ being inducted and the Second and Third Principals being installed. The remaining officers having been elected at the previous meeting were then invested, which included the First and Second Assistant Sojourners their appointment by the Principal Sojourner having been discontinued in practice since 1886. Centenary Jewels were then presented to the Treasurer and Scribe E, 'for services rendered' and a PZ jewel to Harry Nelson Price the Immediate and Installing Principal; in 1897, Queen Victoria's Diamond Jubilee Year, rank in Grand Chapter as PAGDC was awarded to Comp Price, but an almost immediate rank was given to Charles A. Cottebrune, who was invested in April just one month later, in Grand Chapter as Asst Grand Director of Ceremonies.

Before leaving this period in Domatic chapter mention should be made of John Savage, First Principal in 1844 therefore one of the signatories on the application for a Dispensation to permit the Installation of Comp Sherrard, then Third Principal, to succeed as First Principal without having filled the office of Second Principal. It was, of course, declined and as we have seen created that misguided sense of grievance. Only two meetings after the Installation in April 1845, with Sherrard duly installed as Second Principal, the members voted to remove from the Unicorn Tavern, Jermyn Street, to the Falcon Tavern, Fetter Lane, and whilst Savage continued to pay his dues did not make attendances at the new venue. But he was actively engaged in the Royal Arch for we find him as the *Consecrating* First Principal for Enoch Chapter Chapter No 11 on 19 October 1852. Then he was described as 'P.Z. of Nos. 7 and 25' those being Royal York Chapter of Perseverance and Robert Burns Chapter respectively, to which should have been added 'P.Z. of No. 206'. In that Consecration he was assisted by R.G. Alston (Third Grand Principal 1845–54), Alexander Dobie (Grand Registrar 1846) and other Grand Chapter Officers. The founding Principal Sojourner for Enoch Chapter was William Williams and one may wonder whether he was related to his namesake, the provincial Grand Master for Dorset 1812–39 whom we met in earlier pages. Enoch Chapter never strayed far, first meeting at Freemasons' Tavern in Great Queen Street and then in the adjacent Freemasons' Hall.

John Savage was instrumental in the rejection of the proposal to alter the waiting time of twelve months as a Master Mason before entry to the Royal Arch being reduced to one month. That matter was first raised in 1849, but when it was revived in May 1856 Savage was unsuccessful in his resistance and the Resolution in Grand Chapter was passed. He was appointed Grand Sword Bearer in Grand Chapter in 1859.

George Everett of Domatic Lodge and Chapter was appointed Grand Treasurer of both Grand Lodge and Grand Chapter in 1891. Everett was among the fourteen who were proposed in the Chapter in March 1863 and approved by ballot the next meeting but, he never appeared for exaltation. His first appearance in Domatic Chapter was March 1875 when he is shewn as a visitor from 'No. 975' which was the number of Rose of Denmark Chapter. However, he joined Domatic Chapter in October of that year, in 1879 was elected Third Principal and the following meeting, by Dispensation from Grand Chapter, was installed as First Principal being at that time MEZ of Kennington Chapter No 1381.

That meeting in March 1863 also saw a distinguished visitor in Theodore E. Ladd, Director of Ceremonies in Grand Chapter, who kept contact with Domatic Chapter through its Chapter of Instruction in which he was a leading authority in the ritual.

The year 1863 saw the last re-numbering and closing-up on the Registers and Domatic, through whose eyes and experiences we have travelled thus far witnessing some of the developments in Free-masonry in London, which had commenced in 1786 as No 234, became No 293 in 1814, No 206 in 1832, now became No 177 in 1863. In accordance with official instructions the number of the Chapter was automatically changed to No 177 in October of that year. Among the meeting-places of the lodge had been:

Ship Tavern, Little Turnstile 1785
French Horn, High Holborn 1787
Sun, Gate Street, Lincoln's Inn Fields 1787
Plough, Queen Street, Bloomsbury 1790
Robin Hood, Gray's Inn Lane 1791
Pea Hen, Gray's Inn Lane 1791
Six Cans, Little Turnstile 1791
Coach and horses, High Holborn 1800
Hercules Pillars, Great Queen Street 1813
Dover Castle, Weymouth Mews, Portland
Place 1819
The George, Brook Street, Holborn 1820
Half Moon and Stars, Stanhope Street Clare
Market 1832
Red Lion, Houghton Street 1833
Pewter Platter, Charles Street, Hatton Garden 1837
Green Dragon, Fleet Street 1844
Falcon Tavern, Fetter Lane 1845
Anderton's Hotel, Fleet Street 1864

Security of tenure was of the flimsiest until the last-named which was its happy venue until the end of 1938 when the building was demolished to make way for a re-building programme in that area.

The Minutes of 24 January 1850 mark another era for the name 'Domatic' when the following was recorded in the proceedings of the Chapter:

> Comp.n Sigrist having expressed a desire to form a Chapter of Instruction under the Warrant of this Chapter and to be held at the same House in which the Chapter meets every Friday evening the M.E.Z. was pleased to grant his sanction for the same.

A glimpse at the records of this, the oldest surviving Chapter of Instruction in existence, may well furnish a modicum of profit and pleasure.

Domatic Chapter of Instruction

Following the activity of the Chapter of Promulgation the process of standardising for individual Chapters was not easy as there were very few

Si.s. & Brs.   PRINTING OFFICE   .   1844

Durin: the last Six Years my Masonic Works having successfully wended their way in London, to most of the Provinces under the English Constitution, also France, Prussia, America, Scotland, Ireland, the East & West Indies &c. &c. is of itself a sufficient guarantee of their genuineness and worth, and leaves little for me to add in order to prove their value to Freemasons requiring Instruction. But I still deem it necessary to guard the Brethren (particularly the younger part) from the insidious remarks of *some interested brethren*, who say they ought not to be purchased, because in them the secrets of the Order are exposed, to which I answer they are not. The Oath regards the Signs, Tokens, and Words,* and no more. If it were not so, Preston's Illustrations; the Masonic Review. Dr. Oliver's, Works and others might be condemned, as *the whole of them* contain the business of Masonry, and mine does no more. except being calculated to instruct the brethren in their respective duties. and are enabled to perform them, in accordance with the system laid down by the Lodge of Reconciliation; at the Union in 1813.

28 Upper Clifton Street, Finsbury, London.   G. CLARET.

Lectures of the three Degrees, explanation of the Tracing Boards &c.. 1	1	0
Ceremonies of Initiation; Passing & Raising Opening & Closing Installation &c.. 1	1	0
Illustrations; Quarto and Pocket Size 0	7	6
The whole as contained in the above three Books (new Edition) Bound & Gilt 2	0	0
Ditto ditto with Lock & Key 2	5	0
Ditto ditto and Royal Arch. Bound together 3	10	0
Royal Arch Ceremony. Lectures &c. 1	1	0
Signature Book for meetings of Lodges & Chapters. (This Book will serve for twelve Years ..0	10	6
Masonic Minstrel. 200 Songs & Odes. to be used after the Banquet. 0	4	6
Declaration Books, to be signed by all Candidates at Initiation: every Lodge should have them 0	5	0
An Explanation of the First and Second Tracing Boards 0	2	6
Installation of the W. M. and Officers 0 7 6 Opening and Closing in the 3 Degrees 0	5	0
Claret's Masonic Gleanings comprising a Disquisition on the Antiquity; Extent, Excellence		
and Utility of Free-masonry; also some account of the Union. with Anecdotes &c... 0	5	0
An Ornamental Engraved Quarto Post fly leaf, for Summonses 3 0 on good Paper 1	0	0
Letter Press Quarto Post fly leaf ruled divisions for ditto 0	15	0
Japanned Lantern with Star, Lamp and Reflector for the third Degree 0	12	0
Gauntlets per Pair with mock Silver Lace 0 8 0 Ditto with Silver Lace & Kid Gloves 0	16	0
New Edition of the Constitutions half Bound 0 5 0 Whole ditto with Masonic tooling 0	10	0
Working Tools for the 3 Degrees, with Brass Skirritt & Compasses 1	7	6
Badge Cases with Brs name and No. of the Lodge, each from 0	4	0
Tracing Boards in three Coloured Designs, bound in lock Case 0	15	0
The Charge at Initiation stitched Six pence each, or per Dozen 0	5	0

BADGES, JEWELS, COLLARS. LARGE TRACING BOARDS BANNERS &c.

Several Editions of Prestons Illustrations for Sale.

KNIGHTS TEMPLAR IN MANUSCRIPT 2 0 0

Any of the above sent carefully Packed and Sealed, on the receipt of a Bankers or Post Office Order.

Brethren having occasion to send a Post Office Order, will have the goodness to have it made payable at 36 City Road, being near my residence.

* See Oliver's Historical Landmarks No. 2. Page 33. Note 76.

31 *Printed circular from George Claret in 1844 showing the wide range of items he sold*

Chapters of Instruction set up for that purpose. Several experts came to the fore, and their services were much in demand, but there is no evidence that members of Domatic Chapter were among them in the early stage after 1834/5. The Provinces were poorly served and certain of the Royal Arch experts were invited as teachers to make visitations from time to time. It was yet another field of opportunity for George Claret who, from 1838, was supplying written-out copies of Royal Arch ritual which preceded his printed manual published in 1844/5 and priced at £1. 10s. It is worth noting that when 'The Royal Arch Ceremony, Lectures, &c' were bound together with 'Lectures of the three Degrees, explanation of the Tracing Boards, Ceremonies of Initiation, Passing & Raising, Opening & Closing, Installation, and Illustrations, &c.' the price was, in 1844, £3. 10. 0! One would hesitate to translate that figure into its modern value. Claret then described himself as 'P.M. of Lodges 12 and 228 and P.H. of Chapter 12', the latter being United Chapter of Prudence and still bears that number on the Register of Grand Chapter. Claret's Royal Arch manual found its market and served its useful purpose. It was well established by 1850 and knowing his diligence in the cause of uniformity and conformity it would have been faithful to the officially adopted forms. Such was the state when 1850 saw the birth of Domatic Chapter of Instruction, now the oldest teaching authority in the Royal Arch to survive from that important era.

The first Minute Book covers the period from 15 February 1850 to 28 September 1866 and commences with the following:

The Domatic Chapter No 206 having granted their sanction for a Chapter of Instruction to be holden under their Warrant at the Falcon Tavern, Fetter Lane, the following Companions assembled at the above named place, on Friday evening Feby 15 1850, to form themselves into such Chapter of Instruction, and to agree to the necessary Bye Laws for its government

Companions Blackburn, M.E.Z.
Comp^n Crawley H.
Sigrist J.

Smith P.S.
Ireland 1st Assist.
Burgess 2 Assist.
Clark N

1. It was proposed by Comp. Crawley & seconded by Comp. Burgess that this Chapter be called the Domatic Chapter of Instruction and hold its meeting on Friday evening at 8 o clock, at Comp. Ireland's Falcon Tavern, Fetter Lane. carried unanimously.

Then follows ten further Resolutions relating to government and administration.

Expenses in connection with the setting-up were entered at the end of the book and appear in three accounts headed 'Furniture', 'Printing' and 'Books'. (See Appendix F). A brief reference to the furnishing appeared in the *Freemasons' Quarterly Review* of 1850 (p 390):

... The unique set of banners and standards in this Chapter add very much to give effect to the ceremonial.

One year later a celebratory banquet to mark the first year of working was held and from the report published in *FQR* 1851 (p 373) we have the following information:

It was perfectly well known that great difficulty had existed in obtaining instruction in that most beautiful branch of Masonry, the Royal Arch Degree. It is true that an efficient Chapter of Instruction has been in operation at the west end of the town, but Companions living in and about the City were unable to attend. About fifteen months since several Companions resolved to form themselves into a Chapter of Instruction and applied to Domatic Chapter for permission to hold it under the sanction of their Charter; this was granted. By the liberality of Companions Sigrist an unique set of R.A. furniture was obtained and the working of the Chapter was entrusted to the skill and talents of Comp. Blackburn.

That 'unique set of furniture' was kept in constant use and housed at various meeting-places (see Appendix F) right through until October 1980 when, after a weekly tenancy lasting twenty-six years at The Marlborough Head, Drury Lane, where the picture was taken, the accommodation was no longer available. Application to meet in Freemasons' Hall was granted and now the weekly meetings, throughout the year as heretofore, are held in fully furnished Chapter rooms and the redundant miniature equipment preserved for posterity in a grace and favour storage at the Hall.

The banquet was also the means to make a presentation to Blackburn the Preceptor who received a gold watch suitably inscribed on the inner case—'From his Masonic Pupils and Friends', and also bore an engraved triangle within a circle. The presentation was made by Comp Lemanski who had joined at the third meeting and was then described as 'P.M. of Polish National Lodge No. 778'. Tribute was paid by W. Watson of Globe Lodge No 23 and Robert Burns Chapter No 25, who was at one time proprietor of Freemasons' Tavern, Great Queen Street. Watson stated that he had installed Blackburn in the Chairs of two lodges, Globe No 23 and Polish National No 778. Installations, whether in the Craft or the Royal Arch, was a masonic field of activity in which William Watson was renowned as the expert. In a report in *FQR* he was credited with having installed forty-three Masters in twenty-three lodges and ninety-six Principals in various chapters. J.E.N. Walker carried his research a little further and accounted for fifty Masters and one hundred Principals. It is of interest to note that Watson was Exalted in Chapter of Prudence No 12 on 25 June 1840 and was therefore a contemporary with George Claret, and was also a member of Robert Burns Chapter No 25 which in 1850 or earlier had a flourishing Chapter of Instruction, but that one unfortunately did not survive, Watson stated that Blackburn had gained all his knowledge of Royal Arch masonry from Chapter No 25 and that it was mainly because of that the Domatic Chapter of Instruction had made such progress in its first year. Watson died in 1879 and the Royal Arch in London was the poorer for his passing.

Blackburn served as Grand Steward representing Globe Lodge No 23 in 1851 and the following year received a jewel to the value of three guineas in recognition of his efficient services in the Chair and that is the first recorded instance in that lodge of the presentation of a Past Master's jewel. He

made only two appearances in Domatic Chapter in 1849 and 1850 being then described as 'P.Z. 25' but his name does not appear after that. In 1851 he was elected Scribe E, of Domatic Chapter of Instruction, and presumably combined those duties with his Preceptorship. Although he was elected as an Honorary member on 11 September 1856 he remained constant in his attendance at the meetings thereafter. John Crawley, also from Robert Burns Chapter made two attendances at Domatic Chapter meetings and was noted as 'P.Z. No 25'; he was elected to Honorary membership of the Chapter of Instruction on 25 March 1852 and his attendance continued.

Bernard Sigrist, who started it all and supplied the miniature equipment, came from Mount Sinai Chapter No 49 (now No 19) and joined Domatic Chapter on 27 May 1847 being Scribe N at the founding date of the Chapter of Instruction. He was a member of Domatic Lodge becoming Master in 1848 and MEZ of the Chapter in 1852.

George Smith was a member of Domatic Chapter and served as Third Principal for the year ending March 1848 but, owing to straightened circumstances, was unable to progress. Two meetings later, in May, his letter of resignation was read to the members expressing his inability to pay his dues at that time. The dignity of this Companion is shewn by what has been written on the subject:

> Scribe E. read a letter he had received from Comp. George Smith, P.J., expressing his regret at being unable to attend the Convocation in consequence of his inability to pay his dues at present arising from severe losses he had experienced but trusting he should ere long have the power to do so. That the above cause compelled him to tender his resignation as a Member of the Chapter but hoped to have the honor of rejoining when his circumstances became better should he be deemed worthy of acceptance and that he was sorry after being so long time a Member to leave in debt. The resignation of Comp. Smith was accepted and ordered to be entered on the Minutes.

His next appearance was at the meeting of 28 February 1850 when he is listed as assisting in the ceremony, 'Smith as P.S.' for the Exaltation of the WM of Kent Lodge No 15, Bro George Nott. The

32/33 Pages from the minute book of Domatic Chapter of Instruction

Emergency

Domatic Chapter of Instruction

Holden at Comp. Ireland's, Falcon Tavern, Fetter Lane

Tuesday. March 18th 1851

Present

Comp. Blackburn M.E.Z.		Comp. Cox P.S.	Comp. Banks	Comp. Heath
. Selig	H	. Scurell	. Cole	
. Hill	J	. Major	. Dawson	
. Gibbons	J	. Allen	. Kirby	

The Chapter was declared open

The Ceremony was ably worked: Comp. Banks Candidate

The following Companions were unanimously elected Members.

Comp. Banks   N° 7

. D° Major   N° 3

. Cox   N° 12

. Cole   N°

All Business being concluded the Chapter was duly closed, when the Companions partook of an excellent Banquet, furnished by Comp. Ireland, and the evening was spent with masonic harmony and conviviality

Cash Account forward £5. 16. 0

Collected   6. 3

£ 6. 2. 2

following year on 27 March the Minutes have, 'That Comp. George Smith be appointed Janitor and that he do deliver the Summonses and be paid 6s. 0. for each meeting.' He retained that office until 22 January 1857 which was the meeting for election of officers for the ensuing year, when it was noted:

> The Ballot for the Janitor was ordered to stand over to ascertain from Comp. Smith the Janitor, who was also Janitor at another Chapter meeting on the same evening as this Chapter, which of the two Chapters he would elect to act for.

the 'other Chapter' in this case was Cyrus Royal Arch Chapter No 21 whose meetings were held at the London Coffee House, Ludgate Hill, where Smith was actually deputising. However, he stayed with that Chapter, was elected in 1859 and held the office with them for twenty-one years when ill-health and advancing years caused him to resign and he was then presented with Five Guineas in recognition of his faithful service.

Charles Ireland was Exalted in Domatic Chapter on 28 May 1846 being then described 'of Albion Lodge No 9'. At the founding date of the Chapter of Instruction he was First Assistant Sojourner of the Chapter, but although he did not accept higher office was extremely active in Freemasonry in general. His premises in Fetter Lane became known as 'The Masonic Hall' and in addition to the many lodges and Chapters meeting there, celebratory functions were also catered for at the hands of himself and his wife, thus earning a high reputation among London Freemasons. Ireland became Secretary of Royal Jubilee Lodge No 85 (now No 72) and a Lodge of Instruction under their sanction was held at the Falcon Tavern attracting some of the brethren from Domatic Lodge.

Benjamin Burgess was a member of Domatic Chapter until 22 March 1849 but was then erased for non-payment of dues. He appears as a visitor on 23 May 1850 being then described as 'late of 206', which was the number for Domatic at that time, but his name disappears from the records after that.

John Clarke was Exalted in Domatic Chapter on 26 April 1849 whilst he was Junior Deacon of the lodge (*WM* in 1853). When the Chapter of Instruction was founded he was Principal Sojourner in the Chapter and reached the First Principal's Chair in 1855.

The seven founders are thus accounted for but a few other names have to be taken into consideration. Mention has already been made of the expertise of Comp Watson in regard to the Installation of Masters in lodges and Principals in Chapters, but it is quite significant that for eight successive years, from 1845 to and including 1852, the only attendances that he made to Domatic Chapter were on Installation meetings and apparently he rendered valuable service in that connection. It ended, however, when Bernard Sigrist was the Installing MEZ in 1853 and it was on that night Joseph Smith joined 'from Mount Sinai Chapter No 49'. A particular highlight of Watson's masonic career in Globe Lodge No 23 occurred on 5 August 1851 when he had the privilege of initiating HRH Ekbaloddowla, Nawab of Oude, in that lodge. He also rescued Globe Lodge from a moribund state and influenced its return to prosperity by proposing ten members of Robert Burns Lodge No 25 as Joining Members. Seeing that the lodge was, and is, a 'Red Apron Lodge' he thus preserved their privilege; he served as their representative Grand Steward for the year 1848. Although he must have been a moving force behind the founding of Domatic Chapter of Instruction, he did not actually attend a meeting of it until 10 June 1851 and was then elected as a member; he was elected to Honorary Membership on 18 September 1856.

Henry Bridges 'of No 778' (Polish National Chapter now No 534) was one of four elected as Joining Members of the Chapter of Instruction at the second meeting. His competence is shewn by his occupation of the Second Principal's Chair that night and election to occupy MEZ for the following week.

Lemanski, from the same Chapter as Bridges, joined on the night of the third meeting and immediately occupied the Chair as Third Principal.

He was also a member of Globe Lodge, served as Grand Steward in 1852 and during his term of office was elected as Treasurer of the Grand Stewards Lodge.

There are unaccountable gaps in the Minute Book but it would appear that meetings of the Chapter of Instruction were held during those gaps and the Minutes recorded elsewhere have not been preserved. One particular example is the gap between 24 November 1854 and 4 September 1856 yet the Minutes of those two meetings are written on following pages with an attendance of eleven Companions listed for the latter meeting and the Minutes commencing with, 'The Minutes of the last Convocation read and confirmed ...' Among the names recorded for that meeting are Watson, Blackburn, and Ireland. Another gap occurs between September 1864 and that month one year later, but remaining in the Minute Book is a piece of notepaper with a record of three meetings in which the names of Smith, Crawley, Brett, and Pendlebury are among those listed. During that period a number of references to the Domatic Chapter of Instruction appear in issues of the *Freemason's Quarterly Review* as well as *The Freemasons' Magazine* and as an example of its importance and reputation that it had earned by that time the following is quoted from the latter publication issued for 2 August 1862:

A special meeting was held [of Domatic Chapter of Instruction] on July 17th in consequence of the visit of Comp. Younghusband of Liverpool, who was desirous of seeing the working of this Chapter of Instruction as, in his capacity of Preceptor of the Liverpool Chapter, he was anxious to promulgate among those requiring instructions in his province pure and unadulterated working. ... he felt that in accepting the post of Preceptor in his province it was his duty to promulgate pure and correct working only and to enable him to judge what was right, he thought he could not do better than come to the fountain-head and thanked the companions for their kindness.

The MEZ for that meeting was Dr Theodore Ladd, the Preceptor of the Chapter of Instruction. He had joined on 11 September 1856 being then described as 'of No 223' which was Joppa Chapter now No 188. He proposed that the visitor be elected as an Honorary Member and that was warmly carried. Dr Ladd was, undoubtedly, 'the fountain-head' as in that year he was also Grand Director of Ceremonies in Supreme Grand Chapter, one of four to hold that position whose names occur in the Minute Books of the Chapter of Instruction in the second half of the Nineteenth Century. Among those whose names have been mentioned in connection with the Chapter of Instruction and became prominent in Supreme Grand Chapter in that period, are the following:

Name	Chapter No	Appointment in Supreme Grand Chapter	
Joseph Smith	177	Grand Director of Ceremonies	1856–57
Henry Bridges	534	,, ,, ,, ,,	1860
Theodore E. Ladd	188	,, ,, ,, ,,	1862
James Brett	177	,, ,, ,, ,,	1871
Henry Garrod	(not shewn)	Asst ,, ,, ,,	1889
C.A. Cottebrune	177	,, ,, ,, ,,	1893
H. Nelson-Price	177	,, ,, ,, ,,	1897
Henry G. Buss	177	Asst Grand Scribe E.	1880–84
R.A. Pendlebury	975	,, ,, ,, ,,	1887–95
George Everett	177	Grand Treasurer	1891
H.C. Levander	720	Grand Sword Bearer	1881
W.B. Fendick	177	Past Grand Standard Bearer	1897
William Watson	25	Past Deputy Grand Director of Ceremonies	1887
Charles B. Payne	177	Grand Janitor	1857–79
Henry Sadler	177	,, ,,	1879–09

Whilst Ireland had, seemingly, severed connection with both the Domatic Lodge and Chapter, he retained a close association with the Chapter of Instruction even though the Companions heeded the directive to have nothing to do with 'the spurious lodge calling themselves freemasons' meeting at his premises in Fetter Lane. We find reports of Chapter of Instruction meetings at various addresses publicised and reported in masonic periodicals, for example *FQR* wrote of a meeting held on 11 November 1858 at Queen Elizabeth Tavern, Walworth, which appears to have been another establishment in which Ireland had an interest. Another meeting held on 20 May 1859 was covered by *FQR* and *The Freemasons Magazine* stating:—

> Domatic C. of I. moved from City Arms, West Square, St. Georges Road near Elephant and Castle.

In most of the accounts Ireland's name is linked with the Chapter of Instruction, and the movements occurred during the period that gaps arose in the Minute Book. On 6 June 1863 it was reported:

> Domatic C. of I. has removed from the Horns Tavern, Kennington, to Ireland's Masonic Hall, Fetter Lane.

The wanderers had returned to their original meeting-place as it would seem that 'the spurious lodge' had long departed.

It is in this period that Brett was demonstrating his special skills in ritual, a classic illustration of which is in the Minutes of 16 March 1866 when it states he 'ably worked':

1st	Clause	of	the	1st	Section
2nd	..	..	..	..	..
3rd	..	..	..	..	..
1st	..	..	..	2nd	..
2nd	..	..	..	..	..
3rd	..	..	..	..	..
1st	..	..	..	3rd	..
3rd	..	..	..	..	..
1st	..	..	..	4th	..

Reference to the Clauses and Sections, which were First Printed by Lewis Ltd, from 1874 in the *Perfect Ceremonies*, will shew the prodigious effort involved.

The Chapter of Instruction did not remain at Fetter Lane for we have various reports appearing in the masonic press from time to time. The following coverage is from *The Freemasons Magazine*:

> 16 Feb. 1867. Metropolitan. (This has a list of all those attending which included: Little, Pendlebury, Clarke, Foulger with the comment)—'all under the tuition of Comp. Brett.'

> 27 April 1867. Metropolitan. The ceremony of exaltation was ably reheased after which the explanation of the banners was given by Comp. Brett; then the M.E.Z. [Dr. Ladd] illustrated the solids, and was followed by Comp. Brett with the history of the rod of Moses. . . .

> 20 June. 1868. Metropolitan. Comp. Brett P.Z., this able Preceptor of the Chapter, then worked the second and third Sections of the Lecture, including the elaborate explanation of the Royal Arch Banners, and afterwards by special request delivered the famous lecture on the platonic bodies illustrated by diagrams of the Royal Arch jewel and the Triple Tau. The distinguished Masonic writer and archaeologist Comp. W.J. Hughan, of Truro, being present was proposed as a Joining Member by Comp. Little and the proposition seconded by Comp. Brett was carried unanimously. In expressing his acknowledgement to the Companions for his election Comp. Hughan adverted to the fact of his having recently discovered Dr. Dassigny's work in which reference was made to the R.A. degree and which carried back its authentic history as a portion of English speculative Freemasonry to A.D. 1740. The remarks of our diligent and learned Companion were well received with much pleasure and he concluded by paying a well-merited tribute to the consumate ability which Bro. Brett displayed as the foremost Preceptor of Royal Arch Masonry in England. . . .

The following year we find a copy of a Notice which had been circulated entered in the Minutes:

> Dear Sir and Companion,
> You are requested to attend at the 'Horns Tavern',

Kennington, on Monday April 19 at 7 p.m. precisely, to assist in re-opening the above Chapter of Instruction, to determine the days for its future Meetings, and for other & necessary purposes.

[signed] R. Wentworth Little
P.Z. 975, Z. 177. S.E.

At that meeting they decided the meetings should be held fortnightly in the future. What seems to have grown into a somewhat peripatetic behaviour, with a neglect even of the miniature equipment or even its non-use for a spell, caused the sanctioning body to bring the state into proper perspective, as shewn by Domatic Chapter Minutes dated 24 March 1870:

That permission be given to the Chapter of Instruction, which is attached to this Chapter, to be henceforth held at the Metropolitan Railway, Victoria Station, Pimlico, conditionally however that the Chapter, nor the furniture, be not removed or alienated without the consent of this Chapter.

and, the following month the Chapter of Instruction recorded:

4 April 1870. The ceremony of Consecration was then rehearsed by Comp. Little assisted by Comp. Brett who delivered the Oration. Comp. Braid performed the musical parts of the ceremony on the Harmonium. Vote of thanks to Comp. Ward having obtained the furniture and for having it cleaned & renovated.

From the extracts quoted above two items are worthy of comment. Firstly, the word 'Metropolitan' has been mistakenly read having been deemed to be the name of the Chapter of Instruction, whereas it was one of two things; either it was the name of the Railway Restaurant being familiarly used in the reporting, or it was following the custom of that period when London events or masonic happenings were listed under the heading 'Metropolitan' whilst those in the Provinces came under their particular denomination. However, the word was fastened upon by the compilers of the ritual with the title:— *The Holy Royal Arch as practised since 1866 at the Metropolitan Chapter of Improvement*, which was published (n.d.) by W. Straker Ltd, and again in 1920, probably a reprint, by E.E. Alexander. In both rituals the *Foreword*

has the statement:

When a ritual appears in print for the first time it is usually claimed that it is up to date and an 'improvement' upon its predecessors. The virtue claimed for our production is not its novelty or perfection, but its antiquity. We claim that it is the ritual practised in the Metropolitan Chapter of Improvement since 1866 and, we doubt not, for centuries before elsewhere.

It should be noted that the Metropolitan Lodge No 1507 was not founded until 1874 and its Chapter, of that name and number, four years later. Lewis Ltd published *The Metropolitan Working* in 1890 that had no such extravagant claims.

The second item for comment is contained in the report of 20 June 1868 when W.J. Hughan was elected as a Joining Member. This eminent masonic scholar was one of the nine Founders of Quatuor Coronati Lodge No 2076, the premier lodge of masonic research, in 1884 (Consecrated 12 January 1886), which is now known throughout the world through its Correspondence Circle membership. Among the many valuable literary contributions left to posterity by Hughan is his *Origin of the English Rite of Freemasonry*, published by George Kenning in 1884 in which D'Assigny's book, mentioned above, entitled *A Serious and Impartial Enquiry into the Cause of the Present Decay of Free-Masonry in the Kingdom of Ireland*, published in 1744, was fully examined.

The first mention regarding ritual format for Domatic Chapter of Instruction occurred at the meeting on 8 January 1879, in an era when numerous Royal Arch rituals had been printed and in an age when 'improvements' entered the field. It was probably a situation in which terms of reference were advisable, therefore:

It was proposed and carried that Comp. Haslett, Bull, Reed, Wood, & Smallpiece form a committee to agree upon a Ritual to be drafted for Working in this Chapter & that they nominate five of their number to carry into effect at all meetings of this Chapter of Instruction.

If any such draft came into being it has not survived, but, if it had been available what a useful

A

SERIOUS and IMPARTIAL

ENQUIRY

Into the Cause of the present Decay of

FREE-MASONRY

IN THE

Kingdom of *IRELAND*.

Humbly Addrefs'd to all the BRE-
THREN Accepted of before and
fince the *Conftitutions*.

To which are added,

Such Inftructive Remarks as may be
found ufeful to Revive the Honour of that AN-
TIENT CRAFT.

As likewife, by way of APPENDIX, will be inferted
the OLD and NEW REGULATIONS of the *London*
CONSTITUTIONS, by the Confent and Approbation of the GRAND-LODGE of *Ireland*,
and Dedicated to the Right Worfhipful and Right
Hon. the Lord Vifcount ALLEN, Grand-Mafter
of this Kingdom.

The Whole adorned with a Curious Copper-Plate
fuitable to the Order and Defign.

By Fifield Daffigny, M.D. *Author of the Impartial
Anfwer to the Enemies of* FREE-MASONS.

D U B L I N :
Printed by EDWARD BATE in *George's-Lane* near
Dame-Street. M,DCC,XLIV.

Title page from A Serious and Impartial Enquiry . . . . .

link with Claret, Gilkes, Watson, and other great names it would have been.

At the turn of the century a privately printed manual entitled *The Domatic Working of the Ceremonies* met with great success. Unfortunately it proved to be a constant nuisance to the Preceptors correcting the various errors that it perpetuated. Finally, in 1958 it was decided that terms of reference were essential and the Committee approved the typescript manual of their agreed *Ritual of The Holy Royal Arch as Taught by The Domatic Chapter of Instruction No 177* which, in 1960 was printed and made available for all from then on. Whatever changes, mandatory, recommended, or optional, that have arisen in Supreme Grand Chapter since, all have been catered for. An example of that being a demonstration of the *Alternative Installation Ceremonies*, approved by Supreme Grand Chapter 8 November 1961, before what may be viewed as the largest attendance at a private Chapter meeting held in London by the London First Principals' Chapter No 2712, shortly afterwards.

A River Thames Disaster

Minutes of any organisation should not impose blinkers upon those who are to follow and should never fail to include mention of incidents which, although outside its own orbit, may involve its members in some way. it is through such means we have our attention drawn to an item of human interest and the membership taught to keep everything in proper perspective. Londoners were shocked over a maritime disaster that occurred on 3 September 1878 when the pleasure paddle-steamship *Princess Alice*, returning from an excursion and crowded to capacity, was in collision with the collier *Bywell Castle* in Galleon's Reach, Woolwich. Of nearly 900 souls on board only a little over 200 were saved. A full account, from the *Dictionary of Disasters at Sea during the age of Steam 1824-1962*, appears in Appendix J.

The masonic interest in this tragedy emerges in the Minutes of Domatic Chapter of Instruction for the meeting held the next day, 4 September 1878, when the members carried unanimously:

> That a letter of congratulations be sent to Comp. Reed upon his happy deliverance from the dreadful wreck of the Princess Alice off Woolwich.

The letter was sent and a copy affixed to the Minutes states:

> 12 Waterloo Place, S.W.
> 7 September 1878
>
> *Dear Comp.ⁿ Reed,*
> *With infinite pleasure I obey the commands of the Comp.ⁿˢ of the Domatic Chapter of Instruction to offer you their heartiest congratulations upon the Providential deliverance of yourself and Mrs. Reed from the terrible wreck of the Princess Alice. Where so many have perished it is the special cause of thankfulness to Almighty God that you and your wife are saved. Devoutly hoping that the lives of both of you may be long, happy, and prosperous without being disturbed by even the smallest calamity. Receive from each and all heartiest congratulations and in their name, believe me,*
> *Yours faithfully & fraternally,*
> *D.M. Belfrage.*

The reply from Reed, also affixed, was as follows:

> 57 Oxford Street, W.
> 9 Sept
>
> *Dear Comp. Belfrage,*
> *I return on behalf of myself and wife, heartfelt thanks to the Companions of the Domatic Chapter of Instruction for their congratulations on our happy escape at the loss of the Princess Alice. Slowly, but I trust surely, we are recovering from the shock. I trust time will speedily deaden to our memory the appalling sights and sounds of that horrible night. With personal thanks to yourself as our intermedium,*
> *Believe me,*
> *Yours sincerely & fraternally,*
> *Henry Reed.*

119

At the meeting one week later on 11 September, the tragedy having included the loss of one of the members, the Minutes record:

> Ordered to be recorded on the Minutes that a profound expression of regret be expressed for the loss of Comp. Cobham who with his wife and child were lost in the wreck of the Princess Alice on 3 Sept. 1878. Comp. Cobham was buried in Charlton churchyard, left side of North entrance and Comp. Smallpiece attended the funeral.

In 1955 Harold Bevan, Scribe of the Chapter of Instruction was taken ill with what was to be a prolonged illness and the author acted in his stead. The following year, as the situation was unchanged, was then elected in succession. Contact was well maintained with Bevan and, a few years later, when he had recovered sufficiently he paid what was to be his last visit to the Chapter of Instruction. The letter that he wrote following that visit, kept for posterity, may be deemed to be a classic postscript to this subject:

17 Lewisham Park Road, S.E. 15
29 July 1960

Dear Comp. Wells,

On Wednesday last, after a considerable time, I attended the Chapter of Instruction and would like to express my very warm thanks to all members who gave me such a friendly reception. I was particularly delighted to find the Chapter so active. I was very interested in the copy of the letter you showed me regarding the loss of the Princess Alice. My Grandmother, who died in 1904, sometimes spoke of the tragedy. At the time she was living in a house at Erith with the lawn sloping down to the river. She spoke of the quantity of bodies which were washed up on the grassy banks of the garden. It was a great shock to all who lived there and it was seldom you could get the old lady to speak about it; she was 94 when she died. It was the reason my family, brother and sisters were never taken for a sea trip and we were all strictly forbidden to go on one.

With fraternal greetings to you all,
Yours faithfully,
Harold Bevan.

Note: The author is indebted to the library staff of the National Maritime Museum, Greenwich, for their able assistance in research. It is regretted that a picture taken of that portion of the *Princess Alice* which was beached is of a quality that does not justify reproduction here.

Part Three

Into the Twentieth Century
London Rank

As we have now seen, major advances occurred in Freemasonry in general during the nineteenth century, including the recognition of the Royal Arch by the premier Grand Lodge, an action which finally paved the way for the Union in 1813, and the long process of bringing a standard form in both Craft and Royal Arch procedures. Such was the success in masonic organisation that by the end of the century the pattern of behaviour had become well established, and lodge records tended to become stereotyped according to their local and insular interests. The emergence of the twentieth century, however, soon brought the step forward that had been long awaited by Past Masters of London lodges.

For many years London Past Masters had felt a sense of grievance and denial when making comparisons between their own standing and that of their equals in Provinces and Districts. Those brethren had the advantage of appointment to active or Past Rank in their respective Grand Lodges, with promotion as an added incentive for further recognition of continued masonic service. In those ranks brethren were entitled to wear the appropriate dark blue collar and lined apron, and received due recognition in their own areas as officers of the subordinate Grand Lodge. The Past Master in London had only one hope for such distinction and that was by appointment from the Grand Master as an officer, present or past, in the United Grand Lodge of England itself. It was a comparatively rare occurrence, and a District or Provincial Grand Officer had an equal chance of that honour through the recommendation from his Provincial or District Grand Master.

The matter was resolved by the Grand Master at the Quarterly Communication of Grand Lodge in December 1907 when a message from HRH Duke of Connaught and Strathearn was read expressing his desire for power to be given to confer upon a certain number of Past Masters of London Lodges a distinction equivalent to Provincial of District Grand Rank:

> ... the right to wear during the Grand Master's pleasure a distinctive jewel, collar and apron, with the designation of "LONDON RANK" ...

Accordingly, Past Masters of each London Lodge were invited to choose a worthy brother from amongst themselves for recommendation to the Grand Master for this honour, the selection being on grounds of merit and not solely upon order of seniority, but earned 'by long and meritorious service'.

In June 1908 each of the recommended brethren received a Certificate of Appointment stating:

> To All Whom it may concern
>   THIS is to Certify that the
> MOST WORSHIPFUL GRAND MASTER in consideration of Masonic zeal and of service rendered to the Craft in London has been pleased to confer upon Worshipful Brother ..... of the .... Lodge, No. ... the right to wear during the Grand Master's pleasure the distinctive Jewel and Clothing of
> LONDON RANK
> such privileges and subject to such limitations in connection therewith us are now or may hereafter be contained in the Book of Constitution of the Craft in England.

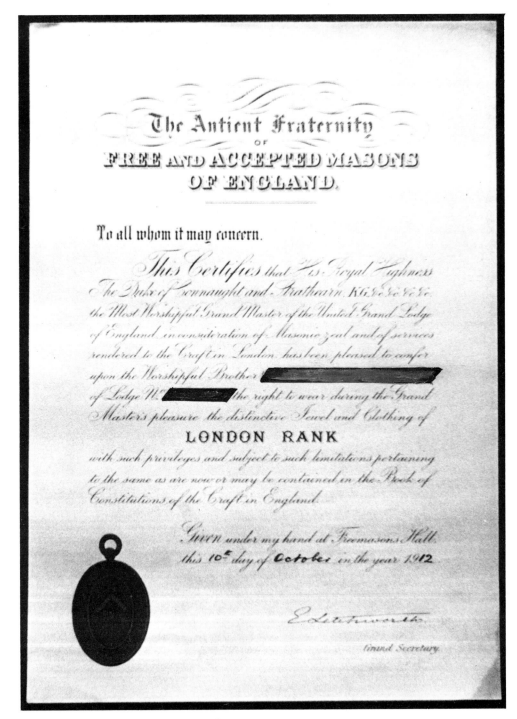

34 *Certificate of appointment to 'London Rank'*

The Certificate was surmounted by the Coat of Arms of the Grand Master and was signed by the Grand Secretary. Certificates in that form, with an appropriate change in the coat of Arms according to the succession of Grand Masters, were issued to each brother so honoured until 1963 when they were discontinued leaving the Letter of Appointment until 1963 when they were discontinued leaving the Letter of Appointment to serve the purpose. Until the commencement of the Annual Investitures, in February 1933, those Certificates were the sole mark of appointment to the honour.

A change in the title was made on 7 June 1939 when the Grand Master, then HRH Prince George, Duke of Kent, granted alteration to the title to LONDON GRAND RANK, and the Certificate was suitably amended.

Addition to the number of annual appointments, and promotion in the Rank, was announced by the Grand Master, HRH Prince Edward, Duke of Kent (son of Prince George) in March 1979. He commented:

London Lodges had always been treated differently when it comes to promotion and that appointments were proportionately fewer than those in Provincial Grand Lodges; the change would mean that a greater number of London Freemasons will receive the honour.

Whereas, after the first appointments to LONDON RANK in 1908, the allocation had been to a ratio of one appointment to every three London lodges, the latest change increased the number to one for every two lodges; and invitation to recommend a worthy Past Master would thus be received by each lodge in alternate years. The total number honoured up to 1958 was 18,615 and from then on to 1982 a further 15,129.

The Grand Master also announced the creation of a new honour, to be known as SENIOR LONDON GRAND RANK, and:

... that regular promotion, although sparing in number, will be made to it. The action would give recognition to those brethren in London who might reasonably have expected further reward for merit; accommodation for which is well provided for in Provincial Grand Lodge structure.

The change in the apron badge and the collar jewel is shewn in Plate No 36. The total number who have received that honour up to 1982 is 711.

Brethren who received LONDON RANK in the first year lost no time in organising themselves and on 29 April 1909 held a celebratory dinner at the Holborn Restaurant with a view to the creation of an Association among themselves in which they could exchange masonic knowledge and opinions on matters of common interest. A Committee and a President were elected and it was agreed that they would dine together as an Association after each Quarterly Communication of Grand Lodge, in much the same manner in which the Grand Stewards meet after Grand Lodge, and those Grand Officers who belong to the Grand Officers' Mess.

A few years later a President's Badge came into being. It is a distinctive gold badge of office suspended from a narrow blue ribbon that is worn on all occasions relating to the Association, and is transferred to each successor. On the reverse the inscription reads:

THE PRESIDENT of the LONDON RANK ASSOCIATION was invested with this PRESIDENTIAL BADGE by V.Wor. Bro. Sir Edward Letchworth Kt., F.S.A., P.G.D., GRAND SECRETARY at the ANNUAL FESTIVAL of the ASSOCIATION on the 31st January 1917.

The first Investiture of London Rank was held in a meeting of the Grand Stewards Lodge specially convened to accommodate Lord Ampthill, pro Grand Master, for that purpose. It has become an annual event but normally with the Assistant Grand Master officiating on behalf of the Grand Master. That meeting is followed by a Festival Dinner, organised by the London Grand Rank Association, with the President as host for the occasion.

The membership of the Association is held at approximately 10,000 and, to cater for those Holders of the rank who have moved away from London, Area Groups have been formed as follows:

Bournemouth (1970), Devonshire (1971), East Sussex (1974), Thanet (1975), West Sussex

United Grand Lodge
OF ANTIENT, FREE AND ACCEPTED MASONS OF ENGLAND

The Right Honourable The Earl of Scarbrough, K.G.
GRAND MASTER.

To All Whom it may concern

This is to Certify that the
Most Worshipful Grand Master in
consideration of Masonic zeal and of services rendered
to the Craft in London has been pleased to confer upon
Worshipful Brother George Frederick Furlong
of the ~ Five Orders Lodge ~ No. 5696
the right to wear during the Grand Master's pleasure
the distinctive Jewel and Clothing of

London Grand Rank

with such privileges and subject to such limitations in
connection therewith as are now or may hereafter be
contained in the Book of Constitutions of this Grand Lodge.
In Testimony whereof I have
hereunto subscribed my name and affixed the Seal
of the Grand Lodge at London this Twenty ninth day
of   October   A.L. 5958 A.D. 1958

James W. Stubbs
Grand Secretary.

35 *Certificate of appointment to 'London Grand Rank'*

(1978), West Midlands (1981), South East Essex (1982).

The quarterly *Bulletin* of the Association, captioned 'Designed to enlighten and entertain' is sent to all members and subscribers around the world and through that, as well as the quarterly meetings, London Freemasonry has an organised voice which has long proved itself helpful and constructive. Its many leaflets and printed talks are available to all Freemasons.

It has been the established custom for Provinces to promote Appeals on behalf of the four main masonic charities, Viz, The Royal Masonic Institution for Girls, the Royal Masonic Institution for Boys, the Royal Masonic Benevolent Institution, and the Royal Masonic Hospital. (note; as at 1982 these are all in process of reorganisation and revised establishment). Several years advance notice is given in the Province sponsoring one of those charities in order to achieve united effort in support of the Provincial Grand Master who presides over his particular Appeal. The Charity jewel, for those who qualify as Stewards for the occasion, usually bears the coat of Arms of the President, if applicable, or that of the Province.

London had not led such an Appeal until 1964. On that subject the President of the Association stated:

> The Royal Masonic Institution for Boys Festival for 1964 was sponsored by the London Grand Rank Association at the express invitation of the M.W. the Grand Master [Earl Scarbrough] ... *This is the first time in history that any such request has been made* ...

At the Investiture, doubtless with the Appeal in mind, the Assistant Grand Master, Maj Gen Sir Allan Adair reminded the brethren:

36 *Apron badge and collar jewel of 'Senior London Grand Rank'*

... London was the acknowledged Masonic Centre of the World, and the World looked to London for example and guidance in masonic matters ...

On behalf of London brethren, RW Bro Rt Hon Earl of Warwick, DL, SGW, Prov Grand Master (Essex) presided over the Festival Dinner for that Appeal and he announced that the total sum of £630,317 had been raised for the Institution. He mentioned the short notice that London had received for the project but praised the effort and support that had been given. The Grand Master, Earl Scarbrough attended the dinner and informed the gathering that Lord Warwick had, only the year before, presided over the Festival for the Appeal on behalf of the Royal Masonic Institution for Girls, organised in the Province of Essex, and the sum raised in that connection had been a total of £396,000. He commented: 'I wonder whether it would be appropriate to look upon Lord Warwick

as a sort of Santa Claus!' (*Masonic Record*, Dec 1964).

That charity venture for London Freemasons was repeated in 1979 when, once more on somewhat short notice, an Appeal, this time for the Royal Masonic Institution for Girls, was organised by the London Grand Rank Association. Sir Lindsay Ring, PJGW, 657th Lord Mayor of London 1975–76, was invited to preside. The total sum raised in that respect was £762,000.

In both cases the Stewards Charity Jewels bore the appropriate pendent replica of coat of Arms of the President, but affixed to the ribbon, blue and yellow stripes for RMIB and plain white ribbon for RMIG, was a miniature London Grand Rank collar jewel. It was a fitting mark of distinction.

London has three lodges especially for Installed Masters where Papers are read, talks and lectures given, and various masonic demonstrations,

37 *President's badge of the London Grand Rank Association*

38 *Sir Lindsay Ring*

39 *Steward's jewel for the 1964 R.M.I.B. festival with LER motif*

40 *Steward's jewel for the 1979 R.M.I.G. festival also showing the LER motif*

usually of historical significance, are organised. Those distinctive lodges are:

Jubilee Masters Lodge No 2712 founded in 1898. This lodge hosts the Investiture of Senior London Grand Rank.

Euclid Lodge of Installed Masters No 7464 founded in 1956.

City of London Lodge of Installed Masters No 8220, founded for Past Masters who are also Liverymen of City Guilds.

In 1923 the First Grand Principal created a further honour to be known as LONDON CHAPTER RANK and Past First Principals of London Chapters were invited to make recommendations for a colleague to be appointed. The first formal Investiture for the Holders for those appointed in that year was in 1934, held in a private Chapter whose offer was accepted and that format has remained through to the present time. The word GRAND was added to the title in 1939 at the same time LONDON RANK was changed.

It seems quite strange to record that the Royal Arch actually forged ahead of the Craft, but in 1970 the First Grand Principal, HRH Prince Edward, Duke of Kent, announced the introduction of promotion in that rank and created SENIOR LONDON GRAND CHAPTER RANK, nine years before its counterpart in the Craft. The annual Investiture for that is conducted in a meeting of London First Principals Chapter No 2712, formed in 1957 and attached to Jubilee Masters Lodge. In 1980 Euclid First Principals Chapter No 7464 was formed, sponsored by the lodge of that name.

As the material for this book was about to go to press Notices of Motion affecting promotion in London Grand Rank were given in Grand Lodge on 9 March 1983 (scheduled to come before the Quarterly Communication of Grand Lodge on 8 June 1983) and, similarly, in Supreme Grand Chapter on 28 April 1983 (to come before the Regular Convocation of Supreme Grand Chapter on 9 November 1983). Rule 60 in the book of *Constitutions* is proposed for amendment to include:

[The Grand Master] may annually at his dis-cretion appoint Brethren who already hold London or Overseas Grand Rank, or Past Provincial or District Grand Officers, to be holders of Senior London Grand Rank.

Royal Arch Regulation 26, dealing with Senior London Grand Chapter Rank, is also to be amended to allow for a similar extension in that appointment.

When confirmed the effect of those two amendments will be that Senior London Grand Rank and Senior London Grand Chapter Rank will be a promotion conferred by the Grand Master (First Grand Principal) as a step between Provincial Grand Rank conferred by the provincial or District Grand Master (or Grand Superintendent) and honours in Grand Lodge or Grand Chapter conferred only by the Grand Master (First Grand Principal). It will set the seal of seniority and mark another form of regular gradation throughout the English jurisdiction of Freemasonry.

Freemasons' Hall—Peace Memorial

No story of Freemasonry in London from 1785 would be complete without some reference to the development of the successive Freemasons' Halls erected in Great Queen Street. Whereas the Antients Grand Lodge meetings had been held in taverns, mainly in the Strand area, the premier Grand Lodge (Moderns), although also having held meetings in taverns had met in various City Livery Halls, however, they came to settle behind, and alongside, the Freemasons Tavern in Great Queen Street. It was but a short step from Lincolns' Inn Fields where this story commenced, across Little Queen Street which many years later was to become absorbed into the present Kingsway.

Two plates of the frontage of Freemasons Tavern are reproduced, an earlier period front from an engraving dated in 1789 and the other 'An artists impression of the 1789 frontage of the Tavern' from a print dated 1811. That subject, with illustrations, was fully examined by Sir James Stubbs in his Inaugural Address following installation as Master of Quatuor Coronati Lodge No 2076 in November 1968. (*AQC* Vol 82 pp 1–32).

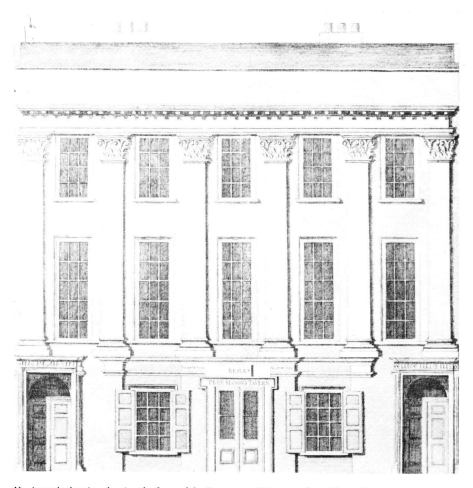

41 *An early drawing showing the front of the Freemasons' Tavern in Great Queen Street*

The first Freemasons' Hall was constructed in 1775-76. It housed a temple designed by Thomas Sandby which was to last until 1932, despite the many hazards to which it was subjected. Various internal alterations were made to Freemasons' Tavern to adapt to the new building but nothing was permanent nor satisfactory, and in 1788 it was decided to demolish the house, brethren having been invited to contribute to an extensive building fund. The names of 82 brethren and 26 lodges who contributed £25 each as a loan without interest were printed annually in *The Free-Masons Calendar* from 1787 to 1813. A medal was struck for each and those few which have survived from that limited issue are highly prized. One hundred years later, to commemorate that event a replica was struck by Messrs. Toye, Kenning and Spencer, Great Queen Street, and officially approved. A full account of the original medal and an historical study by T.O. Haunch appears in *AQC* Vol 82, pp 21-32, following the Inaugural Address mentioned above.

42 *An artist's impression of the Freemasons' Tavern in Great Queen Street c1789*

The foundation stone of that first Freemasons' Hall was laid by the Grand Master, Lord Petre, in 1775, and the Hall was dedicated on 23 May 1776. Sir James Stubbs recalled that the highlight of that dedication ceremony was an inspiring oration by the Grand Chaplain, the Rev William Dodd, who unfortunately came to an untimely end the following year when he was hanged at Tyburn (Marble Arch) having been convicted of forgery, which was then a capital offence.

Acquisitions of property in Great Queen Street from time to time afforded opportunities for expansion. Regarding that subject we find an item in the Minutes of Domatic Lodge dated 19 February 1816:

A Vollentary Subscription for to Defray the Expenses of the purchase of the Two Houses enjoining the Hall.

Whereas the former building projects had been affairs of the Brethren under the Moderns jurisdiction, the United Grand Lodge had now brought the matter into concern for those who were formerly under the Antients; all were involved.

It would appear that those 'Two Houses' would have been Nos 62 and 63 which were acquired with the assistance of Sir John Soane. He was Grand Superintendent of Works from 1813 to 1836, an architect responsible for the rebuilding of the Bank of England, and a prolific collector of artifacts of archaeological interest. To preserve his collection he presented his house in Lincoln's Inn Fields with its art treasures to the nation and they are there to be seen in what is now known as the Soane Museum.

The foundation stone for the second Freemasons' Hall was laid on 27 April 1865 and the building opened by the Earl of Zetland, Grand Master, on 14 April 1869. A disastrous fire occurred in 1883 which gave opportunity for further expansion.

A third building was planned which was intended to be a memorial to King Edward VII, who died in 1910, having been grand Master, as HRH Prince of Wales, from 1874 until his accession in 1901. A fund had been set up for that purpose and a comprehensive scheme was devised but, in the words of Sir James Stubbs, in reality it was but a bold attempt to knit together into a coherent whole the patchwork of previous buildings ranging along the one side of Great Queen Street. Fortunately, that scheme was never achieved because of the removal of the labour force in 1917; the requirements of the Great War of 1914–18 halted all efforts.

In those War years the Minute Books of all lodges and chapters had entries similar to the following:

Belgian Fund	£1. 1. 0
Prince of Wales Fund	4. 4. 0
Red Cross Fund	1. 1. 0
War Savings Certificates (@ 15. 6d each)	1. 11. 0
„ „ „	2. 6. 6
„ „ „	3. 17. 6
War Loan	100. 0. 0
Freemasons War Hospital	10. 0. 0
Masonic Nursing Home	5. 5. 0

The last two items referred to the Freemasons' Hospital and Nursing Home, Fulham Road, which was opened in August 1916. It was the predecessor of the Royal Masonic Hospital named as such and opened on 12 July 1933 by HM King George V accompanied by HM Queen Mary.

At the Especial Grand Lodge held at the Royal Albert Hall on 27 June 1919 the Fund in hand was incorporated into the launching of the Masonic Million Memorial Fund. A special jewel, a Peace medal, was struck for that occasion and worn by those who attended. Later that year the wearing of the jewel was extended to all brethren who although qualified to attend that Especial Grand Lodge were unable to do so owing to the limitation of the accommodation; 7,500 brethren took lunch on that day and the event was whimsically described by Sir James Stubbs as 'the largest knife-and-fork gathering of Freemasons in this or probably any other country!'

Consideration was given to siting the new Hall between the Strand and the Embankment, but tradition held sway and it was resolved to stay in

43 *Examples of Freemasons' Hall Jewel, Hall Stone Jewel and Peace Memorial jewels*

44 *Freemasons' Hall, London*

Great Queen Street. Speaking at the Masonic Festival at Olympia on 8 August 1925, the pro Grand Master, Lord Ampthill stated:

> Our new Temple will rise not only as a Memorial to the dead but also as a sign and inspiration to the living, so that the new generation may persist with renewed zeal in the building of that invisible temple not made with hands which is the ultimate and highest object of our Fraternity.

Competitive entries from architects were invited and the final selection was made in 1926. On 14 July the following year, at the Royal Albert Hall, a symbolic foundation stone was laid with simultaneous remote control over the lowering of a real foundation stone on the site. The foundation stone for the building itself had been presented by the three lodges still in existence from those which formed the original Grand Lodge in London in 1717, namely, The Lodge of Antiquity No 2, the Royal Somerset House and Inverness Lodge No 4, and the Fortitude and Old Cumberland Lodge No 12; it was indeed a tangible link. The ceremony was performed by HRH The Duke of Connaught, Grand Master, who used the Christopher Wren maul, the treasured possession of The Lodge of Antiquity No 2 offered on loan for the occasion.

The Masonic Million Memorial Fund was far exceeded by the cost of the building but those members and lodges who raised the £1,330,000, the approximate cost, in measures prescribed as qualification, received the commemorative Hall Stone Jewel. They numbered 53,000 individual subscribers, and 1,321 lodges. Two Districts and one Province were responsible for rooms Nos 11, 12 and 17, appropriately named 'Japan', 'Burma', and 'Buckinghamshire' in commemoration of their efforts.

At the end of 1938 the Masonic Million Memorial Fund officially closed and the Committee was dissolved. The following March, HRH The Duke of Connaught retired as Grand Master and was succeeded by HRH Prince George Duke of Kent who was formally installed in July 1939 by His Majesty King George VI, Past Grand Master, in the presence of 12,000 brethren at Olympia. By the time the next Quarterly Communication of Grand Lodge was due, and called for September 1939, a mere few months only, war was declared and within three years, on 23 August 1942 the united Grand Lodge of England lost its Grand Master who was killed on active service. It is noteworthy that HM King George VI, who was appointed Past Grand Master on 3 March 1937, personally installed three successive Grand Masters:

19 July 1939 at Olympia ... HRH Prince George Duke of Kent
1 June 1943 at F.M. Hall ... 6th Earl of Harewood
23 March 1948 at Royal Albert Hall ... Duke of Devonshire

Illness prevented him from installing the next Grand Master, the Earl of Scarbrough, that ceremony being performed by the 18th Earl of Derby, Deputy Grand Master, on 6 November 1951. King George VI died on 6 February 1952 but his memory will live long in the annals of English Freemasonry and in the hearts of its members.

At the outbreak of hostilities of what was to be known as 'The Second World War', the expectation of destruction of life and property, which had been suitably rehearsed in other countries not the least of which were Ethiopia and Spain, could not be properly assessed. At first all theatres and cinemas were closed and meetings of any kind were discouraged, but for one year there was very little activity affecting London and whilst remaining alert a resumption of entertainment and gatherings was achieved, albeit a little modified. The 'phoney war' in Europe, and what an unfortunate term that was—for in reality it could be compared only with an interval between rounds before the contest continued, London life was resurrected on a modest scale. Then events were shaping up for reality, following the evacuation of Allied forces from Dunkirk, the threat of invasion and the 'softening-up' process in bombing raids became imminent. A typical example of letters being sent out by Secretaries of London lodges and Chapters can be seen in those sent by the Scribe E, of Domatic Chapter No 177:

Dear Sir & Companion,   *September 1940*

In view of the abnormal conditions and possible danger due to Air raids and threatened Invasion, it has been decided to postpone the Convocation due to be held on October 3rd next, and possibly that on November 1st. The usual Summons will be sent to you for the next meeting when a suitable date has been arranged.

By command of the M.E.Z.,

Joseph Ritson, P.Z., P.G.St.B.
Scribe E.

That letter not only reflects the conditions, but gives a hint of confidence in the use of the word 'when' the suitable date is arranged! But then the London 'Blitz' followed the pattern that had already affected cities throughout the country and once again we turn to the same source for another example common to masonic history for the period:

Dear Sir and Companion   *18 November 1940*

I regret to inform you that on October 15th last the premises of Pagani's Restaurant were struck by a German bomb and the greater part burned out. I understand the Masonic Temple is almost intact and some of the Chapter and Lodge boxes with their contents have been saved. Unfortunately there is at present no trace of the box belonging to Domatic Chapter containing the Officers' collars, bible, signature book, staves, etc., and I am afraid they have all been destroyed. Claims for compensation will be made in due course. The old Chapter Charter and the Centenary Warrant, with Minute books, Account books, etc., are safe at the above address [Comp. Ritson's home address in Weybridge, Surrey]. Other older Minute books and records were deposited several years ago at Freemasons' Hall and I understand are still there.

I am consulting with the Principals and Past Principals as to the most suitable place at which to hold our future meetings, and shall be glad if Companions will kindly let me have their suggestions. The dates of meetings may have to be altered for a time, but I hope everything may be satisfactorily arranged for our next meeting in January.

Yours faithfully and fraternally,

Joseph Ritson, L.G.C.R., P.G.St.B.
Scribe E.

P.S.

Signature book was with Scribe E. and saved with other records. J.R.

The spirit contained in that letter was indeed the common spirit throughout the country. The war history of the nation, and of London in particular, is known to all; the individual experiences of lodges and Chapters has been recorded according to interest and ability in their separate histories, together with accounts of their members serving national interests in or out of uniform.

Freemasons' Hall itself, bears a few scars from shell splinters, and bomb fragments, and sustained minor fire damage, but the Peace Memorial stood to celebrate another victory with admirable dignity, still to house the mother of all Grand Lodges throughout the world; at least those whose practise of Freemasonry is such that it justifies Recognition.

Certain London Lodges

The 'Four Old Lodges' involved in the formation of the premier Grand Lodge in London in 1717 were listed in the following order by Rev James Anderson on p 109 of his 2nd edition of the book of *Constitutions* which was published in 1738:

1 At the *Goose* and *Gridiron* Ale-house in St. Paul's Church-Yard.

2 At the *Crown* Ale-house in *Parker's Lane*, near *Drury Lane*.

3 At the *Apple-Tree* Tavern in *Charles-Street*, *Covent Garden*.

4 At the *Rummer* and *Grapes* Tavern in *Channel-Row*, *Westminster*.

No 2 failed to survive and lasted only about twenty years after the Grand lodge was formed. An application to restore it to the Register in 1752 was rejected. The remaining three lodges have been classified as 'Time Immemorial' and two of them, listed as 1 and 4 above, have the distinction of working without a Warrant.

In a Paper entitled 'The Time Immemorial lodges', given to the London Grand Rank Association in 1968, R.W. Bro Erskine Simes, QC, Past Grand Warden, Grand Registrar, raised some very interesting points, some of which have been incorporated below. On the assumption that the 'Four Old Lodges' in 1717 were composed similarly in the year 1723 when lists of members were compiled, there were differences between them both in size and in the social status of their members. No 1 had twenty-two members and the master and wardens were described as 'Mr'; No 2 had fifteen members and No 3 had twenty-one with 'Mr' used in the same manner but no other titles appeared; No 4 had seventy-one members which included 10 noblemen, 3 'Honourables', 4 Baronets or Knights, 2 generals, 10 colonels, 4 officers below field rank, and 24 Esquires among the titles that were listed. It appears to have been wholly speculative in its masonic construction, whereas, according to Erskine Simes, the other lodges contained a number of probable operative masons.

No 1 which met at the 'Goose and Gridiron Ale-house' possesses a copy of the 'Old Charges' dated 1686 and claims to be the oldest lodge. Tradition asserts that Sir Christopher Wren, architect of St. Paul's Cathedral, was Master of this lodge in 1680 but there is no evidence in support and his membership itself can be treated only as circumstantial; he presented three mahogany candlesticks to the lodge. Their treasured possession also is a mason's maul which was used at the laying of the foundation stone of St. Paul's Cathedral and in consequence is known as the 'Wren maul'. It is the custom of that lodge formally to present it for use at all major masonic functions and it was used by Grand Lodge at the Royal Albert Hall on the occasion of the Installation of the Duke of Kent in June 1967; the 250th Anniversary of the founding of the premier Grand Lodge. That lodge did have members who were operative masons and their Master in 1721 is recorded as such. In the year 1759 it took the name 'West India and American Lodge' when many of its members came from the Western Hemisphere, and it was given precedence as No 1 from the inception of the official *List of Lodges* compiled by the Moderns. In 1769 it took the name Lodge of Antiquity, by which name it is known today, but because of the balloting arrangements between the two Grand Lodges at the Union in 1813 for positioning of lodges for the new *Register*, No 1 fell to the Antients first lodge (Grand Masters No 1), Lodge of Antiquity became No 2. It was in this lodge that a schism arose among its membership in 1778 that resulted in the setting-up of yet another Grand Lodge, this time under the title of 'Grand Lodge of England South of the River Trent'. It lasted only ten years but in that time actually constituted two new lodges. It was the outcome of an incident in which William Preston was involved, the same brother who formulated ritual lectures was so dedicated to the dissemination of masonic knowledge that he bequeathed an Annuity of £300 in Consols as an endowment for the annual appointment of a lecturer by Grand Lodge—now known as 'The Prestonian Lecturer' for the year. William Preston died in 1818 and is buried in St Paul's Cathedral.

HRH the Duke of Sussex, Grand Master of the United Grand Lodge of England from 1813 to 1843, was elected annually as Master of Lodge of Antiquity from 1809 to his death in 1843. In 1812 he instituted the 'Royal Medal' which was presented to members of the lodge who shewed themselves to be proficient; in 1834, to mark his 25th year as Master of the lodge he gave permission to have gold jewels, the Grand Stewards nominated by the lodge to have gold tassels on their aprons, and Past Grand Stewards and officers of their lodge to have gold cord on their collars.

Lodge No 4 on Anderson's list had the distinction of providing three of the first four Grand Masters: George Payne in 1718, Dr John Theophilus Desaguliers in 1719, and re-election of George Payne in 1720. The venue for this lodge, 'The Rummer and Grapes', was featured by William Hogarth in his painting 'Night' shewing the Master being escorted by the Tyler; an intriguing cameo of freemasonry of the 1738 period. The lodge appeared on the *List of Lodges* as No 3, later as No 2, but at the Union was allocated No 4 on the new *Register* and bears the name Royal Somerset House and Inverness lodge.

Lodge No 3 on the original list, 'upon some difference', lost its place and that resulted in the members accepting a Warrant dated 27 February 1723 'tho' they wanted it not' and they were relegated to 11th place—although the second position was left vacant on the 1729 *List*. Despite their

45 *William Hogarth's engraving* 'Night' (1738) *featuring The Rummer and Grapes Inn*

protests they remained in the tenth position until 1756 when the lodge was placed at No 6; at the Union it became No 12 and is known today as Lodge of Fortitude and Old Cumberland and duly acknowledged as 'Time Immemorial'. The following is an extract from Anderson's 1738 list printed on pp 184-5:

A list of the Lodges in and about *London* and *Westminster*

Many *Lodges* have by accidents broken up, or are partition'd, or else removed to new Places for their conveniency, and so, if subsisting, they are called and known by those new Places or their *Signs*.

But the *subsisting* Lodges, whose *Officers* have attended the GRAND LODGE of *Quarterly Communication* and brought their Benevolence to the General Charity within 12 months past, are here set down according to their Seniority of *Constitution*, as in the *Grand Lodge-Books* and the *Engraved List*.

Signs of the Houses	Date of *Constitution*
1. KINGS-ARMS Tavern in St. Paul's Church-Yard, removed from the Goose and Gridiron. meeting in form.	- - - - -

This is the *Senior Lodge*, whose Constitution is immemorial.

2. HORN Tavern in *New Palace Yard, Westminster*, the Old Lodge removed from the RUMMER and GRAPES, *Channel-Row*, whose *Constitution* is also immemorial, it being one of the *four Lodges* mention'd Page 109.	- - - - -

10. QUEEN'S-HEAD in *Knave's-Acre*. This was one of the *four Lodges* mention'd Page 109, viz. the Apple-Tree *Tavern* in *Charles-Street, Covent Garden*, whose *Constitution* is immemorial; but after they removed to the Queen's *Head*, upon some Difference, the members that met there came under a *new Constitution*, tho' they wanted it not, and it is therefore placed at this Number. N.B. The Crown in *Parker's-Lane*, the Other of the *four* old Lodges, is now extinct.

27 Feb. 1923

The first Grand Master at the foundation of the premier Grand Lodge, Anthony Sayer, came from the lodge listed at No 10 above, but No 3 on the original list.

The Grand Stewards Lodges which have been mentioned many times in this work served their Grand Lodges in slightly different ways. That of the Moderns arose from 'A Grand Steward to prepare the Feast in the best manner'—remembering that at the inaugural meeting in 1717 the brethren 'resolv'd to hold the *Annual* Assembly and Feast ...' According to Rev Anderson (1738 Edn) it was at Grand Lodge on Lady Day 1721 the brethren agreed that the General Assembly required more room and arrangements were to be made for the next one to be held at Stationer's Hall, Ludgate Street. He also recorded:

Then the *Grand Wardens* were order'd, as usual, to prepare the Feast, and to take some *Stewards* to their Assistance, Brothers of Ability and Capacity, and to appoint some Brethren to attend the Tables; for that no Strangers must be there. But the *Grand Officers* not finding a proper Number of Stewards, our Brother Mr. Josiah Villenau, Upholder in the Borough of Southwark, generously undertook the whole himself, attended by some Waiters, Thomas Morrice, Francis Bailey, &c.

Villenau was appointed Senior Grand Warden in 1721, whilst one of the 'Waiters', Thomas Morrice, having served as Junior Grand Warden for 1718 and 1719 was re-appointed for 1721. A direct appointment of 'Stewards' was made by the Duke of Richmond, Grand Master on 24 June 1724:

ORDERED. That the Stewards do prepare a List (for the Grand Masters perusal) of twelve fitt persons to Serve as Stewards at the next Grand ffeast, And that they do make up their Accounts with all Convenient Speed that the Same may be Audited.

It was during his Grand Mastership that we find use of the term 'Grand Steward' in the Minutes of 'a Generall Meeting held at Merchant Taylors Hall' on 27 December 1725:

After the Generall healths were over, One was drank to the Grand Steward Viz! John Heidegger, & his two Deputys Viz! John Potter and Mr Lambert

46 *Sir James Stubbs*, KCVO, *PSGW, Grand Secretary 1958–80*

with thanks for their handsome and Elegant Entertainment.

It seems that the number of 'twelve fitt persons' could not be sustained for we find the subject as a resolution for Grand Lodge on 26 November 1728 when Dr Desaguliers moved:

> To revive the *Office* of *Stewards* to assist the *Grand-Wardens* in preparing the *Feast*, and that their Number should be 12 which was readily agreed to.

The number remained at twelve until the Union when their ranks were increased to eighteen. In 1904 that was further increased to nineteen which remains to this day.

The following nineteen lodges, all meeting in London, have the privilege of nominating one subscribing member for appointment as Grand Steward; with the exception of the first one on the list all are from the former Moderns Grand Lodge:

Grand Master's Lodge No 1, founded 1756
Lodge of Antiquity No 2—'Time Immemorial'
Royal Somerset House and Inverness Lodge No 4—
    'Time Immemorial'
St. George's and Cornerstone Lodge No 5, founded
    1730
Lodge of Friendship No 6, founded 1721
British Lodge No 8, founded 1722
Tuscan Lodge No 14, founded 1722
Lodge of Emulation No 21, founded 1723
Globe Lodge No 23, founded 1723
Castle Lodge of Harmony No 26, founded 1725
Old Kings Arms Lodge No 28, founded 1725
St. Alban's Lodge No 29, founded 1728
Old Union Lodge No 46, founded 1735
Lodge of Felicity No 58, founded 1737
Lodge of Peace and Harmony No 60, founded 1738
Lodge of Regularity No 91, founded 1755
Shakespear Lodge No 99, founded 1757
Jerusalem Lodge No 197, Warrant dates from 1771
Prince of Wales's Lodge No 259, founded 1787

The Stewards Lodge as it was named was constituted No 117 on the Moderns Register in 1735. On the various re-numbering it became Nos 115, 70, 60, 47, but in April 1792 it was ordered to be placed at the head of the *List of Lodges* without number and that is its position to this day. It has

no power to 'Make, Pass and Raise' masons its membership being restricted to those who have served or are serving as Grand Stewards. It is generally accepted that the crimson for the regalia follows that of the Order of the Bath and was included amongst specific Regulations at the Quarterly Communication of Grand Lodge held on 17 March 1731 when Dr Desaguliers 'taking Notice of some Irregularities in wearing the Marks of Distinction which have been allowed by former Grand Lodges, Proposed':

> ... That those Brethren that are Stewards shall wear their aprons lined with red Silk and their proper Jewels pendant to red Ribbons. That all those who have served the Office of Steward be at Liberty to wear Aprons lined with red silk and not otherwise.

Whilst Domatic Lodge has the distinction of being the only *Antients* lodge on record to have been formed as an 'operatives' lodge, even though that claim was made by its membership at that time and not substantiated by the Warrant which was issued to them, an account does exist of an 'operatives' lodge under the premier Grand Lodge (Moderns) which was dated about twenty years earlier.

The history of *Bedford Lodge No 157 from 1766 to 1966* was compiled by A.F. Christlieb and on p 5 he commented:

> ... the Lodge was operative when formed and must have grown out of some body—whether regularly formed or not—and, according to some authorities, The Bedford Lodge is one of the only two existing Lodges known to have been operative when constituted.

From the first known attempt at a history of the lodge, written about 1798 under the title *Memorandums of the Bedford Lodge of Free-Masons* which contains all that is known about the lodge in the period before 1766, Christlieb quoted:

> How long this Lodge has been incorporated as an Operative Lodge of Free Masons is uncertain; from the information of an aged brother, Master of this Lodge in 1772, it was in reputable circumstances about the years 1739 and 1740; but no documents of its transactions are preserved from that period until

the beginning of the year 1766, when it conformed to the Rules of the Grand Lodge of England, and was constituted by Lord Blaney, then Grand Master, on the 17th of May, under the denomination of the Operative Lodge of Free and Accepted Masons No. 364, to be holden at the Mitre Tavern, Union Street, Cripplegate, on the first and fourth Wednesday in every month; none but Operative Masons were admitted members before this period.

Thus, into the period of 'organised Freemasonry' we have the counterbalance of an operatives lodge in each of the two Grand Lodges. There is even a link somewhat remotely forged between Domatic Chapter and Bedford Lodge by membership in both of Arthur Loutherburgh Thiselton in the 1820's. Mention was made earlier of his occupation as scene painter at Drury Lane, and through his efforts the setting up of the Chapter of Promulgation for creating uniformity in the Royal Arch. According to the Minutes of Bedford Lodge, 29 December 1824, Thiselton had submitted drawings of Lodge Boards for the three degrees to Bedford Lodge and the Committee had deliberated only so far as to request the Secretary:

> ... to wait upon one of the Grand Secretaries to know if any Plan or Design is sanctioned by the Grand Lodge, or if the Boards now used by the Grand Stewards Lodge are to be considered as the standard that other Lodges are to go by, and that he do report to the lodge at its next meeting the result of such interview.

In April 1826, Thiselton having ceased membership of Bedford Lodge another brother was appointed to paint Lodge Boards.

In the Introduction to this book an examination of the words Domatic and Geomatic, as well as their use in masonic context was presented, the one representing references to 'Operative Freemasons' and the other 'Speculative Freemasons'.

Such was the confidence of brethren in Domatic Lodge at the conclusion of the Second World War in 1945 that they petitioned for a daughter lodge to be founded and, of the forty-three lodges formed in that year they were granted Warrant for Lodge No 6214 to bear the name Geomatic. It

was Consecrated on 22 February 1946 by the Assistant Grand Master, Brig-Gen William Harry Darell, *CB, CMG, DSO*.

A Royal Arch Chapter to bear the same name under the sanction of the lodge followed very shortly afterwards and was Consecrated in 1950.

The London Masonic Centre

Enemy bombers and destructive rockets launched against the capital city in the Second World War took great toll of its buildings and amongst those losses were a number of hotels and restaurants which had provided masonic accommodation. Owing to increasing pressures in that connection, masonic boundaries for London lodges were extended to permit those who so desired to meet in fringe Provincial areas but still remain under the direct administration of the Grand Secretary at Freemasons' Hall.

Although new lodges and chapters were constituted in the early post-war years, even at an somewhat advanced rate, the numbers recorded for London in no way reflected the true growth as some lodges, in order to escape rising costs and the general effects of raging inflation, transferred to adjoining Provinces. The following table will give useful comparative data:

Number of lodges on the Register

	1936	1946	1956	1966	1976	1982
London	1,221	1,376	1,593	1,690	1,693	1,677
Provinces	2,990	3,580	4,361	5,039	5,405	5,706

Numbers of chapters on the Register

	1936	1946	1956	1966	1976	1982
London	496	592	684	729	717	704
Provinces	1,082	1,302	1,532	1,743	1,897	2,044

Rising costs pinched to such an extent that some lodges seemed to be moving from place to place in their attempts to stem the tide for their senior members struggling on fixed incomes.

It was the closure in 1967 of the masonic accommodation and catering provided by Lyons Corner House at Tottenham Court Road that triggered action that was to prove helpful. That closure affected 65 lodges and an item in the masonic press may be said to have fired the imagination of those and many other brethren:

> Lodges faced with rising costs and insecurity of tenure are invited to communicate with P.J. Rodwell, Brook Cottage, Wickhambrook, Newmarket, Suffolk.

A meeting was arranged, a committee was formed, and to provide for working costs to explore for properties that might be adapted for masonic purposes in the London area, the interest from a returnable deposit of £50 from supporting lodges would be used. Within a very short time the project gained the support of 259 lodges.

The London Grand Rank Association gave every support to the venture by providing a platform for meetings open to all London brethren, as well as publicity in the *Bulletin*, the members of the Association bringing this to the notice of brethren at lodge meetings. But, this was an age of opportunity for property developers with whom that committee could not compete, the various planning projects and major schemes officially sponsored accounted for other affected structures; it was also the age of soaring costs for reconstruction.

Among the properties brought under consideration were:

The Hall, lower ground floor, City Temple, Holborn Viaduct.

47 *The Middlesex Sessions House was built in 1782*

143

Former school premises of Royal Masonic Institution for Boys, Wood Green.

St. Giles Church School, Endell Street.

Sir John Lyon House, Upper Thames Street.

For various reasons they all proved unsuitable, but each had provided a useful exercise and tested many capabilities, not the least of which was the endurance of some of the brethren involved. Patience was eventually rewarded when the Middlesex Sessions House, Clerkenwell Green, came under review.

The Sessions House was built in 1779-82 and had served London well. it was last used as a Court of Justice in December 1920 and from then on had been used at various times for such commercial purposes as offices and/or storehouse. But for some years it had been unoccupied with both interior and exterior protected under an official Preservation Order, which is still in existence. For that reason there was no encouragement whatsoever for the interest of developers. It was in a delapidated condition and undoubtedly was a daunting project for the Committee to consider and to place before London Brethren. A non-profit making company was set up—The Central London Masonic Centre Limited—and the freehold was purchased. The conversion, with many set-backs en route, resulted in seven temples complete with their own ante-rooms and dining rooms, with full catering facilities, as well as committee rooms, accommodation for lodges of Instruction, and lounges and licensed bars. Whilst such figures had not been dreamed of at the commencement of the enterprise it became another Million Pound venture, which now provides accommodation for 200 Craft lodges and 60 chapters.

The importance to London Freemasonry of this building was suitably marked by the manner in which the Dedication Ceremony was conducted on Thursday 5 June 1980. The assistance of the Grand Stewards Lodge was requested and a specially convened meeting under the mastership of Norman A· Powers, Past Junior Grand Deacon, was called by its Secretary J.N. Gems, Past Assistant Grand Director of Ceremonies, to receive the Dedicating Officer RW Bro Sir James Stubbs, KCVO, PGSW, Grand Secretary.

London Grand Rank Association was very well represented in that two Committee members had been appointed to the Board of Trustees at its founding and both were invited by the Dedicating Officer to assist in the ceremonial, Nigel T. Haines, PAGDC as Senior Warden and Roy A. Wells, PAGDC as Junior Warden. Others engaged in the ceremony of Dedication were:

Rev F.G.W.W. Heydon Past Grand Chaplain

Alan F. Ferris Grand Director of Ceremonies

Cdr M.B.S. Higham, RN Deputy Grand Secretary

E. Osborne, Past Grand Standard Bearer (Chairman of Trustees)

A.R. Craddock, PGStB Grand Tyler

E.S. South, Past Grand Organist (Musical Director)

The ceremony took place in the largest lodge room situated on the first floor with just over 100 brethren present, but the whole proceedings were televised on a closed circuit to other lodge rooms where seating had been arranged for easy viewing. The total attendance of 450 brethren was carefully controlled by ticket applications. A fitting conclusion was the celebration luncheon over which Derek Clark, Chairman of the Board of Directors of The Central London Masonic Centre Ltd, presided.

A photograph of the members of the Council, standing at the foot of the 'Judges Staircase'—some of whom were originators of the enterprise from 1967—is now on display in the Reception Hall. It commemorates the patience and assiduity of those brethren who, when faced with a formidable problem, applied themselves to the utmost of their powers, and will see others enjoy the fruits of their labours.

An appropriate postscript on the efforts of all London brethren, continuing from the organisation in 1717 might well be:

May Brotherly Love, Relief, and Truth, in conjunction with Temperance, Fortitude, Prudence, and Justice, distinguish Free and Accepted Masons till time shall be no more

48 *The Middlesex Sessions House was opened as the London Masonic Centre in 1980*

49 *Council Members of the London Masonic Centre at Clerkenwell Green in 1980:* left to right; *front row, F.L. Rourke, C.E. Smart, R. Wyatt, E.W. Osborne, B.A. Cheeseman; second row, H.D. Thomas, H.R.P. Owen, J. Gibson; back row, B. Ross, D.H. Clarke*

146

Appendix A

A DISPENSATION GRANTED BY THE ANTIENTS GRAND LODGE DATED 29 JULY 1775

To all whom { Seal of the / the Antients / Grand Lodge } it may Concern

WHEREAS,

Our Trustry & well-beloved Brother Thomas Grogan, Past Master of the good Lodge No. 128 has made Application to us for a Dispensation to make Free Masons according to the most Ancient Custom of the Craft.

And Whereas it appears that the said Thomas Grogan is well qualified for the due Execution of such Dispensation and that his great love for the Craft is the only motive which induced him to this undertaking, therefore We do hereby Authorise and Impower our well-beloved Brother Thomas Grogan as aforesaid, to Congregate and Form a Lodge at the Coach & Horses in Duke Street, Saint James's London. And in the said Lodge when duly Congregated, To Admit & make Free Masons according to the most Ancient & Hon[ble] Customs of the Royal Craft in all Ages and Nations throughout the known World. Whereby our Trusty and well-beloved Brother Tho.[s] Grogan may Congregate and Select a sufficient number of worthy Brethren to be Constituted in good order and time; With the design of promoting the Society by the increase of worthy members, We have given this our Dispensation to hold in full force and Virtue for the space of Thirty Days from the Date hereof, Earnestly requesting all Master Masons under the Ancient Constitution to be aiding and Assisting the said Tho[s] Grogan in the due Execution hereof, as far as Time & Convenience may Permit.

Providing, that all Admissions & Makings (under this Dispensation) shall be faithfully Transacted according to the Expressed directions in the Book of Constitutions Intitled Ahiman Rezon (under the Title of Philacteria) otherwise to forfeit all rights to Constitution of Registry.

Given under our hands and Seal of the Grand Lodge in London the Twenty ninth day of July In the Year of our Lord One Thousand seven hundred & seventy five And in the Year of Masonry Five Thousand Seven Hundred Seventy and Five.

[Signed]   W. Dickey G. Sec.   Lau. Dermott D.G.M.

The only differences between that Dispensation and the one granted to Charles Fenwick would have been his name instead of Thomas Grogan, the venue 'to Congregate and Form a lodge' would have been stated as 'The Sign of the Ship, Little Turnstile, Lincoln's Inn Fields, and instead of the signature of William Dickey, Grand Secretary, it would have been John McCormick who succeeded.

Appendix B

WARRANT OF THE DOMATIC LODGE No 234 ANTIENTS (now No 177 on the Register of United Grand Lodge of England).

_____

GRAND MASTER *Antrim*

Laurence Dermott D.G.M.

John Feakins S.G.W   Thomas Harper J.G.W.

0

0

0

To all whom it may concern

We the Grand Lodge of the Most ANCIENT and HONOURABLE Fraternity of Free and Accepted Masons (according to the old Constitutions granted by His Royal Highness Prince Edwin at York, Anno Domini Nine Hundred twenty six, and in the year of Masonry Four Thousand nine Hundred twenty and six) in ample Form assembled, viz., The Right Worshipful Most Potent and Puissant Lord the Right Honourable Randal William McDonnell Earl and Baron of Antrim Lord Viscount Lord Dunluce, Lord Lieutenant of the County of Antrim in the Province of Ulster and Kingdom of Ireland, Knight of the most honourable Military Order of the Bath, one of his Majesty's most honourable Privy Council and in that part of Great Britain called England and Masonical Jurisdiction thereunto belonging Grand Master of Masons, The Right Worshipful Laurence Dermott Esq. Deputy Grand Master, and the Right Worshipful John Feakins Esq. Senior Grand Warden, and the Right Worshipful Thomas Harper Esq. Junior Grand Warden (with the Approbation and Consent of the Warranted Lodges held within the Cities and suburbs of London and Westminster) Do hereby authorise and impower our Trusty and Well beloved Brethren viz. The Worshipful John Wood one of our Master Masons, The Worshipful Charles Broad his Senior Warden and the Worshipful John Perkins his Junior Warden, to Form and Hold a Lodge of Free and Accepted Masons aforesaid at the sign of the Ship Little Turn-style Holborn in the Parish of St. Giles in the Fields (or elsewhere) in London upon the last Monday of each Callender Month and on all Seasonable Times and lawful Occasions: And in the said lodge (when duly congregated) to admit and make Free Masons according to the most Ancient and Honourable Custom of the Royal Craft in all Ages and Nations throughout the Known World. And we do hereby farther authorise and impower our said Trusty and Well beloved Brethren John Wood Charles Broad and John Perkins (with the consent of the Members of their Lodge) to nominate, chuse, and install their Successors, to who they shall deliver this Warrant, and invest them with their Powers and Dignities as Free masons &c. And such Successors shall in like manner nominate, chuse, and install their Successors &c &c &c. Such Installations to be upon (or near) every St. John's Day during the continuance of this Lodge for ever, Providing the above named Brethren and all their

No.

CCXXXIII

Successors always pay due Respect to this Right Worshipful Grand Lodge, otherwise this Warrant to be of no Force nor Virtue. Given under our Hands and Seal of our grand Lodge in London this Seventh day of February in the Year of our Lord One thousand seven hundred eighty and six being the fourth year of the Grand Mastership of the Right Honourable Earl of Antrim.

John McCormick, Grand Sect.[ry]

(Note—This Warrant is registered in the Grand Lodge Vol 6 letter F.)

Appendix C

WARRANT OF LODGE No 258 (now Lion and Lamb Lodge No 192) the additional Warrant that was held by Domatic Lodge for a period of six years from 1789 to 1795.

ANTRIM GRAND MASTER
Jas. Perry D.G.M.

Thos. Harper S.G.W.

Jas. Agar J.G.W.

To all whom it may concern

We, the Grand Lodge of the most ANCIENT and HONOURABLE Fraternity of Free and Accepted Masons (according to the Old Constitutions granted by His Royal Highness Prince Edwin, at York, Anno Domini Nine hundred twenty and six, and in the Year of Masonry Four thousand Nine hundred twenty and six) in ample form assembled, viz., The Right Worshipful and Puissant Prince Randal William McDonnell, Marquis, Earl and Baron of Antrim, Lord Viscount Dunluce, Lieutenant of the County of Antrim, in the Province of Ulster and Kingdon of Ireland, Knight of the most honourable Military Order of the Bath, one of His Majesty's most honourable Privy Council and in that part of Great Britain called England, and Masonical jurisdiction thereunto belonging, GRAND MASTER OF MASONS, The Right Worshipful James Perry Esq. Deputy Grand Master, The Right Worshipful Thomas Harper, Esq. Senior Grand Warden, and The Right Worshipful James Agar, Esq. Junior Grand Warden (with the approbation and consent of the Warranted Lodges held within the Cities and Suburbs of London and Westminster), Do hereby authorise and impower our Trusty and Well-beloved Brethren, viz. The Worshipful Sir Watkin Lewis one of our Master Masons, the Worshipful Edward Cook his Senior Warden, and the Worshipful Thomas Abbott his Junior Warden, to Form and Hold a Lodge of Free and Accepted Masons aforesaid, at the Sign of the Sun, in Gate Street, Lincoln's Inn Fields, in the Parish of St. Giles in the Fields, or elsewhere in London, and to meet the second Thursday in each Kallendar Month, on all seasonable and lawful occasions: and in the said Lodge (when duly congregated) to admit and make Freemasons according to the most Ancient and Honourable Custom of the Royal Craft, in all Ages and Nations throughout the Known World. And we do hereby further authorise and impower our trusty and well-beloved brethren Sir Watkin Lewis Kt, Edward Cook and Thomas Abbott (with the Consent of the Members of this Lodge) to nominate, chuse, and install their successors, to whom they shall deliver this Warrant, and invest them with their Powers and Dignities as Freemasons, &c. And such successors shall in like manner nominate chuse, and install their successors, &c., &c., &c. Such installations to be upon (or near) every St. JOHN's DAY, during the continuance of this Lodge, for ever. Provided the above named brethren, and all their successors, always pay due respect to this Right Worshipful Grand Lodge, otherwise this Warrant to be of no Force nor Virtue.

No. 258

Given under our hands and Seal of our Grand Lodge in London, this twenty-fourth day of December, in the Year of our Lord One Thousand Seven Hundred Eighty and Nine, and in the year of Masonry Five Thousand Seven Hundred Eighty and Nine.

John McCormick,
Grand Secretary.

Note.—This Warrant is Registered
in the Grand Lodge, Vol 6
Letter F.

Appendix D

To His Royal Highness the Duke of Sussex Grand Master of the United Grand Lodge of Ancient Free Masons of England.

The Humble Memorial of the Masters, Past Masters, Officers and Brethren of divers Lodges assembled under the government of your Royal Highness.

SHEWETH

That in pursuance of the union which has been happily effected under the auspices of your Royal Highness and your August Brother the Duke of Kent, eighteen brethren were selected to form a lodge, under the name or title of 'The Lodge of Reconciliation' to revise the different modes of Workmanship, and from them to form a system for the general use and government of the Craft.

That the Lodge of Reconciliation having been formed accordingly, and having 'arranged the various points referred to their consideration' the brethren of the lodges of both Fraternities, were by the Command of your Royal Highness, frequently summoned to attend the meetings of the said lodge, in order that your Memorialists 'might be instructed in the forms and Ceremonies to be in future, used throughout the Craft.'

That signal success attended their labours, which combine purity of language with a strict adherence to the Ancient Landmarks of our Honorable order, and while they attract the attention of the Scholar, they are not above the Comprehension of every Brother who has received a common Education.

That from the moment of its being made public to the Society, a general spirit of Emulation pervaded the whole Masonic Body, and such have been the commendable industry and laudable attention of the Brethren in general, that the number of expert Masters has increased in the proportion of nearly five to one.

That the system so promulgated by the lodge of Reconciliation is not only firmly established in London, but has been eagerly received by the Brethren in most of the Counties of England and Wales, in Scotland and Ireland, and has even been extended to East and West Indies.

That with the most painful concern we lament to state to our gracious and venerated Grand Master, that a few individuals have lately insinuated to the Fraternity that the whole of what they have been so instructed in and taught by the Lodge of Reconciliation, ought not to be practised, as another system would soon be presented to them, under the sanction of your Royal Highness. This Intelligence has been received by your Memorialists and the Members of their respective lodges with the utmost astonishment and grief, and if persisted in will assuredly be attended with more injurious consequences than the unhappy division of 1752.

Your Memorialists therefore most humbly solicit, that your Royal Highness will be pleased to declare your Sanction to the System of Free Masonry practised taught and promulgated by the Lodge of Reconciliation prior to the first of December 1815.

Note: For some days previous to presenting the Memorial, a copy of the following notice was left at all Committee Rooms:

The Brethren are respectfully informed, that the Memorial to be presented to HRH the Duke of Sussex, our MW Grand Master, will lie for signatures, at the Crown Tavern, St. Martins Lane, Charing Cross, until 8 o'clock next Saturday Evening, and not after that time, as it must be presented to the Grand Master on Sunday 29th Instant.

[January 1816]

Appendix E

Details from a circular printed by George Claret in 1844 which shews the extent to which his masonic printing and trading had developed.

Sirs & Brs.   PRINTING OFFICE   1844

During the last Six Years my Masonic Works having successfully wended their way in London, to most of the Provinces under the English Constitution, also France, Prussia, America, Scotland, Ireland, the East and West Indies &c. &c. is of itself a sufficient guarantee of their genuineness and worth, and leaves little for me to add in order to prove their value to Freemasons requiring Instruction. But I still deem it necessary to guard the Brethren (particularly the younger part) from the insidious remarks of *some interested brethren*, who say they ought not to be purchased because in them the secrets of the Order are exposed, to which I answer they are not. The Oath regards the Signs, Tokens, and Words* and no more. If it were not so, Preston's *Illustrations*; the Masonic Review, Dr. Oliver's Works and others might be condemned as *the whole of them* contain the business of Masonry, and mine does no more, except being calculated to instruct the brethren in their respective duties, and are enabled to perform them, in accordance with the system laid down by the Lodge of Reconciliation, at the Union in 1813.

28 Upper Clifton Street, Finsbury, London.   G. Claret.

Lectures of the three Degrees, explanation of the Tracing Boards, &c.	1. 1. 0
Ceremonies of Initiation: Passing & Raising: Opening & Closing Installation &c.	1. 1. 0
Illustrations; Quarto and Pocket Size	7 6
The whole as contained in the above three Books (new Edition) Bound & Gile	2 0 0
ditto ditto with Lock & Key	2 5 0
ditto ditto and Royal Arch Bound together	3 10 0
Royal Arch Ceremony, Lectures &c.	1 5 0
Signature Book for meetings of Lodges & Chapters (this Book will serve for twelve Years)	10 6
Masonic Minstrel, 200 Songs & Odes, to be used after the Banquet	4 6
Declaration Books, to be signed by all Candidates at Initiation; every Lodge should have them	5 0
An Explanation of the First and Second Tracing Boards	2 6
Installation of the W.M. and Officers 0 7 6 Opening and Closing in the 3 Degrees	5 0
Claret's Masonic Gleanings comprising a Disquisition on the Antiquity; Extent; Excellence and Utility of Freemasonry; also some Account of the Union with Anecdotes &c.	5 0
An Ornamental Engraved Quarto Post fly leaf, for Summonses 3 0 on good Paper	1 0 0
Letter Press Quarto Post fly leaf ruled divisions for ditto	15 0
Japanned Lantern with Star, Lamp and Reflector for the Third Degree	12 0
Gauntlets per Pair with mock silver lace 0 8 0 ditto with Silver Lace & Kid Gloves	16 0
New Edition of the Constitutions half-bound 0 5 0 Whole ditto with Masonic tooling	10 0
Working Tools for the 3 Degrees, with Brass Skirritt & Compasses	1 7 6
Badge Cases with Brs name and No of the Lodge each from	4 0

* See Oliver's *Historical Landmarks* No 2 Page 33. Note 76.

Tracing Boards in three Coloured Designs bound in lock Case   15   0
The Charge at Initiation stitched Six pence each or per Dozen   5   0

BADGES, JEWELS, COLLARS, LARGE TRACING BOARDS BANNER &c
SEVERAL EDITIONS OF PRESTON'S ILLUSTRATIONS FOR SALE
Knights Templar in Manuscript 2   0   0

Any of the above sent carefully Packed and Sealed, on the receipt of a Bankers or Post Office Order.

Brethren having occasion to send a Post Office Order, will have the goodness to have it made payable at 36 City Road, being near my residence.

Appendix F

Plate No. 22 is the Frontispiece of Thomas Harper's edition of *Ahiman Rezon* published in 1807 and the following is the 'explanation of the Frontispiece' printed in that book:

———————

The design is a prostyle Temple of the Doric Order, and bears an historical view of Ancient Masonry; by this is understood, that kind of history which is universally received and acknowledged in Ancient Lodges.

Upon the dome are pourtrayed, whole length figures of the three great Masters of the Tabernacle in the Wilderness. The two crown'd figures, with that on the right, represent the three Masters of the Holy Lodge at Jerusalem; And the figures on their left represent the three Great Masters of the second Temple, at Jerusalem.

This fabric is supported by three Noble Columns, bearing masonic badges, with the Arms of England, Ireland, and Scotland, depicted thereon; thereby denoting the triple union, which in the year 1772 was formed by those three Grand Lodges, to promote the honour and dignity of the Ancient Craft.

The ascent to the building, alludes to the five Orders in Architecture, and also to the summit and perfection of Ancient Masonry.

Upon the pediment above, are the Armorial Bearings of the Fraternity, taken from Holy Writ; and is thus emblazoned. ARMS. Quarterly per squares, counterchanged *vert*; First quarter, *azure*, a Lion rampant, *or*; second, *or*, an Ox passant *sable*: third, *or*, a Man with hands uplifted *proper*, robed in crimson and ermine: fourth, *azure*, an Eagle displayed *or*. CREST. The Holy Ark of the Covenant *proper*. SUPPORTERS. Two Cherubims with wings extended. MOTTO. [Hebrew] or Holiness to the Lord.

Appendix G

Existing Royal Arch Chapters *in London* possessing Charters of Confirmation establishing a founding date prior to the Union of 1817

Name	Date	Antient or Modern	Number Formerly: Now		Founded in or now attached to Lodge:
Mount Moriah Chapter	1783	A	241	143	Middlesex Lodge
St. George's Chapter	1785	A	5	5	St. George's & Cornerstone
Chapter of Fidelity	1786	A	3	3	Lodge of Fidelity
St. George's Chapter	1786	M	49	140	St. George's Lodge
Chapter of St. James	1788	M	2	2	Lodge of Antiquity
Domatic Chapter	1793	A	293	177	Domatic Lodge
Royal York Chapter of Perseverance	1801	A	7	7	Royal York Lodge of Perseverance
United Chapter of Prudence	1808	M	12	12	Lodge of Fortitude and Old Cumberland
Mount Sion Chapter	1810	A	241	22	Neptune Lodge
Mount Sinai Chapter	1811	A	56	19	Royal Athelstane Lodge
Cyrus Chapter	1811	M	22	21	Lodge of Emulation
British Chapter	1812	M	8	8	British Lodge
Moira Chapter	1813	M	143	92	Moira Lodge

Of the above thirteen Chapters it will be seen that seven were from the Antients jurisdiction and six from the Moderns. Only five could establish an earlier date than that granted to Domatic, and of those three were Antients.

Royal Arch Regulations published in 1823, six years after the 1817 Union, listed seventeen Chapters for London:— Nos. 2/3/5/6/8/9/12/16/22/56/122/143/241/281/293/308/493. Comparison will shew that the list omits Nos 7 and 49 and it should be noted that No 6 did not qualify for a founding date until 1824; No 9 fell by the wayside and did not achieve a date until 1889; of No 16 there is no trace. Mount Sinai was attached to No 56 which became No 37 on the closing up of the Register but that lodge was erased in 1859 at which date it came under the sanction of No 19, but that did not affect the founding date; No 122 was the number held by United Lodge of Prudence but there is no record of a Chapter; the same applies to No 281; No 308 became Tranquility Chapter No 185 but the date granted was 1818, after the Union; No 493 is now Prince of Wales's Chapter No 259 and did not achieve a date until 1824; No 281 is Chapter of Temperance dated 1862.

There is the possibility that Chapters may have been held under those numbers quoted above but regularity could not be established for them and although perhaps on the Registers, were unacceptable for the new Register and were not recognised. The later dates for them were probably granted when they became properly organised. One classic example of neglect can be seen in the experience of Grand Master's Chapter No 1 which was actually holding meetings in 1817 but unfortunately failed to apply for a Charter of Confirmation and remained outside the Regulations in that respect. It had to apply, eventually, to be newly Constituted and as a result did not achieve a date until 1886.

Holding occasional meetings, often not minuted, was insufficient to warrant earlier dates than those granted which was done only upon evidence of regular meetings. Domatic Chapter had met at the Hercules Pillars, Great Queen Street, in 1789 but regularity of meetings could not be proved until 1793 and that was the earliest date acceptable. Occasional Chapter meetings, not associated with a particular lodge also were unacceptable.

Appendix H

Domatic Chapter of Instruction

Comp Sigrist's Furniture Account

Bible square & Comp.	2.6
Flooring board & doble cube Pedestal	2. 6.6
brass letters on top & front of	
Pedestal	7.6
3 scepters Pick Crow & shovel	6.0
3 greater lights Trowel & sword	9.6
making mounting & japanning	2.17.0
japanning doble Cube white	3.0
5 principal Banners	1.15.0
plate of pure gold	5.0
2 brass sockets 5 spiers & mounting	
to hang principal banners on	15.0
Case with lock 2 handles for flooring	
box	7.0
4 Jewels 8/- & rep (?) pedestal 3/-	11.0
	£10. 5.0

Printing Account

500 note Circulars	15. –
100 supper cards	3. –
100 cards & 50 notices	4.6
500 cards	5.0
	£1. 7.6

Book Account

To 6 numbers of the quarterly Review		18.0
by private subscription	5.0	
by fees and fines collected	6.10	
	11.10	

Appendix J

An account of the loss of the Princess Alice, in collision with Bywell Castle in the River Thames on 3 September 1878, extracted from *Dictionary of Disasters at Sea, during the age of Steam 1824-1962*, Vol 11, Charles Hocking, published by Lloyd's Register of Shipping, 1969. (Courtesy of National Maritime Museum)

――――――――――

PRINCESS ALICE
London Steamboat Co: 1865; J. Caird & Co.; 251 tons; 219-2 X 20-1 X 8-4; 140 i.h.p.; 12 knots; oscillating engines.
The *Princess Alice* (Capt. W. Grinstead) was, for her time, a large and commodious river steamship. On the day on which the disaster occurred the weather was fine and warm, attracting many excursionists, and the vessel left London at about 10 a.m. on September 3rd, 1878, with a full load, bound for Gravesend and Sheerness. At about 6 p.m. she left Gravesend on the return trip, being crowded almost to capacity, the number of passengers and crew being estimated at nearly 900. The evening was fine and clear.

At 7.40 p.m. while in Galleon's Reach, about one mile below Woolwich, the *Princess Alice* met the collier *Bywell Castle*, 1,376 tons, Capt. T. Harrison, proceeding upon an opposite course, being at the time in charge of a Thames pilot. The collier was high out of the water, having discharged her coal and returning in ballast. This circumstance made her deck almost inaccessible to the drowning passengers after the collision.

As the two vessels approached each other there were a few moments of fatal indecision on the part of Capt. Grinstead. There were warning shouts from both ships and then the pleasure steamship ran athwart the bows of the collier; being struck on the starboard sponson aft of the paddle-box.

The collier's bow drove into the other's engine-room, almost cutting her in two. The bow portion of the *Princess Alice* sank immediately, taking with it all those passengers sitting there. The tide was at two hours ebb, and the *Bywell Castle* under the force of this, and the way from her engines, was swept some distance down before she could stop and drop anchor.

For a few minutes there were scenes of indescribable horror and utmost confusion. According to a statement by Capt. Harrison three boats were got out by the *Bywell Castle*, one of these being a large ship's lifeboat which took some time to lower, and this delay coupled with the distance which the ship had drifted from the wreck, greatly retarded the work of rescue. The pleasure steamship *Duke of Teck*, belonging to the same company as the *Princess Alice*, arrived about ten minutes after the disaster and took on board some survivors. From the moment of the collision to when the vessel foundered was only a brief four to five minutes, allowing scant time for ships in the vicinity to send aid.

The number lost is generally assumed to be 640 persons, including Capt. Grinstead. Those saved numbered a little over 200.

INDEX

Page numbers in *italics* denote illustrations and captions. This index does not include names, places or lodges etc mentioned within quoted passages. An * placed after a lodge or chapter number means that it is no longer on the English Register; q indicates a quoted passage. The following abbreviations are used:

GM—Grand Master
(A)—Atholl or 'Antients' Grand Lodge
(P)—Premier or 'Moderns' Grand Lodge

INDEX

'Makings' 5, 38
'Making Cloth' 24, *27*
Marlborough Head, The 110
Masonic Million Memorial fund 132, *133*, 135
Masonic Record, The 126
McCann, James 65, 81
McCormick John GSec(A) (1785–90) 11, 15, 22, 78
Memorandums of the Bedford Lodge of Free-Masons (c1798) 141–2
Mendoza, Harry 92
Metropolitan Lodge and Chapter No 1507, 117
Metropolitan Royal Arch ritual 117
Middlesex Sessions House, Clerkenwell *143*, 144, *145*
Mivart, James 45, 63, 65, 66
Moderns Grand Chapter 72, 82, 87
Moderns Grand Lodge (or Premier GL): and the Antients' 37–8; certificates 33; Grand Stewards 139, 141; meeting places 129; Royal Arch 3, 26, 82–4; the Union 1, 45, 51–64, 137
Moira, Earl of 84
Montgomery, Andrew *20*
Morgan, George 67
Morning Advertiser, The (1794) q90
Morrice, Thomas 139
Mount Moriah Lodge No 34, 16, 80
Mount Sinai Chapter No 19, 87, 97, 111, 114
Mount Sinai Lodge No 121, 57
Mountnorris, Earl of 84

Neptune Lodge No 22, 38, 77
'*Night*', William Hogarth 137, *138*
Nine Worthies (*see* Excellent Masters)

Old Charges 137
Old King's Arms Lodge No 28, 141
Old Union Lodge No 46, 141
Orbis Miraculum (rev. Samuel Lee), 93
Origin of the English Rite (Hughan) 117
Osborne, E. 144, *146*
Owen, H.R.P. *146*
Oxford Royal Arch Ritual 100

Parker, Joshua 14, 19
Parker, Sir Peter DepGM(P) (1787–1811) 83
Parkinson, R.F. q90
Payne, C.B. 106
Payne, George GM(P) (1718, 1720) 137
Peace and Harmony Lodge No 60, 141
Peace Memorial Jewel *133*
Pendlebury, R.A. 107, 115
'Penny Black' postage stamp 95

Perfect Ceremonies ritual 116
Perkins, John 16–17, 21, 77
Perry, James DepGM(A) (1787–90) 38, 40–1
Petrie, Lord 132
Phoenix Lodge No 173, 58, 60, 79
Polish National Chapter No 534, 114
Powers, Norman 144
Premier Grand Lodge (*see* Moderns GL)
Preston, William 137
Price, H.N. 107
Prince of Wales's Lodge No 259, 141
Princess Alice 119, 159
Promulgation, Lodge of 56–7, 64, 81

Quatuor Coronati Lodge No 2076, 106, 117, 129
Queen Elizabeth Tavern 116
Queens Head, Soho 48

Ranger 'Bro' 34
Read, James 78
Reconciliation, Lodge of, 44–5, 50–1, 57, 59, 64–5, 81, 93–95
Records of Mount Sinai chapter No 19 93
Red Apron Lodge 114
Regalia, costs to Domatic Lodge 15
Register of Members of the Royal Arch 79
Regularity, Lodge of, No 91, 141
Richmond, Duke of 139
Ring, Sir Lindsay 126, *127*
Rite of Memphis 104
Ritual of the Holy Royal Arch as Taught by Domatic Chapter of Instruction No 177 3
Robert Burns Chapter No 25, 107, 111
Robert Burns Lodge No 25, 114
Roberts Manuscript (1722) 32
Rose of Denmark Chapter No 975, 108
Ross, B. *146*
Rourke, F.L. *146*
Royal Albert Lodge No 907, 103
Royal Alpha Lodge No 16, 93
Royal Arch: Acceptance by Moderns 82–5; attachment to lodge 87, 89; certificates 75, 77, earliest *76*; jewels 89; qualifications 70–3; ritual 89–90, 92–3, 101, 110, Claret 3, Moderns ritual 70; Tracing Board *100*; Union 55, 69–74, 82–3, 87
Royal Arch Regulations 87, 89, 101
Royal Athelstane Lodge No 19, 87
Royal Cumberland Chapter No 18*, 90
Royal Jubilee Lodge No 72, 114
Royal Masonic Benevolent Institution 47, 125